THE DRIVING FORCE OF THE MARKET

FOUNDATIONS OF THE MARKET ECONOMY

Edited by Mario J. Rizzo, *New York University* and Lawrence H. White, *University of Georgia*

A central theme of this series is the importance of understanding and assessing the market economy from a perspective broader than the static economics of perfect competition and Pareto optimality. Such a perspective sees markets as causal processes generated by the preferences, expectations and beliefs of economic agents. The creative acts of entrepreneurship that uncover new information about preferences, prices and technology are central to these processes with respect to their ability to promote the discovery and use of knowledge in society.

The market economy consists of a set of institutions that facilitate voluntary cooperation and exchange among individuals. These institutions include the legal and ethical framework as well as more narrowly "economic" patterns of social interaction. Thus the law, legal institutions and cultural or ethical norms, as well as ordinary business practices and monetary phenomena, fall within the analytical domain of the economist.

Other titles in the series

CAPITAL IN DISEQUILIBRIUM
The role of capital in a changing world
Peter Lewin

PRICES AND KNOWLEDGE
A market-process perspective
Esteban F. Thomsen

KEYNES' GENERAL THEORY OF INTEREST
A reconsideration
Fiona C. Maclachlan

LAISSEZ-FAIRE BANKING
Kevin Dowd

EXPECTATIONS AND THE MEANING OF INSTITUTIONS
Essays in economics by Ludwig Lachmann
Edited by Don Lavoie

PERFECT COMPETITION AND THE TRANSFORMATION OF ECONOMICS
Frank M. Machovec

ENTREPRENEURSHIP AND THE MARKET PROCESS
An enquiry into the growth of knowledge
David Harper

ECONOMICS OF TIME AND IGNORANCE
Gerald O'Driscoll and Mario J. Rizzo

DYNAMICS OF THE MIXED ECONOMY
Toward a theory of interventionism
Sanford Ikeda

NEOCLASSICAL MICROECONOMIC THEORY
The founding Austrian vision
A.M. Endres

THE CULTURAL FOUNDATIONS OF ECONOMIC DEVELOPMENT
Urban female entrepreneurship in Ghana
Emily Chamlee-Wright

RISK AND BUSINESS CYCLES
New and Old Austrian perspectives
Tyler Cowen

THE DRIVING FORCE OF THE MARKET

Essays in Austrian economics

Israel M. Kirzner

London and New York

First published 2000
by Routledge
11 New Fetter Lane, London EC4P 4EE

Simultaneously published in the USA and Canada
by Routledge
29 West 35th Street, New York, NY 10001

Routledge is an imprint of the Taylor & Francis Group

Typeset in Garamond by
BC Typesetting, Bristol
Printed and bound in Great Britain by
St Edmundsbury Press, Bury St Edmunds, Suffolk

British Library Cataloguing in Publication Data
A catalogue record for this book is available from the British Library

Library of Congress Cataloging in Publication Data
Kirzner, Israel M.
The driving force of the market: essays in Austrian economics/
Israel M. Kirzner.
p. cm. – (Foundations of the market economy)
Includes bibliographical references and index.
1. Austrian school of economists. I. Title. II. Foundations of the market economy series.
HB98.K558 2000
330.15′7–dc21 99-056937

ISBN 0–415–22823–9

B'EZRAS HASHEM

CONTENTS

PREFACE

As the twentieth century draws to a close, the Austrian tradition in economics has, it appears, begun to attract a significantly increased volume of attention. Long thought to be a relic of a once-prominent school that had been swept from the professional stage soon after the end of the first third of the century, Austrian economics has recently enjoyed something of a renaissance. Younger economists are discovering validity in Austrian critiques of mainstream, late-twentieth-century economics; they are finding many of the positive Austrian insights to be of substantial help in achieving economic understanding. This volume collects a bundle of papers written during the past decade, which seek either to explicate the Austrian perspective to economists not yet familiar with it, or to use this perspective substantively to pursue our task of expanding and deepening economic understanding. In particular this writer has consistently sought in these papers to deploy the entrepreneurial emphasis of Austrian economics to illuminate key theoretical issues both in positive and in normative economics.

Several papers in this volume focus specifically on the work of Ludwig von Mises and Friedrich Hayek. This is no accident. Each of these Austrian economists had a research and publishing career covering almost seven decades in this century. Most of these years were years in which Mises and Hayek found themselves treated virtually as intellectual outcasts offering unfashionable, indeed, old-fashioned, doctrines, based on a thoroughly outmoded methodology. Modern Austrian economists understand, however, that some of the published work of Mises and of Hayek during the mid-century decades were, while certainly consistent with earlier Austrian (and broadly neoclassical) economics, in fact pathbreaking theoretical contributions which significantly deepened and extended the Austrian economic tradition—in ways which decisively challenged the new orthodoxy which began to dominate the profession at that very same time. It is only now, at the very end of the century, that these contributions of Mises and Hayek are beginning to be appreciated more widely in the economics profession. It is because so much in this book owes a significant intellectual debt to those contributions, that it has seemed appropriate to include, as an appendix to these papers, obituary remarks contributed by the author on Mises and on Hayek, which draw specific attention to their intellectual legacies in economics. A third obituary contributed by the author is also included in this volume. This is the obituary for Ludwig M. Lachmann. Lachmann's role in the renaissance of the Austrian tradition was a crucially important one. Although this writer differed with Lachmann for many years on many foundational aspects of modern Austrian economics, he believes that his own understanding of the economic process would have been far poorer and far less satisfactory, had he not had the privilege of crossing intellectual swords over the years with that gracious (but remarkably tenacious) scholar.

Many of these papers were presented at Austrian Economics Colloquium sessions at New York University. The author is grateful to all colloquium participants both for their critical and their positive comments on those presentations. He particularly recalls the helpful and critical comments of Peter Boettke, Roger Koppl, Mario Rizzo, Joseph Salerno, and Douglas G. Whitman.

The research invested in these papers was supported by funding generously provided by the Sarah Scaife Foundation. The author gratefully acknowledges this support (and also the crucially important role played by a great admirer of both Mises and Hayek, Richard M. Larry).

Israel M. Kirzner
September, 1999

ACKNOWLEDGMENTS

The author and publishers would like to thank the following for permission to reproduce copyright material in this work:

American Economic Association for "Entrepreneurial Discovery and the Competitive Market Process: An Austrian Approach" from *Journal of Economic Literature*, March 1997, XXXV, pp. 60–85.

Routledge for "The Subjectivism of Austrian Economics" from G. Meijer (ed.) (1995) *New Perspectives on Austrian Economics*, Routledge.

South African Journal of Economics for "Subjectivism, Freedom and Economic Law" from *South African Journal of Economics*, 1992, 60(1).

Nomos Verlag for "The Limits of the Market: The Real and the Imagined" from W. Möschel, M.E. Streit and U. Witt (eds) (1994) *Marktwirtschaft und Rechtsordnung*, Nomos.

Institut für Weltwirtschaft, Kiel University and Mohr Siebeck for "The Ethics of Competition" from H. Siebert (ed.) (1994) *The Ethical Foundations of the Market Economy*, J.C.B. Mohr.

The University of Chicago Press, Robin A. Cowan and Mario J. Rizzo for "The Nature of Profits: Some Economic Insights and their Ethical Implications" from Robin A. Cowan and Mario J. Rizzo (eds) (1995) *Profits and Morality*, University of Chicago Press. Copyright © 1995 The University of Chicago.

Kluwer Academic Publishers for "Coordination as a Criterion for Economic 'Goodness'" from *Constitutional Political Economy*, 1998, 9, pp. 289–301.

The Mises Institute for "Reflections on the Misesian Legacy in Economics" from *Review of Austrian Economics*, 1996, 9(2), pp. 143–54.

Cato Journal for "Mises and His Understanding of the Capitalist System" from *Cato Journal*, forthcoming.

Journal des Economistes et des Etudes Humaines for "Hedgehog or Fox? Hayek and the Idea of Plan-Coordination" from *Journal des Economistes et des Etudes Humaines*, June/September 1999, IX(2/3), pp. 217–37.

Editions ECONOMICA for "Competition and the Market Process: Some Doctrinal Milestones" from J. Krafft (ed.) (1999) *Le processus de concurrence*, Editions ECONOMICA.

Hillsdale College Press and Richard Ebeling for "The Driving Force of the Market: The Idea of 'Competition' in Contemporary Economic Theory and in the Austrian Theory of the Market Process" from R. Ebeling (ed.) (1997) *Austrian Economics; Perspectives on the Past and Prospects for the Future*, Hillsdale College Press.

Kluwer Academic Publishers for "Creativity and/or Alertness: A Reconsideration of the Schumpeterian Entrepreneur" from *Review of Austrian Economics*, 1999, 11, pp. 5–17.

Edward Elgar Publishing Ltd for "Rationality, Entrepreneurship, and Economic 'Imperialism'" from Sheila C. Dow and Peter E. Earl (eds) (1999) *Economic Organisation and Economic Knowledge: Essays in Honor of Brian J. Loasby*, Edward Elgar.

National Review for "Tribute to von Mises: On the Market" from *National Review*, November 9, 1973, pp. 1246, 1260. © 1973 by National Review, Inc. www.nationalreview.com. Reprinted by permission.

Critical Review for the obituary of F.A. von Hayek from *Critical Review*, 1992, 5(4). © Center for Independent Thought.

Institute for Humane Studies for the obituary of Ludwig M. Lachmann from Institute for Humane Studies, *Institute Scholar*, 1991, 10(2–3).

Every effort has been made to contact copyright holders for their permission to reprint material in this book. The publisher would be grateful to hear from any copyright holder who is not here acknowledged and will undertake to rectify any errors or omissions in future editions of this book.

Part I

THE CHARACTER OF AUSTRIAN ECONOMICS

1

ENTREPRENEURIAL DISCOVERY AND THE COMPETITIVE MARKET PROCESS

An Austrian approach

I

The Austrian tradition is represented in modern economics by a "very vocal, feisty and dedicated subset of the economics profession" (Vaughn, 1994, p. xi). Much of the work of this group of scholars is devoted to the most fundamental problems of microeconomics.[1] This Austrian work, therefore, differs in character and content from a good deal of neoclassical theory which, despite widespread and growing awareness of its limitations, continues to serve as the analytical core of mainstream economics. This paper sets forth the outlines of one important approach within modern Austrian economics, an approach offering a perspective on microeconomic theory which (while it has generated a considerable literature of its own) is not ordinarily well-represented either at the (mainstream) textbook level, or in the (mainstream) journal literature. Although the author subscribes to and has contributed to this approach, the purpose of this chapter is exposition, not advocacy. References to criticisms of mainstream microeconomics which have been discussed in the Austrian literature should be understood here not as arguments in favor of the Austrian approach, but as clues that may be helpful in understanding what the Austrians are saying, and how what they are saying is to be distinguished from the approach taken by other modern economists.

This chapter does not offer anything like a survey of modern Austrian economics. It does not deal at all with such major areas within it, such as cycle theory, monetary theory, capital theory. Within its chosen scope of microeconomics, it does not claim to represent a universally accepted Austrian position (or even to cover its entire range of topics). Nonetheless, the approach described here is arguably central to the reviving contemporary interest in Austrian ideas, and has been treated as such in a number of recent general surveys of modern Austrian economics (Littlechild, 1986; Caldwell and Boehm, 1992; Vaughn, 1994).[2]

During the past two decades modern Austrian economics has emerged out of the classic earlier "subjectivist" traditions[3] (which began in the late nineteenth century with Carl Menger, Eugen von Boehm-Bawerk, and Friedrich von Wieser),[4] particularly as that tradition came to be represented in the mid-century contributions of Ludwig von Mises and Friedrich Hayek.[5] The early work of the Austrian School until the 1930s was correctly perceived as simply one variant of the dominant early twentieth century mainstream approach to economic understanding (often loosely referred to as "neoclassical"). But the work of Mises and Hayek from the 1930s on, steered the Austrian tradition in a direction sharply different from that being taken at that time by mainstream neoclassical microeconomics.[6] By 1950 both Mises and Hayek had crystallized separate, definitive, statements of their disagreements with mainstream microeconomics, and of their own substantive approaches. These were indeed separate statements, differing from one another certainly in style and, no doubt, to some degree also in substance. But it can be argued that they are best understood as both overlapping and complementary, rather than as contrasting alternatives. It was these contributions of Mises and Hayek which, while almost entirely ignored by the mid-century mainstream of the profession, have nourished the Austrian revival of the past two decades, and which have generated the modern Austrian approach to understanding the competitive market process set forth in this chapter.

At the basis of this approach is the conviction that standard neoclassical microeconomics, for which the Walrasian general equilibrium model (in its modern Arrow-Debreu incarnation) is the analytical core, fails to offer a satisfying theoretical framework for understanding what happens in market economies. This conviction is rooted (a) in criticisms of the lack of relevance in models which seek to explain market phenomena as if they were, at each and every instant, strictly equilibrium phenomena, and (b) in the belief that it is a methodologically legitimate demand to be made of a theory of the market, that it not merely begin with the instrumentalist assumption of already-attained equilibrium, but also realistically offer a plausible explanation of how, from any given initial set of nonequilibrium conditions, equilibrating tendencies might be expected to be set into motion in the first place. As will be noted below, such criticisms are not (or, at any rate, no longer) *exclusively* "Austrian" criticisms. In fact, a good deal of recent non-Austrian work in microeconomics has in some fashion attempted to grapple with these difficulties. What stamps the entrepreneurial discovery approach as Austrian is not these criticisms themselves, but rather the specific positive elements of the approach.

These positive elements focus on the role of knowledge and discovery in the process of market equilibration. In particular this approach (a) sees equilibration as a systematic process in which market participants acquire more and more accurate and complete mutual knowledge of potential demand and supply attitudes, and (b) sees the driving force behind this systematic process in what will be described below as entrepreneurial discovery. Although, of course, much contemporary mainstream work in microeconomics takes its point of departure from the imperfection of knowledge (relaxing the older standard neoclassical assumption of complete, universal information), the Austrian approach set forth in this paper has little in common with this work.

For the mainstream, imperfect information is primarily a circumstance constraining the pattern of attained equilibrium (and introducing a new "production" cost, that of producing or searching for missing information). For the Austrian approach imperfect information is seen as involving an element which cannot be fitted at all into neoclassical models, that of "sheer" (i.e., unknown) ignorance. As will be developed below, sheer ignorance differs from imperfect information in that the discovery which reduces sheer ignorance is necessarily accompanied by the element of surprise—one had not hitherto realized one's ignorance. Entrepreneurial discovery is seen as gradually but systematically pushing back the boundaries of sheer ignorance, in this way increasing mutual awareness among market participants and thus, in turn, driving prices, output and input quantities and qualities, toward the values consistent with equilibrium (seen as the complete absence of sheer ignorance).

What will emerge from this chapter is thus the exposition of an Austrian way of understanding the systematic character of markets which, while sharply differing from the mainstream competitive equilibrium model, does not necessarily see that model as totally irrelevant. (Many practical questions, such as those regarding the effects of price controls, minimum wage laws, and the like, can be answered quite adequately without going beyond simple competitive supply-and-demand equilibrium models.) The dynamic competitive process of entrepreneurial discovery (which is the driving element in this Austrian approach) is one which is seen as tending systematically toward, rather than away from, the path to equilibrium. Therefore, the standard, competitive equilibrium model may be seen as more plausible as an approximate outcome, in the Austrian theory here presented.[7] This aspect of the entrepreneurial discovery approach troubles a number of the Austrian economists who have not accepted it. In order to clearly locate the entrepreneurial discovery perspective within the range of modern Austrian theoretical points of view, it will be necessary briefly to identify more precisely the various disagreements which other Austrians have had with this approach.

Section II of this chapter will review the Austrian criticisms of the equilibrium emphasis of the neoclassical models. Section III will develop the Austrian understanding of the market process, based upon the twin concepts of sheer (i.e., unknown) ignorance and entrepreneurial discovery. Section IV will survey several areas of applied microeconomics (antitrust economics, welfare economics, the theory of justice, and the possibility of socialist economic calculation), taking special note of the significant differences which the Austrian approach entails in regard to policy recommendations in these areas. Section V will note the various criticisms to the entrepreneurial discovery theory developed in this chapter, offered by several contemporary Austrian economists. Section VI concludes the chapter by clearing up certain misunderstandings concerning the Austrian approach.

II

Mainstream microeconomics interprets the real world of markets as if observed phenomena represent the fulfilment of equilibrium conditions.[8] Markets consist of successfully maximizing agents whose decisions are held to fit in together perfectly, in the sense that each maximizing decision being made correctly anticipates, in effect, at least, all the other maximizing decisions being made simultaneously. It is this latter condition which mathematically constrains the attained values of the key decision variables. For this condition to be fulfilled, only that set of input and output prices and quantities can prevail which simultaneously satisfies the relevant equations of supply and demand (themselves constructed by aggregating the selling and buying decisions consistent with maximizing under a range of hypothesized states of affairs). It is this aspect of modern neoclassical economics which accounts for its characteristic emphasis upon: (a) the constrained maximization pattern imposed by the theory upon individual decision making, and (b) the mathematics of simultaneous equation systems. Valiant attempts have been made to enrich the realism of these equilibrium microeconomic models by building into them assumptions acknowledging imperfections in competition. Nonetheless, the dominant trend has been to concentrate upon models of competitive equilibrium, that is upon models in which both prices and product/resource qualities are taken as given to each decision maker, and as being independent of the decisions made. Not only do these competitive models (like all equilibrium models) assume complete mutual knowledge (in the relevant sense), they also assume, in effect, that the crucial market variables of price and quality are somehow presented to each decision maker as an external fact of nature. Neoclassical economics operates on the assumption that the world reflects the relationships that would prevail in such equilibrium models—with the model of competitive equilibrium being the favorite one. While Austrians have not been alone in criticizing this approach to understanding markets, their criticisms have been both pioneering and trenchant.

Austrian dissatisfaction with this standard approach to understanding real world market phenomena emerged most clearly in the forties. Both Mises and Hayek expressed dismay at models labeled as competitive, in which market participants are forbidden, as it were, from competing (in the sense in which, in everyday discourse and experience, market participants compete by bidding higher prices or by offering to undersell competitors, by offering consumers better quality merchandise, better service, and the like; see Mises, 1949, p. 278fn; Hayek, 1948, pp. 92–118). Their unhappiness with models of so-called perfect competition ultimately stemmed from their unwillingness to surrender the economists' insights into the dynamic character of active markets to equilibrium models, in which all decisions have somehow been pre-reconciled, held as at all times governing market phenomena. It seems accurate to understand their impatience with the neoclassical preoccupation with equilibrium models as arising from (a) the blatantly false nature of the assumption that market conditions are at all times in equilibrium, and (b) methodological unease with an instrumentalist mode of theorizing and empirical analysis that finds it useful to presume that equilibrium always prevails, while recognizing no obligation to account theoretically for any equilibrative process (from which equilibrium might be explained as emerging).

Modern presentations of the entrepreneurial discovery approach have echoed these criticisms of equilibrium economics, and have deployed these criticisms in seeking to demote the concept of perfect competition from its position of dominance in modern neoclassical theory, in order to replace it by notions of dynamic competition (in which market participants are, instead of exclusively price takers, competitive price—and quality—makers). Within the two broad bases for Austrian (as well as for non-Austrian) criticism, several strands of difficulty with the neoclassical competitive equilibrium paradigm may be distinguished. The clear identification of these strands will help us understand the Austrian character of the positive approach, based on entrepreneurial discovery, to be developed in Section III.

(a) Criticisms of the unrealistic character of neoclassical theory relate both to the way in which individual decisions are modeled in that theory, and the way in which that theory sees real world market outcomes as satisfying the conditions for equilibrium.

(i) At the individual level Austrians have taken sharp exception to the manner in which neoclassical theory has portrayed the individual decision as a mechanical exercise in constrained maximization. Such a portrayal robs human choice of its essentially open-ended character, in which imagination and boldness must inevitably play central roles. For neoclassical theory the only way human choice can be rendered analytically tractable, is for it to be modeled as if it were *not* made in open-ended fashion, as if there was *no* scope for qualities such as imagination and boldness. Even though standard neoclassical theory certainly deals extensively with decision making under (Knightian) risk,[9] this is entirely consistent with absence of scope for the qualities of imagination and boldness, because such decision making is seen as being made in the context of known probability functions. In the neoclassical world, decision makers know what they are ignorant about. One is never surprised. For Austrians, however, to abstract from these qualities of imagination, boldness, and surprise is to denature human choice entirely.[10]

Now we should emphasize that a good deal of critical attention has been directed in recent years by non-Austrians at the neoclassical assumption of perfect information. A significant literature has shown how imperfect information may, as a consequence of entailed externalities, render the equilibrium outcomes of market economies inefficient in terms of Paretian criteria. It is however necessary to dispel a certain confusion which has arisen in this regard. Joseph Stiglitz (1994, pp. 24ff.) who has been a central contributor to this critical literature, has taken note of what he believes to be the parallel Austrian concern with imperfect information. He has also (1994, p. 43) drawn attention to what he understands as the contrary Austrian view, namely, that it claims informational efficiency for the price system. We should emphasize that, on both these points, he has missed the crucial element that sharply distinguishes the unknown ignorance (with which Austrians have been concerned) from the imperfect information (central to the critical literature in which Stiglitz himself has been a pioneer). For Stiglitz "imperfect information" refers to known-to-be-available information which it is costly to produce. But for Austrians the focus is upon what has been termed "previously unthought-of knowledge" (Thomsen, 1992, p. 61). In Section III we shall return to see how, as a consequence of this distinction, Austrian appreciation for the discovery potential of market processes does not at all imply that "informational efficiency" for market outcomes which Stiglitz has denied.

(ii) At the market level, Austrians have rebelled against a microeconomics which can find coherence in markets and can explain market phenomena only by asserting that markets are, at all times, to be treated as if already in the attained relevant state of equilibrium.

Such a picture of the world Austrians find simply false, not merely in the sense that an explanatory theoretical model may, obviously, not offer a photographic representation of the richly complex reality it is being used to explain, but in the sense that this picture falsely labels important features of reality. For Austrians it is unacceptable to claim that, at each and every instant, the configuration of production and consumption decisions currently made, is one which could, in the light of the relevant costs, not possibly have been improved upon. To claim that, at any given instant, all conceivably relevant available opportunities have been instantaneously grasped, is to fly in the face of what we know about real world economic systems. It is one thing to postulate rapid equilibrating processes as imposing systematic order upon markets; it is quite another thing (in the absence of any theory of equilibrative processes!) to treat the world as at all times already in the attained state of equilibrium.[11]

(b) The basic methodological foundation for Austrian unhappiness with mainstream neoclassical preoccupation with equilibrium models, has not so much to do with the false and misleading picture of real markets, which standard deployment of these models entails, as with the instrumentalist view of theory which the neoclassical equilibrium-preoccupation came to express. Austrians, in this version of their criticism, need have no quarrel with equilibrium models as such. No doubt significant features of real world market economies can indeed be illuminated by use of such models. But, the Austrian criticism runs, we are surely entitled to demand a theoretical basis for the claim that equilibrating processes systematically mold market variables in a direction consistent with the conditions postulated in the equilibrium models. If competitive markets are to be explained in terms of Marshallian supply and demand diagrams, surely we are entitled to a theoretical process-"story" which might account for the economists' confidence in the special relevance of the intersection point in that supply and demand diagram. In our undergraduate freshman classes we do offer such stories: if above equilibrium prices prevail, this generates surplus of supply over demand; these surpluses force prices downwards, etc., etc. But strictly speaking, these plausible stories are, within the neoclassical framework, quite illegitimate. That framework requires us simply to accept equilibrium models as the only explanatory tool necessary for understanding prices and outputs. This, for Austrians, is methodologically unacceptable. What, we must ask, accounts for the powerful equilibrating tendencies which economists believe to be operating in markets? If, at any time, real world limitations upon the perfection of information possessed have prevented instantaneous attainment of equilibrium, why should we have confidence in any possible equilibrative process?[12] And how, if we do observe such equilibrating processes, can we understand what has generated them?[13]

Kenneth Arrow's well known paper of 1959 offers an excellent illustration of (a) how a foremost exponent of the neoclassical approach perceptively recognized one aspect of the problem upon which this latter Austrian criticism has focused, and (b) how this led him to develop an analytical dynamics from which the standard competitive equilibrium model emerges only as the outcome of a process. Arrow focused his attention upon the Marshallian perfectly competitive supply and demand model in the single commodity market, and especially, upon the requirement of this model that supply equal demand. He draws attention to the logical gap in the perfectly competitive model:

> Each individual participant in the economy is supposed to take prices as given and determine his choices as to purchases

> and sales accordingly; there is no one left over whose job it is to make a decision on price.
>
> (Arrow, 1959, p. 43)

He overcomes this difficulty by proposing that it be recognized "that perfect competition can really prevail only at equilibrium" (Arrow, 1959, p. 41). In disequilibrium each supplier faces a downward sloping demand curve and, acting "monopolistically," seeks an optimal price-quantity combination. The equilibrating process operates through each supplier discovering that (as a result of the comparable activities of his fellow "monopolists") his demand curve is shifting "at the same time as he is exploring it" (Arrow, 1959, p. 46).

Arrow recognized that the very notion of a perfectly competitive market in disequilibrium is incoherent. And he recognized an obligation to offer a model that might account for the emergence, out of initial disequilibrium, of an equilibrating process. His critique of the core of neoclassicism, illustrates well the vulnerability of mainstream theory to the Austrian criticisms discussed in this section. A number of non-Austrian writers have followed Arrow's critique, and Franklin Fisher's (1983) important contribution attracted a modest amount of professional attention. Nonetheless, the mainstream has proceeded by virtually ignoring these criticisms, and operating as if its core paradigm was, by and large, as relevant as ever.

Austrians maintain that a theoretical framework for understanding the equilibrative process is available. This framework offers its explanation not by denying the operation of competition in disequilibrium but *per contra* (and in sharpest contrast to Arrow's labeling system), by reformulating the notion of competition to make it utterly inconsistent with the equilibrium state.

III

The entrepreneurial discovery approach which has emerged in modern Austrian economics during the past quarter of a century was developed out of elements derived from Mises and from Hayek. From Mises the modern Austrians learned to see the market as an entrepreneurially driven process. From Hayek they learned to appreciate the role of knowledge and its enhancement through market interaction, for the equilibrative process. These two distinct elements have been welded into an integrated theoretical framework which, on the one hand, is consistent with and, on the other hand, is articulated in a manner more explicit than the earlier Austrian expositions.[14]

Mises' conception of the market as an entrepreneurially driven process pervades his mature theoretical work.

> The driving force of the market process is provided neither by the consumers nor by the owners of the means of production—land, capital goods, and labor—but by the promoting and speculating entrepreneurs . . . Profit-seeking speculation is the driving force of the market as it is the driving force of production.
>
> (Mises, 1949, pp. 325–6)

"The activities of the entrepreneur are the element that would bring about the unrealizable state of the evenly rotating economy if no further changes were to occur" (Mises, 1949, p. 335). "In the imaginary construction of the evenly rotating economy there is no room left for entrepreneurial activity . . ." (Mises, 1949, p. 253). The focus here is on the market *process*, as opposed to the "imaginary construct" of the "evenly rotating economy" (corresponding roughly to the state of general market equilibrium).

Entrepreneurial activity has no place at all in neoclassical equilibrium microeconomics (because it is inconsistent with the conditions satisfied in the equilibrium state; Baumol, 1993, ch. 1). But for Austrians the entrepreneurial role provides the theoretical key with which to account for the market as a process. For Mises, the economist

> shows how the activities of enterprising men, the promoters and speculators, eager to profit from discrepancies in the price structure, tend toward eradicating such discrepancies . . . He shows how this process would finally result in the establishment of the evenly rotating economy. This is the task of economic theory. The mathematical description of various states of equilibrium is mere play. The problem is the analysis of the market process.
>
> (Mises, 1949, pp. 352–3)

Hayek's emphasis on the role of knowledge and its enhancement in the course of the market process goes back to his work in the thirties. It was Hayek who insisted that

> the concept of equilibrium merely means that the foresight of the different members of the society is . . . correct . . . in the sense that every person's plan is based on the expectation of just those actions of other people which those other people intend to perform and that all these plans are based on the expectation of the same set of external facts . . . Correct foresight is then . . . the defining characteristic of a state of equilibrium.
>
> (Hayek, 1948, p. 42)

In his pioneering discussion of the equilibrating process Hayek pointed out that, "if we want to make the assertion that, under certain conditions, people will approach (the equilibrium state), we must explain by what process they will acquire the necessary knowledge" (Hayek, 1948, p. 46).

For Hayek the equilibrating process is thus one during which market participants acquire better mutual information concerning the plans being made by fellow market participants. For Mises this process is driven by the daring, imaginative, speculative actions of entrepreneurs who see opportunities for pure profit in the conditions of disequilibrium. What permits us to recognize that these two perspectives on the character of the market process are mutually reinforcing, is the place which each of these two writers assigns to competition in the market process. The Austrian approach includes a concept of competition which differs drastically from that encapsulated in the label "competitive" as used in modern neoclassical theory.

For neoclassical economics the maximum possible degree of competition is represented by the equilibrium notion of perfect competition, in which all traces of rivalry are absent. Anything less than perfect elasticity in the supply/demand curves faced by potential buyers/sellers corresponds, in neoclassical terminology, to some degree of monopolistic power.[15] Mises rejected this nomenclature, in that it implies that monopoly prices are somehow determined without that competitive process which constitutes for Mises the essence of the market. "Catallactic competition is no less a factor in the determination of monopoly prices than it is in the determination of competitive prices . . . On the market every commodity competes with all other commodities" (Mises, 1949, p. 278). He cites Hayek's critique of the doctrines of imperfect or monopolistic competition (Mises, 1949, p. 278fn), and emphasizes that competition (far from being defined, as in the perfectly competitive model, as the state in which all participants face identical prices) "manifests itself in the facts that the sellers must outdo one another by offering better or cheaper goods and services and that the buyers must outdo one another by offering higher prices" (Mises, 1949, p. 274). In other words, the essence of competition is precisely that dynamic rivalry which the neoclassical equilibrium notion of competition is at great pains to exclude. Hayek's path-breaking critique of the dominance of the perfectly competitive model (and hence also of the corollary doctrines of imperfect and monopolistic competition) takes as its point of departure precisely this feature of the model. That model, he points out deals

> with a state of what is called "competitive equilibrium" in which it is assumed that the data for the different individuals are fully adjusted to each other, while the problem which requires explanation is the nature of the process by which the data are thus adjusted.
>
> (Hayek, 1948, p. 94)

For Hayek, on the other hand, "competition is by its nature a dynamic process whose essential characteristics are assumed away by the assumptions underlying static analysis" (ibid.). "Competition," he insists

> is essentially a process of the formation of opinion . . . a process which involves a continuous change in the data and whose significance must therefore be completely missed by any theory which treats these data as constant.
>
> (ibid., p. 106)

In other words the role of competition in economic theory must, for both Mises and Hayek, focus not on the state of affairs at the end of the market process, but upon the character of that process itself. More recently Hayek has emphasized the nature of competition as a "discovery procedure"—i.e., as generating "such facts as, without resort to it, would not be known to anyone . . ." (Hayek, 1978, p. 179).

For the modern Austrian approach, this perception of competition as the dynamic, driving force for discovery in the market process has become central. The key to an explanation of the equilibrative process is to recognize the pivotal role of dynamic competition in that process. This equilibrative process of competition is at work even in markets in which one firm may enjoy monopolistic privilege. This is because even a monopolistic equilibrium can be approached, in a world of uncertainty, only through a process whereby market participants can become better aware of one another's attitudes and plans. Only the process of competition can achieve this.[16]

We have thus placed our finger on the key interrelated analytical concepts with which the modern Austrian entrepreneurial discovery theory of the market process operates. These concepts are: (a) the entrepreneurial role; (b) the role of discovery; (c) rivalrous competition. Each of these requires some brief discussion.

(a) The *entrepreneurial role*: In standard neoclassical equilibrium theory there is, by its very character, no role for the entrepreneur. In equilibrium there is no scope for pure profit: there is simply nothing for the entrepreneur to do. (If textbooks do speak of the entrepreneur in the theory of the firm this turns out to refer simply and imprecisely to the owner of the firm who, operating in equilibrium markets, is indeed able to "maximize," but who has no opportunity to sell output at a price exceeding costs.)[17] If the entrepreneur grasps the opportunities for pure entrepreneurial profit created by temporary absence of full adjustment between input and output markets, the neoclassical market in full equilibrium can, of course, find no room for him. In Austrian theory the entrepreneur is an agent whose character has been carefully explored.

For Mises the term "entrepreneur" refers to "acting man in regard to the changes occurring in the data of the market" (Mises, 1949, p. 255). Entrepreneurship is human action "seen from the aspect of the uncertainty inherent in every action" (Mises, 1949, p. 254). The Misesian concept of human action thus implies the open-ended framework within which all decisions made must necessarily partake of the speculative character essential to the notion of entrepreneurship. "In any real and living economy every actor is always an entrepreneur" (Mises, 1949, p. 253). By freeing microeconomic analysis from the constrictions of the equilibrium state, Austrian theory is able to recognize the speculative element in all individual decision making, and to incorporate the activity of the real world business man into a theoretical framework that provides understanding of the market process. In focusing upon the entrepreneurial decision in a Knight-uncertain world, Austrian theory thus diverges sharply from the notion of the individual decision that constitutes the analytical building block of neoclassical microtheory. For neoclassical microtheory each decision, whether made by consumer, firm, or resource owner, is made within a definitely known framework made up of a given objective function, a given set of resource constraints, and a given set of technologically or economically feasible ways of transforming resources into desired objectives. (Uncertainty, while of course recognized as surrounding each decision, expresses itself in the form of known probability distributions relating to the given elements of this known framework.) In this neoclassical context, there is no room for entrepreneurship not only in the sense (mentioned earlier) that no opportunities for pure profit can possibly exist, but also in the sense that the model precludes all Knightian uncertainty that might affect the character of the individual decision. Boldness, imagination, drive are characteristics which are simply irrelevant to individual decision making in neoclassical microtheory.

This Austrian emphasis on the entrepreneur is fundamental.[18] Whereas each neoclassical decision maker operates in a world of *given* price and output data, the Austrian entrepreneur operates to *change* price/output data. In this way, as we shall see, the entrepreneurial role drives the ever-changing process of the market. Where shortages have existed, we understand the resulting price increases as driven by entrepreneurs recognizing, in the face of the uncertainty of the real world, the profit opportunities available through the expansion of supply through production, or through arbitrage. Except in the never-attained state of complete equilibrium, each market is characterized by opportunities for pure entrepreneurial profit. These opportunities are created by earlier entrepreneurial errors which have resulted in shortages, surplus, misallocated resources. The daring, alert entrepreneur discovers these earlier errors, buys where prices are "too low" and sells where prices are "too high." In this way low prices are nudged higher, high prices are nudged lower; price discrepancies are narrowed in the equilibrative direction. Shortages are filled, surpluses are whittled away; quantity gaps tend to be eliminated in the equilibrative direction. In a world of ceaselessly changing tastes, resource availabilities, and known technological possibilities, this entrepreneurial process cannot guarantee rapid (or slow) convergence to a state of equilibrium. But it does at each moment guarantee profit-incentives tending to nudge the market in what, from the perspective of that moment, must be recognized as the equilibrative direction.

The critical question for an entrepreneurial theory of market process, is how to understand, in the existence of such profit-incentives, the existence also of a systematic tendency for entrepreneurial errors to be replaced by profit-making entrepreneurial corrections. For this aspect of the entrepreneurial discovery theory we must postulate a tendency for the profit opportunities generated by earlier entrepreneurial error, to be noticed and grasped. The Austrian approach indeed includes such a postulate. To appreciate this we turn to the second of the above listed three key analytical elements in this approach.

(b) *The role of discovery*: We have already seen that Hayek pioneered in interpreting the equilibrative market process as a process of mutual discovery. In the course of this process market participants become better informed of the plans being made by other participants. Whereas some initial plans must, as a result of initial entrepreneurial error, turn out to have been mistaken, these errors tend systematically to become eliminated as market experience reveals the infeasibility of some (hitherto sought after) courses of action and the (hitherto unnoticed) profitability of other courses of action. In the world of static equilibrium, a chosen course of action, because it was pronounced mathematically to have been the optimal course of action within the given decision framework, cannot fail to be chosen again and again, so long as that given framework prevails. In the market-process world of entrepreneurial discovery, on the other hand, flawed plans (i.e., those made on the basis of an erroneously imagined decision framework) can be expected to tend to be corrected through the responsiveness of alert, imaginative entrepreneurs to the opportunities revealed as a result of the initially flawed plans. In other words, this approach postulates a tendency for profit opportunities to be discovered and grasped by routine-resisting entrepreneurial market participants.

In the neoclassical context a decision can never be corrected—because no decision can ever be truly mistaken. The reason for a change in a decision, thus can be found only in an exogenously generated change in the relevant decision-framework. But in the Austrian context a decision can be corrected as a result of the decision-maker's discovery of an earlier error in his view of the world. Whereas earlier plans had overlooked available profit opportunities (as, for example, where some buyers buy goods at high prices, that were being sold elsewhere in the same market for lower prices), subsequent plans can be expected to reflect discovery of the profit opportunities implicit in (and constituted by) the earlier plans. We should acknowledge that, from the neoclassical perspective, it is not at all obvious why we should expect such discoveries to be made.

After all, it may be objected from the mainstream economist's point of view, if an available opportunity for profit was universally overlooked yesterday, why should we expect that opportunity to be noticed today? It is not as if that profit opportunity was the object of systematic search (in which case it might be expected that a time consuming search process would identify it sooner or later). An opportunity for pure profit cannot, by its nature, be the object of systematic search. Systematic search can be undertaken for a piece of missing information, but only because the searcher is aware of the nature of what he does not know, and is aware with greater or lesser certainty of the way to find out the missing information. In the economics of search literature, therefore, search is correctly treated as any other deliberate process of production. But it is in the nature of an overlooked profit opportunity that it has been utterly overlooked, i.e., that one is not aware at all that one has missed the grasping of any profit. From the neoclassical perspective, therefore, a missed opportunity might seem (except as a result of sheer, fortuitous good luck) to be destined for permanent obscurity.

It is here that the Austrian perspective offers a new insight, into the nature of surprise and discovery. When one becomes aware of what one had previously overlooked, one has not produced knowledge in any deliberate sense. What has occurred is that one has discovered one's previous (utterly unknown) ignorance. What distinguishes discovery (relevant to hitherto unknown profit opportunities) from successful search (relevant to the deliberate production of information which one knew one had lacked) is that the former (unlike the latter) involves that surprise which accompanies the realization that one had overlooked something in fact readily available. ("It was under my very nose!") This feature of discovery characterizes the entrepreneurial process of the equilibrating market. What accounts for a systematic tendency toward that succession of wholesome surprises which must constitute the equilibrative process, is not any implausible series of happy accidents, but rather the natural alertness (Kirzner, 1973, pp. 35ff., 65ff.) to possible opportunities (or the danger of possible disaster) which is characteristic of human beings. In the world of uncertainty such natural alertness expresses itself in the boldness and imagination which Austrian theory ascribes to entrepreneurs in the context of the market. Entrepreneurial alertness refers to an attitude of receptiveness to available (but hitherto overlooked) opportunities. The entrepreneurial character of human action refers not simply to the circumstance that action is taken in an open-ended, uncertain world, but also to the circumstance that the human agent is at all times spontaneously on the lookout for hitherto unnoticed features of the environment (present or future), which might inspire new activity on his part. Without knowing what to look for, without deploying any deliberate search technique, the entrepreneur is at all times scanning the horizon, as it were, ready to make discoveries. Each such discovery will be accompanied by a sense of surprise (at one's earlier unaccountable ignorance). An entrepreneurial attitude is one which is always ready to be surprised, always ready to take the steps needed to profit by such surprises. The notion of discovery, midway between that of the deliberately produced information in standard search theory, and that of sheer windfall gain generated by pure chance, is central to the Austrian approach.[19] The profit opportunities created by earlier entrepreneurial error do tend systematically to stimulate subsequent entrepreneurial discovery. The entrepreneurial process so set into motion, is a process tending toward better mutual awareness among market participants. The lure of pure profit in this way sets up the process through which pure profit tends to be competed away. Enhanced mutual awareness, via the entrepreneurial discovery process, is the source of the market's equilibrative properties.

Austrians are careful to insist (i) that continual change in tastes, resource availabilities, and known technological possibilities always prevent this equilibrative process from proceeding anywhere near to completion; and (ii) that entrepreneurial boldness and imagination can lead to pure entrepreneurial losses as well as to pure profit. Mistaken actions by entrepreneurs mean that they have misread the market, possibly pushing price and output constellations in directions not equilibrative. The entrepreneurial market process may indeed reflect a systematically equilibrative tendency, but this by no means constitutes a guaranteed unidirectional, flawlessly converging trajectory. What the Austrian entrepreneurial discovery process seeks to explain is not any imaginary mechanical sure-fire convergence to equilibrium, but rather the existence and nature of those important tendencies which markets display toward continual discovery and exploitation of pure profit opportunities thus tending to nudge the market in the equilibrative direction. In this process the capacity of market participants to discover earlier error, is central.[20]

(c) *Rivalrous competition*: What drives the market process is entrepreneurial boldness and imagination; what constitutes that process is the series of discoveries generated by that entrepreneurial boldness and alertness. Austrians are at pains to emphasize the dynamically competitive character of such a process. The process is made possible by the freedom of entrepreneurs to enter markets in which they see opportunities for profit. In being alert to such opportunities and in grasping them, entrepreneurs are competing with other entrepreneurs. This competition is not the competitive state achieved in neoclassical equilibrium models, in which all market participants are buying or selling identical commodities, at uniform prices. It is, instead, the rivalrous process we encounter in the everyday business world, in which each entrepreneur seeks to outdo his rivals in offering goods to consumers (recognizing that, because those rivals have not been offering the best possible deals to consumers, profits can be made by offering consumers better deals).[21]

It is from this perspective that Austrians stress (i) the discovery potential in rivalrous competition, and (ii) the entrepreneurial character of rivalrous competition. The competition that characterizes the market process reveals information which no one was aware of its having been lacking. (This, as we shall see in Section IV, will be of importance in assessing the possibility of the deliberate engineering, in a socialist economy, by central planners, of the kinds of outcomes yielded in a capitalist economy by the competitive market process.) This is what Hayek had in mind when he referred to competition "as a discovery procedure" (Hayek, 1978, p. 179). The competitive process is an entrepreneurial one in that it depends crucially on the incentives provided by the possibility of pure entrepreneurial profit. From this perspective profit emerges most importantly not as evidence of entrepreneurial error (which it certainly is), but as the powerful incentive to keep down the incidence of entrepreneurial error.

As noted in Section II, Stiglitz saw Austrians as claiming "informational efficiency" (in the Paretian sense) for this "discovery procedure" of the market. This is not the case. The knowledge gained through the discovery process of the market refers to the "unthought-of knowledge" with which Austrians have been concerned. Ignorance of this unthought-of knowledge is responsible for failure to attain equilibrium. Attainment of equilibrium, imagined as the eventual outcome of an uninterrupted process of market discovery, does not attribute informational efficiency to that state of equilibrium. The informational inefficiency which Stiglitz and his colleagues have attributed to equilibrium states, relates, on the other hand, to "known ignorance," that is, to "known-to-be-available" information which it is costly to produce.[22]

IV

The entrepreneurial discovery approach offers a theoretical framework for understanding how markets work. This framework has important practical implications for applied economics and for economic policy. We briefly take note of four areas of application where the Austrian approach implies sharply different practical conclusions from those usually derived from neoclassical economics. A number of additional areas of application might also have been explored here. Examples of such areas, omitted here because of space constraints are: law and economics (see for example Rizzo, 1979), and the economics of transition (see for example Boettke, 1993). The four areas examined are: (a) antitrust policy; (b) the applicability of accepted theories of economic justice; (c) welfare economics; (d) the workability of central planning under socialism.

(a) *Antitrust policy*: Standard economics, built upon neoclassical insights into the Pareto-efficiency qualities of perfectly competitive equilibrium, has for most of this century been deployed to support antitrust policy limiting firm size (both absolutely and relative to the industry). Despite the healthy dose of realism introduced into antitrust economics in recent decades, and despite the substantive theoretical improvements introduced into our understanding of competition by the theory of contestable markets, it remains the case that standard microeconomics sees the ideal degree of competition as represented by the perfectly competitive model. The Austrian view sees matters quite differently.

For the Austrian approach competition is socially beneficial primarily in a dynamic sense. Coordination tends to be induced among the decisions made in the market place under the pressure of rivalrous entrepreneurs alert to the profit-opportunities created by initial discoordination. To harness the entrepreneurial initiative intrinsic to this kind of dynamic competition, we do not require fulfillment of the classic Knightian conditions for perfect competition—in fact those conditions *preclude* scope for (and, in fact, any need for) entrepreneurial initiative. The perfect knowledge requirement central to the perfectly competitive model can in fact be satisfied only by assuming away the need for any coordinative process. To induce dynamic entrepreneurial competition we require the fulfillment of only one condition: guaranteeing free entrepreneurial entry into any market where profit opportunities may be perceived to exist. Most of the insights of contestable market theory turn out not only to be consistent with the entrepreneurial discovery approach, but in fact to be implied by that approach. To limit the size of firms (for example by obstructing mergers) is, in the entrepreneurial discovery approach, to block entrepreneurial entry, and is thus *anti*-competitive in the relevant sense. Conversely, many aspects of real-world business activity, involving such practices as advertising, or any of innumerable forms of product differentiation, set down as imperfectly competitive or even as "monopolistic" in the standard framework (because they imply less than perfectly elastic demand curves facing firms), are precisely the kinds of entrepreneurial initiative which make up the dynamic competitive process.[23]

(b) *Economic justice*: There are many policy issues which hinge upon public perceptions of economic justice or injustice. In recent decades economists have explored the economic justice of alternative economic policies. In this they have been following a venerable tradition in economics. When John Bates Clark wrote his *Distribution of Wealth* almost a century ago, his motivation, in developing the tools of marginal productivity theory, was to demonstrate the consistency of capitalism with economic justice. One significant implication of the entrepreneurial discovery approach has been that it appears to cast crucial aspects of the capitalist system in a drastically different ethical light, than has traditionally emerged from the neoclassical perspective.

Neoclassical economics asks us to rule on the justice of the method through which or the pattern in which a given (known-to-be-knowable) pie is distributed among the potential claimants to it. This may be seen as a pie of given output; or, in more sophisticated versions, it may be seen as the yet-to-be-determined pie to be baked out of given inputs. This "given-pie" framework for discussion of economic justice restricts us to considering the justice of capitalist earnings or receipts in regard only to already existing goods (including already existing inputs with the capability of generating alternative outputs). From the Austrian perspective, such restriction places blinders upon our ethical assessment of capitalist incomes.

In the Austrian perspective there must be afforded the possibility, at least, of considering the justice also of *discovered* income. A discovered income is one gained not by earning or otherwise receiving a share of any given pie, but one gained by discovering the existence of something valuable, the very existence of which was hitherto wholly unknown. Discovery would include not only one of hitherto unknown natural resources (as in an oil discovery) but also of new kinds of output (as through entrepreneurial product-innovation), or of new additional productivity (of known outputs) available from known inputs (as when an entrepreneur innovates a new productive technique). The earmark of a genuine discovery is that it reveals the existence of something concerning which one had not been merely ignorant, but in fact *utterly* ignorant (in the sense that one was not even aware of one's ignorance). All kinds of discovery essentially create something genuinely new, something simply not present (as far as human knowledge up until now could fathom) in the pie of available inputs and outputs given just prior to the moment of discovery.

The making of a genuine discovery is not an act of deliberate production (in this it differs also from a successful deliberate search). Neither is it simply the fortuitous outcome of a stroke of wholly undeserved luck. Discovery is attributable, at least in significant degree, to the entrepreneurial alertness of the discoverer. A theory of justice built upon a perspective which compels us to refrain from considering and therefore recognizing the moral character of discovered gain must, from the Austrian perspective, appear seriously incomplete if not wholly misconceived.

All this has, of course, particular relevance to judging the justice of pure entrepreneurial profits. Such profits simply do not fit into the neoclassical distributional scheme, and, therefore, defy any justification within standard theories of justice otherwise sympathetic to capitalist distribution patterns.[24] For the Austrian viewpoint, however, pure entrepreneurial profits emerge clearly as the wholly discovered gains, which accompany entrepreneurial creation and discovery in the sphere of production. An understanding of pure profits in this manner permits the economist to explain more accurately (to the philosopher, citizen, or statesman engaged in moral judgments concerning capitalist justice) the true economic character of what they are evaluating.[25]

(c) *Welfare economics*: Neoclassical economics includes an analytical framework designed to assess the social efficiency of alternative arrangements, policies, and events. The Austrian approach to understanding markets outlined in this chapter, implies a certain dissatisfaction also with the neoclassical approach to welfare economics. The cause for this dissatisfaction can be identified in straightforward fashion.

Standard welfare theory considers the allocation pattern governing the uses made of society's resources at a given instant (or, by strict extension, to a given intertemporal allocation pattern being irrevocably adopted at that instant). The theory then analyzes that pattern from a perspective of imagined omniscience, against the socially optimal allocative pattern implied by the data. Austrian economists along with many other economists are of course deeply concerned by the well-understood analytical difficulties (especially for methodological individualists) of defining what "socially optimal allocation" is to mean, within the neoclassical framework.[26] But the Austrian dissatisfaction of interest to us in the present context has a different root. The entrepreneurial discovery approach reminds us that the degree of achieved social efficiency (or even the degree of efficiency that will be achieved in the equilibrium state toward which a market may be converging) is not the only dimension along which to judge the economic success of a social system. Just as important, surely, is the speed and accuracy with which the system is able to identify and overcome the waste and discoordination of disequilibrium situations. Standard welfare theory provides no scope for considering this dimension, because this discoordination involves that sheer ignorance which cannot be incorporated into neoclassical analysis (so that intertemporal welfare analysis cannot grapple with, or even consider, the question of how rapidly—or whether—the volume of sheer ignorance is being reduced).

Up to now, it must be acknowledged, Austrian economics has—with one important exception to be noted below—not done much more than to identify this serious shortcoming of standard welfare economics. But this identification (and its being related to the social function of the entrepreneurial discovery process) must be considered already a significant step forward.[27] As a result of this step, Austrian economists are not satisfied to ask, in regard to issues such as tax policy and the like, merely what impact will a given program have upon the allocative efficiency of the system (as an exercise, say, in applied comparative statics). They also ask what impact it will have in regard to the stimulation of those acts of entrepreneurial discovery upon which the equilibrative process must depend. The one area in which Austrian economics has not merely raised new questions but has in fact fruitfully pursued the entrepreneurial discovery approach to its full welfare-economic implications, is in the modern version of its long-standing Misesian critique of central planning. To this we now turn.

(d) *Central planning under socialism*: In a famous 1920 article Mises asserted on theoretical grounds, the "impossibility" of rational economic calculation under socialism and hence the impossibility of central planning. In a series of essays during the 1930s, Hayek supported Mises' contention and responded to several attempted solutions by socialist economists to refute that contention. Out of all these attempted solutions, the "decentralized" solution of Oskar Lange and Abba P. Lerner became the most famous. For decades the mainstream literature on comparative systems routinely cited these solutions by Lange and Lerner as having definitively laid to rest the critiques of the possibility of socialist calculation argued by Mises and Hayek.

During the past 15 years, largely as a result of the resurgence of interest in the Austrian tradition, a different assessment of the inter-war calculation debate has emerged.[28] Especially as an implication (or application) of the entrepreneurial discovery approach to understanding the market process, it has come to be recognized that Lange and Lerner had not, in fact, refuted the theoretical challenge leveled by Mises and Hayek. The history of the economic calculation debate is not our concern here. What is important is that a modern Austrian understanding of the market process is able to show the limitations of the Lange-Lerner solution. In seeking to simulate, through decentralized socialist production, the conditions satisfied in a perfectly competitive equilibrium market system, that solution in fact misses the difficulties which Mises had seen for the possibility of socialist planning.

The Lange-Lerner solution requires the central planning authority to announce non-market prices for resources and commodities. Working with these prices as "parameters" (see Lange, 1938, p. 70)—as if they corresponded to the prices under perfectly competitive equilibrium—decentralized socialist managers would then plan their resource "purchases" (from state suppliers), their output production and input mix, in a manner designed to equalize marginal cost and marginal revenue (as if maximizing firm "profit" under perfectly competitive conditions). The extent to which the announced prices in fact diverged from the "correct" values would be revealed in the surpluses and shortages generated for the various resources, thus permitting the central authority to adjust prices accordingly in the directions necessary to achieve resource market clearing. The entire scheme is based, explicitly, on the view that the capitalist market economy operates in this way; that resource and output prices are given to entrepreneurs, and that firms then use these prices parametrically to maximize the excess of revenue over cost. The Austrian entrepreneurial discovery approach sees the market economy quite differently, and therefore sees the problem facing the socialist central planning authority quite differently.

The economic problem facing any society, in this view, is primarily that of how, in a world of incessant changes in tastes, resource availabilities, and technological possibilities, to generate mutually sustaining expectations on the part of agents in the economy, such that (a) the series of actions taken are in fact able to be completed as planned, and (b) that that series of actions tends to reveal and exhaust all the available opportunities for social economic gain. Under the imagined conditions of perfectly competitive equilibrium this problem does not exist, not because it has already been successfully solved, but because the equilibrium state has been constructed to avoid the problem in the first place. Whether under socialism or under capitalism, reference to the equilibrium state offers no clues as to how to solve the problem; it offers only a picture of a world in which the problem has never existed.

From this perspective the Austrians understand that whatever social efficiency may be achieved in the market economy is not achieved at all by its participants behaving as if they were agents in a perfectly competitive equilibrium state—but precisely by their behaving entrepreneurially and (dynamically) competitively, under conditions of disequilibrium. The Lange-Lerner solution, in which the socialist managers are instructed to act as perfectly competitive agents, and in which resulting resource surpluses and shortages lead the central authority to adjust resource prices, is simply *not* a simulation of how markets actually operate under capitalism. This solution has *not* successfully incorporated the techniques to which any capitalist successes may be attributed. Central adjustment of non-market prices in response to resource surpluses and shortages (generated by socialist managers having mistakenly behaved as if the originally announced prices were in fact "correct") corresponds to nothing that occurs in capitalist markets (despite its similarity to certain highly dubious textbook stories of how perfectly competitive market clearing prices are arrived at). The Lange-Lerner solution offers no scope whatsoever for anything in socialism that might correspond to the pure profit motivated entrepreneurial acts of discovery which drive the capitalist market process.[29]

V

It remains to relate the entrepreneurial discovery approach outlined in this paper to alternative viewpoints within the universe of modern Austrian economists. The entrepreneurial discovery approach embraces elements, especially elements in its criticisms of neoclassical microeconomics, with which all Austrian economists broadly agree. But the specific framework of the entrepreneurial discovery approach—seeing the market process as consisting of systematic equilibrating tendencies, made up of episodes of mutual discovery and learning (by market participants)—has been rejected by a number of modern Austrian economists. These economists emphasize, more than does the entrepreneurial discovery approach, the radical uncertainty of the future, with which market participants must contend. We may distinguish two groups of Austrians who have, as result of such emphasis, dissented from the entrepreneurial discovery approach: (a) those who object radically to the asserted equilibrative character of the market process, and (b) those who object to the emphasis of the entrepreneurial discovery approach upon systematic mutual learning as the key feature in the market process (as well as to what they believe to be the implication of the entrepreneurial discovery approach, that the market in fact successfully attains *approximate* equilibrium).

(a) Those who object to the asserted equilibrative character of the market process (as explained in the entrepreneurial discovery approach), have been led by one of the leading figures in the modern Austrian revival, Ludwig Lachmann. A significant number of younger "Austrian" economists have followed Lachmann in this regard, and their debates with exponents of the entrepreneurial discovery approach have enlivened and enriched Austrian economics during the past decade. A careful exposition and analysis of these critics of the entrepreneurial discovery theory is beyond the scope of this chapterer. The following thumbnail sketch of the Lachmann position undoubtedly fails to do justice to the subtleties of that position, and is offered here only to identify, at least, a stream of Austrian dissatisfaction with the entrepreneurial discovery approach. Lachmann (1986, 1991) saw the market process as one not only in ceaseless motion (on which the entrepreneurial discovery theorists would be in thorough agreement) but in a ceaseless motion in which at no time is there any assurance that the equilibrative forces are stronger than the disequilibrative forces (set in motion by changes in the independent variables of the system)—so that one may not presume to say that the market process even tends to promote mutual discovery among market participants. Following on the later work of George Shackle (Lachmann, 1976) this group of Austrians has questioned the very meaningfulness of any equilibrium concept at all. They have deplored an approach (the entrepreneurial discovery approach) which appears to them simply as an attempt to rescue what they believe to be an unsalvageable way of understanding markets, viz. within the neoclassical paradigm. In a world of incessant change, they argue, it is precisely those acts of entrepreneurial boldness which must frustrate any discovery efforts made by fellow entrepreneurs. The entrepreneurial character of the market process (which is not disputed) must virtually guarantee, indeed, that that process must fail to be characterized as a systematic procedure of mutual discovery.[30]

Some followers of Lachmann, as well as others, have questioned, not so much the meaningfulness of the equilibrium concept itself (or of the notion of an equilibrating tendency), as the idea that we can, even in principle, identify an equilibrium position. In an open-ended world there is, these critics argue, no equilibrium position "out there" that can serve as a reference point for discussion of the presence or absence of "equilibrating tendencies" (see for example, Buchanan and Vanberg, 1991).

(b) Those who object to the systematic learning character of the market process (as claimed by the entrepreneurial discovery approach) have been led by Murray Rothbard (1994; a foremost late twentieth century exponent of Austrian economics) and by Joseph Salerno (1993, 1994). Although their position is a relatively new one and has not yet generated sustained debate within the Austrian camp, it has already elicited a good deal of attention, and seems likely to stir up vigorous discussion in the immediate future. Rothbard and Salerno's understanding of the market process sees it not as a continual process of knowledge acquisition, but as a continual process of entrepreneurial decision making which, at each moment, encourages the most perceptive entrepreneurs to make their best judgments in a world of incessant change, through the use of monetary calculation of estimated profits and losses. The degree to which the market achieves coordination is attributed, in the Rothbard-Salerno view, not to any systematic process of knowledge enhancement (through entrepreneurial alertness or anything else), but to the ability of shrewd entrepreneurs, using money prices as tools for calculation, to deploy resources at each moment, in what they believe to be their most urgently demanded uses—as judged ultimately by the consumers. At each moment, it is then claimed, the market has generated that "constellation of resource prices" which always reflects the circumstance that existing resources are devoted to their most valuable uses (Salerno, 1993, p. 124). Rothbard and Salerno do not deny that the entrepreneurial approach accurately captures the insights pioneered by Hayek in his papers on knowledge (Hayek, 1937, 1945, 1948). Their position is simply that this approach differs sharply from a distinctly Misesian paradigm, a paradigm which they endorse.

One important implication of this position is the assertion that, because of the incessant changes in the external data of the market, it leads to the denial of any actual progression in historical time toward long-run equilibrium (Salerno, 1993, p. 122). This assertion claims, it appears, not merely that exogenous changes prevent the equilibrating process in any given period of time, from going very far (a claim which, it is recognized, the entrepreneurial discovery approach would certainly endorse), but also that unless one "invokes the ideas of quiescent calendar periods which separate successive exogenous shocks" (an invocation attributed by Salerno to the entrepreneurial discovery approach; Salerno, 1993, p. 129), exogenous changes are continually frustrating any tendencies toward eventual equilibration.

The brief remarks in this section concerning debates within the "Austrian camp" should help dispel any illusion (possibly created by this chapter) that the entrepreneurial discovery approach is seen as a cut-and-dried, completed body of Austrian doctrine. Most "Austrians" see this approach as an important but still debated development in work still in progress. They see it as inviting further exploration and application to such areas as: law and economics (see, for example, Rizzo, 1979), the interface between Austrian and mainstream neoclassical paradigms, and the evaluation of mainstream neoclassical attempts to confront the kinds of concerns which have motivated Austrian economics. The theory of entrepreneurial discovery is thus seen as embodying a set of ideas able to inspire several new research programs, rather than as constituting any kind of definitive orthodoxy.

VI

These concluding observations take up briefly the question of whether there exists any necessary relationship between an Austrian approach (such as the entrepreneurial discovery perspective discussed here) and support for a policy of uncompromising laissez faire. A complete and careful discussion of this relationship is beyond the scope of this chapter (and, if it were to be successful in expounding the relevant nuances, would require far more space than is here available). Nonetheless it seems useful to offer the following outline for such a discussion. This will (a) respond to frequently expressed (and fully justified) curiosity concerning this relationship, and

(b) perhaps provide necessary further clarification of the Austrian position presented in this chapter.

It is true that, in their policy judgments, economists in the Austrian tradition have tended overwhelmingly to favor market solutions for solving society's economic problems. Certainly, this tendency is largely rooted in a shared and appreciative understanding of the coordinative properties of the entrepreneurial market process. There are, indeed, Austrian grounds for arguing that government regulation of market activity is likely to obstruct and frustrate the spontaneous, corrective forces of entrepreneurial adjustments. Yet to conclude that Austrian economics by itself rigorously entails adoption of unbridled laissez faire as the scientifically endorsed economic policy for nations, is a far too oversimplified—and inaccurate—conclusion.

Let us not forget that traditionally the economic case for laissez faire depended, for whatever its worth, on the claim that spontaneously achieved outcomes are, in a relevant sense, efficient (and can therefore only be worsened, not improved, by regulatory interference). Austrian economics cannot, strictly speaking, possibly offer a case for laissez faire based on this claim. After all, Austrian economics makes no claim that the market outcomes at any given date are efficient and socially optimal (in any sense in which traditional neoclassical welfare theory would use these terms). It is therefore certainly a misreading of the Austrian theory to construe it as claiming that the entrepreneurial discovery process ensures an unerring trajectory toward the attainment of that complete mutual awareness which is necessary for any notion of social optimization. What the Austrian theory argues is the far more nuanced thesis that the unbridled market tends to offer the incentives likely to stimulate movement in the direction of complete mutual awareness. To the extent that a case for laissez faire must rest on the claim that the market attains complete mutual awareness, Austrian economics provides no basis for such a case.

In addition it should be emphasized that, although the entrepreneurial discovery approach throws significant light on the incentives which stimulate movements in the direction of full mutual awareness, this does not amount to the assertion that all movements must be in that direction. Still less is it the case that entrepreneurial discovery is claimed successfully to attain full mutual awareness. As was noted in Section III entrepreneurial decisions may be entirely mistaken; they may in fact be more mistaken than those other entrepreneurial judgments they are replacing. So that, instead of correcting the earlier misallocations of resources, the entering entrepreneurs may be making matters even worse. And such errors may generate still more errors. Moreover, even if one imagined that, in a world of stable resource availabilities and consumer preferences, entrepreneurial judgments tend to avoid new errors, the possibility of volatile changes in resource supply and consumer demand conditions must inevitably prevent the entrepreneurial discovery process from proceeding very far toward complete mutual awareness by market participants.

If the Austrian theory claims that entrepreneurial discovery can account for a tendency toward equilibrium, that vague-sounding term "tendency toward" is used deliberately, advisedly, and quite precisely. Such a tendency does exist at each and every moment, in the sense that earlier entrepreneurial errors have created profit opportunities which provide the incentives for entrepreneurial corrective decisions to be made. These incentives offer rewards to those who can better anticipate precisely those changes in supply and demand conditions which we have seen to be so disconcertingly possible. What our understanding of the entrepreneurial discovery process provides, is not conviction that an unerringly equilibrative process is at all times in progress, but rather appreciation for the economic forces which continually encourage such equilibrative movement.

Such Austrian appreciation for the market forces encouraging the equilibrative tendency certainly does offer support for laissez faire. It is no accident that Austrian economists have tended to see economics as showing the unwisdom of government regulation. For, although entrepreneurs can, as noted above, make errors, *there is no* ***tendency*** *for entrepreneurial errors to be made*. The tendency which the market generates toward greater mutual awareness, is not offset by any equal but opposite tendency in the direction of diminishing awareness. Understanding how government regulation of entrepreneurial activity is likely to frustrate the coordinative tendency toward error-correction, is often believed sufficient to permit the Austrian economist roundly to condemn such interventions.[31]

NOTES

The author is deeply grateful to Mario Rizzo, Peter Boettke, and Yaw Nyarko, for extensive and helpful comments on an earlier draft. Further helpful comments were provided by Joseph T. Salerno, and by other members, of the Austrian Economics Colloquium at New York University. Several anonymous referees provided many additional valuable suggestions. The author is grateful to the Sarah Scaife Foundation for research support.

1. The emphasis here on microeconomics expresses the focus of the present chapter, not the scope of modern Austrian economics. For important modern Austrian contributions to macroeconomic and to monetary theory, see Garrison (1978, 1984), White (1984), Selgin (1988), Selgin and White (1994), Horwitz (1992). See also Snowdon, Vane, and Wynarczyk (1994, ch. 8). For a link between Friedrich Hayek's macroeconomics and the Austrian microeconomics set forth in this chapter, see Schmidtchen and Utzig (1989).
2. For an authoritative, encyclopedia-style set of surveys of modern Austrian economics, see Boettke (1994).
3. For discussions of Austrian subjectivism (and also on its influence on other schools of economic thought) see Coats (1983), Wiseman (1983, 1985), O'Driscoll and Rizzo (1985, ch. 2), Buchanan (1982), Lachmann (1982).
4. For general surveys of the history of the Austrian tradition, see Hayek (1968), Vaughn (1994), Kirzner (1992). For collections of papers representing the work of the Austrian School from 1870 to the present see Littlechild (1990), Kirzner (1994).
5. Among the principal relevant works are Mises (1949), Hayek (1941, 1948, 1978).
6. For the thesis that these developments in the work of Mises and Hayek stemmed from their participation in the interwar debate on the possibility of socialist economic calculation, see Kirzner (1992, ch. 6).
7. For a critique of the use by Austrian economists (such as Mises and Murray Rothbard) of a concept (the "evenly rotating economy") which parallels that of the equilibrium state, see Cowen and Fink (1985).
8. It has been strongly argued by Machovec (1995) that the great neoclassical economists of the period before 1930 did *not* proceed in this manner.
9. Frank Knight developed his classic distinction between risk and uncertainty in Knight (1921).
10. See for example, Pasour (1982) and Moldofsky (1982); see also Shackle (1972); Buchanan (1979).
11. For examples of Austrian literature critical of the standard equilibrium approach see Rizzo (1979), Ikeda (1990). For a mainstream reaction to this literature see Phelan (1987). See also Loasby (1994), Harper (1994a).
12. This confidence has, in recent literature, been challenged also on the grounds of possible path-dependency. See for example Arthur (1989), Cowan (1990).
13. For literature on the role of process theory in economics, see particularly High (1990), Lachmann (1986), Ikeda (1990, 1994), Kerber (1994). For a pioneering contribution see Richardson (1960).
14. For excellent modern Austrian expositions of the approach developed in this section see Vihanto (1989, 1994). For discussions which are at least partly critical of the Austrian approach see Loasby (1989, ch. 10) and Loy (1988).
15. See Stigler (1957) for the emergence of the view that explicitly rejects rivalrousness as an ingredient in competitive analysis.
16. It follows that monopolistic (or monopolistically competitive) equilibrium states, are entirely compatible with the notion of dynamic competition (which might in fact bring about such states).

17. The statement in the text presumes that rents earned by firms who own scarce, non-reproducible resources used in their production operations, are (although included in accounting "profit") properly to be included in the firms' economic costs. These firms certainly enjoy an advantage over other firms who, not owning these resources, must produce with resources of lower productivity. But this advantage consists, for the economist (as distinct from the accountant), not in entrepreneurial profit won by the fortunate firms, but rather in rental income earned through asset ownership. The entrepreneur is considered as hiring these resources from himself as owner, and should then include this rental income as part of his (implicit) economic costs. For a full and classic discussion of the sense in which differential rent on assets owned are properly included in the firm's economic costs, see Fritz Machlup (1952, pp. 237ff., 288ff.).
18. For an example of Austrian work in an applied field in which this emphasis on entrepreneurship is central, see Baird (1987). For general discussion of this Austrian emphasis, see also Runde (1988). A work which (while on the whole sharply critical of the Austrian approach) provides a very insightful exposition of it, is Ioannides (1992, especially chs. 3, 4, 5). Other valuable recent critical discussions of Austrian entrepreneurial theory include Ricketts (1993), Vaughn (1994, pp. 141ff.), Harper (1994b).
19. For further discussion of the Austrian concept of discovery see Kirzner (1989, ch. 2). See also Littlechild (1982a), Beesley and Littlechild (1989), Streit (1992).
20. For clarification of possible misunderstandings concerning this claim for equilibrative tendencies in markets, see Section VI below.
21. For the existence of a long tradition in economics in which rivalrous competition was recognized, see McNulty (1967), Ekelund and Hébert (1981). For modern Austrian (or Austrian-influenced) discussions of dynamic competition see Boudreaux (1994), Armentano (1978), Addleson (1994), Arthur (1994), Kunz (1989).
22. The paragraph in the text has the objective of making clear the distinction between the quite separate aspects of imperfect information treated respectively by Stiglitz and by the Austrians. It does not have the objective of providing an Austrian critique of Stiglitz's position. For such a critique see Thomsen (1992, ch. 3). See also Boehm (1989, pp. 208ff.), and Thomsen (1994).
23. For an excellent example of non-Austrian appreciation for these considerations, see Fisher, McGowan, and Greenwood (1983), Brozen (1982). Among Austrian (or Austrian-inspired) writers on this issue see Armentano (1986), Beesley and Littlechild (1989), DiLorenzo and High (1988), DeBow (1991).
24. See for example Clark (1899, p. 201). For a discussion of Robert Nozick's (1974) theory of justice in regard to profit, see Kirzner (1989, p. 69ff.).
25. These observations on an Austrian view of economic justice have been advanced by the present writer (Kirzner, 1989). They do not substantially overlap with the observations concerning justice expressed either by Mises or by Hayek.
26. For Austrian critiques of standard notions of social efficiency, see Rizzo (1979), Rothbard (1979).

27. Roy Cordato (1992) has done valuable work exploring this avenue for Austrian normative economics. For a critique of Cordato's work see Prychitko (1993). See also Vihanto (1989, pp. 86ff.), Hamlin (1992), Sugden (1992) and White (1992, pp. 263ff.).
28. Major contributions to this literature have been Lavoie (1985), Vaughn (1980), Boettke (1993, ch. 3), see also Keizer (1989) and de Soto (1992).
29. For a valuable non-Austrian paper independently recognizing much of what is here argued in the text, see Makowski and Ostroy (1993).
30. Among those who have been deeply influenced by Lachmann's position, see Torr (1981), O'Driscoll and Rizzo (1985), Lavoie (1994), Wiseman (1989), Loasby (1992). See also Lewin (1994). For critical reaction to Lachmann's position, see O'Driscoll (1978), Garrison (1987).
31. For an example of such a belief, see Kirzner (1985).

REFERENCES

Addleson, Mark (1994) "Competition," in Peter J. Boettke (ed.) (1994), pp. 96–102.

Arrow, Kenneth J. (1959) "Toward a Theory of Price Adjustment," in Moses Abramowitz *et al.* (eds) *The Allocation of Economic Resources*, Stanford, CA: Stanford University Press, pp. 41–51.

Armentano, Dominick T. (1978) "A Critique of Neoclassical and Austrian Monopoly Theory," in Louis M. Spadaro (ed.) (1978), pp. 94–110.

—— (1986) *Antitrust Policy: The Case for Repeal*, Washington, DC: Cato Institute.

Arthur, Thomas C. (1994) "The Costly Quest for Perfect Competition: Kodak and Nonstructural Market Power," *New York University Law Review* 69(1), pp. 1–76.

Arthur, W. Brian (1989) "Competing Technologies, Increasing Returns, and Lock-In by Historical Events," *Economic Journal* 99(394), pp. 116–31.

Baird, Charles W. (1987) "Labor Law and Labor-Management Cooperation: Two Incompatible Views," *Cato Journal* 6(3), pp. 933–50.

Baumol, William J. (1993) *Entrepreneurship, Management, and the Structure of Payoffs*, Cambridge, MA and London: MIT Press.

Beesley, Michael E. and Littlechild, Stephen C. (1989) "The Regulation of Privatized Monopolies in the United Kingdom," *Rand Journal of Economics* 20(3), pp. 454–72.

Boehm, Stephan (1989) "Hayek on Knowledge, Equilibrium and Prices," *Wirtschaftspolitische Blatter* 36(2), pp. 201–13.

Boettke, Peter J. (1993) *Why Perestroika Failed*, London and New York: Routledge.

—— (ed.) (1994) *The Elgar Companion to Austrian Economics*, Aldershot: Edward Elgar.

Boettke, Peter J. and Rizzo, Mario J. (eds) (1994) *Advances in Austrian Economics*, Vol. I, Greenwich, CT and London: JAI Press.

Boudreaux, Don (1994) "Schumpeter and Kirzner on Competition and Equilibrium," in Peter J. Boettke and David L. Prychitko (eds) *The Market*

Process: Essays in Contemporary Austrian Economics, Aldershot: Edward Elgar, pp. 52–6.

Brozen, Yale (1982) *Concentration, Mergers, and Public Policy*, New York and London: Macmillan.

Buchanan, James M. (1979) "Natural and Artifactual Man," in *What Should Economists Do?*, Indianapolis: Liberty Press, pp. 93–112.

—— (1982) "The Domain of Subjective Economics: Between Predictive Science and Moral Philosophy," in Israel M. Kirzner (ed.) *Method, Process, and Austrian Economics: Essays in Honor of Ludwig Von Mises*, Lexington, MA and Toronto: Heath, Lexington Books, pp. 7–20.

Buchanan, James M. and Vanberg, Viktor J. (1991) "The Market as a Creative Process," *Economic Philosophy* 7(2), pp. 167–86.

Caldwell, Bruce J. and Boehm, Stephan (1992) *Austrian Economics: Tensions and New Directions*, Boston: Kluwer.

Clark, John Bates (1899) *The Distribution of Wealth*, New York and London: Macmillan.

Coats, Alfred W. (1983) "The Revival of Subjectivism in Economics," in Jack Wiseman (ed.) *Beyond Positive Economics*, London: Macmillan, pp. 87–103.

Cordato, Roy E. (1992) *Welfare Economics and Externalities in an Open-ended Universe: A Modern Austrian Perspective*, Boston/Dordrecht/London: Kluwer.

Cowan, Robin (1990) "Nuclear Power Reactors: A Study in Technological Lock In," *Journal of Economic History* 50(3), pp. 541–67.

Cowen, Tyler and Fink, Richard (1985) "Inconsistent Equilibrium Constructs: The Evenly Rotating Economy of Mises and Rothbard," *American Economic Review* 75(4), pp. 866–9.

Debow, Michael E. (1991) "Markets, Government Intervention, and the Role of Information: An 'Austrian School' Perspective, with an Application to Merger Regulation," *George Mason University Law Review* 14(1), pp. 31–98.

DiLorenzo, Thomas J. and High, Jack C. (1988) "Antitrust and Competition, Historically Considered," *Economic Inquiry* 26(3), pp. 423–35.

Ekelund, Robert B., Jr and Hébert, Robert F. (1981) "The Proto-History of Franchise Bidding," *Southern Economic Journal* 48(2), pp. 464–74.

Fisher, Franklin (1983) *Disequilibrium Foundations of Equilibrium Economics*, Cambridge: Cambridge University Press.

Fisher, Franklin M., McGowan, John J. and Greenwood, Joen E. (1983) *Folded, Spindled and Mutilated: Economic Analysis and U.S. v. IBM*, Cambridge, MA: MIT Press.

Garrison, Roger W. (1978) "Austrian Macroeconomics: A Diagrammatical Exposition," in Louis M. Spadaro (ed.) (1978), pp. 167–204.

—— (1984) "Time and Money: The Universals of Macroeconomic Theorizing," *Journal of Macroeconomics* 6(2), pp. 197–213.

—— (1987) "The Kaleidic World of Ludwig Lachmann," *Critical Review* 1(3), pp. 77–89.

Hamlin, Alan P. (1992) "On the Possibility of Austrian Welfare Economics," in Bruce J. Caldwell and Stephan Boehm (eds) (1992), pp. 193–206.

Harper, David (1994a) "A New Approach to Modeling Endogenous Learning Processes in Economic Theory," in Peter J. Boettke and Mario J. Rizzo (eds) (1994), pp. 49–79.

—— (1994b) *Wellsprings of Enterprise: An Analysis of Entrepreneurship and Public Policy in New Zealand*, Wellington: NZ Institute of Economic Research.

Hayek, Friedrich A. von (1937) "Economics and Knowledge," *Economica*, N.S., Feb., 4, pp. 33–54.

—— (1941) *The Pure Theory of Capital*, Chicago: University of Chicago Press.

—— (1945) "The Use of Knowledge in Society," *American Economic Review* 35(4), pp. 519–30; reprinted in *Individualism and Economic Order* by Friedrich A. Hayek (1948) London: Routledge and Kegan Paul.

—— (1948) *Individualism and Economic Order*, London: Routledge and Kegan Paul.

—— (1968) "Economic Thought VI: The Austrian School," in David L. Sills (ed.) *International Encyclopedia of the Social Sciences*, Vol. 4, New York: Macmillan, pp. 458–62.

—— (1978) "Competition as a Discovery Procedure," in *New Studies in Philosophy, Politics, Economics and the History of Ideas*, Chicago: University of Chicago Press, pp. 179–90.

High, Jack (1990) *Maximizing, Action, and Market Adjustment: An Inquiry into the Theory of Economic Disequilibrium*, Munich: Philosophia.

Horwitz, Steven (1992) *Monetary Evolution, Free Banking, and Economic Order*, Boulder, CO: Westview Press.

Ikeda, Sanford (1990) "Market-Process Theory and 'Dynamic' Theories of the Market," *Southern Economic Journal* 57(1), pp. 75–92.

—— (1994) "Market-Process," in Peter J. Boettke, (ed.) (1994), pp. 23–9.

Ioannides, Stavros (1992) *The Market, Competition, and Democracy: A Critique of Neo-Austrian Economics*, Aldershot: Edward Elgar.

Keizer, Willem (1989) "Recent Reinterpretations of the Socialist Calculation Debate," in J.J. Krabbe, A. Nentjes, and H. Visser (eds) *Austrian Economics: Roots and Ramifications Reconsidered*, Part 2, Bradford: MCB University Press, pp. 63–83.

Kerber, Wolfgang (1994) "German Market Process Theory," in Peter J. Boettke (ed.) (1994), pp. 500–7.

Kirzner, Israel M. (1973) *Competition and Entrepreneurship*, Chicago: University of Chicago Press.

—— (1985) "The Perils of Regulation: A Market-Process Approach," in *Discovery and the Capitalist Process*, Chicago: University of Chicago Press, pp. 119–49.

—— (1989) *Discovery, Capitalism, and Distributive Justice*, Oxford: Basil Blackwell.

—— (1992) *The Meaning of Market Process: Essays in the Development of Modern Austrian Economics*, London and New York: Routledge.

—— (ed.) (1994) *Classics in Austrian Economics: A Sampling in the History of a Tradition*, London: William Pickering.

Knight, Frank H. (1921) *Risk, Uncertainty and Profit*, Boston: Houghton Mifflin Co.

Kunz, Harald (1989) "Der Wettbewerb Als Entdeckungsverfahren," *Wirtschaftspolitische Blatter* 36(2), pp. 214–19.

Lachmann, Ludwig M. (1976) "From Mises to Shackle: An Essay on Austrian Economics and the Kaleidic Society," *Journal of Economic Literature* 14(1), pp. 54–62.

—— (1982) "Ludwig von Mises and the Extension of Subjectivism," in Israel M. Kirzner (ed.) *Method, Process, and Austrian Economics: Essays in Honor of Ludwig von Mises*, Lexington, MA and Toronto: D.C. Heath, pp. 31–40.

—— (1986) *The Market as an Economic Process*, Oxford: Basil Blackwell.

—— (1991) "Austrian Economics as a Hermeneutic Approach," in Don Lavoie (ed.) *Economics and Hermeneutics*, London: Routledge, pp. 134–46.

Lange, Oskar (1938) "On the Theory of Socialism," in Benjamin E. Lippincott (ed.) *On the Economic Theory of Socialism*, Minneapolis: University of Minnesota Press, pp. 55–143.

Lavoie, Don (1985) *Rivalry and Central Planning: The Socialist Calculation Debate Reconsidered*, Cambridge: Cambridge University Press.

—— (1994) "Introduction: Expectations and the Meaning of Institutions," in Don Lavoie (ed.) *Expectations and the Meaning of Institutions: Essays in Economics by Ludwig Lachmann*, London and New York: Routledge, pp. 1–19.

Lewin, Peter (1994) "Knowledge, Expectations, and Capital: The Economics of Ludwig M. Lachmann," in Peter J. Boettke and Mario J. Rizzo (eds) (1994), pp. 233–56.

Littlechild, Stephen C. (1982) "Controls on Advertising: An Examination of Some Economic Arguments," *Journal of Advertising* 1, pp. 25–37.

—— (1978) *The Fallacy of the Mixed Economy: An Austrian Critique of Conventional Mainstream Economics and of British Economic Policy*, London: Institute of Economic Affairs.

—— (1990) *Austrian Economics*, Vol. I, *History and Methodology*; Vol. II, *Money and Capital*; Vol. III, *Market Process*, Aldershot: Edward Elgar.

Loasby, Brian J. (1989) *The Mind and Method of the Economist: A Critical Appraisal of Major Economists in the 20th Century*, Aldershot: Edward Elgar.

—— (1992) "Market Co-ordination," in Bruce J. Caldwell and Stephan Boehm (eds) (1992), pp. 137–56.

—— (1994) "Evolution Within Equilibrium," in Peter J. Boettke and Mario J. Rizzo (eds) (1994), pp. 31–47.

Loy, Claudia (1988) *Marktsystem und Gleichgewichtstendenz*, Tubingen: J.C.B. Mohr (Paul Siebeck).

Machlup, Fritz (1952) *The Economics of Sellers' Competition: Model Analysis of Sellers' Conduct*, Baltimore: Johns Hopkins University Press.

Machovec, Frank M. (1995) *Perfect Competition and the Transformation of Economics*, London and New York: Routledge.

Makowski, Louis and Ostroy, Joseph M. (1993) "General Equilibrium and Market Socialism: Clarifying the Logic of Competitive Markets," in

Pranab K. Bardhan and John E. Roemer (eds) *Market Socialism: The Current Debate*, New York and Oxford: Oxford University Press, pp. 69–88.

McNulty, Paul J. (1967) "A Note on the History of Perfect Competition," *Journal of Political Economy* 75(4), pp. 395–9.

Mises, Ludwig von (1949) *Human Action*, New Haven, CT: Yale University Press.

Moldofsky, Naomi (1982) "Market Theoretical Frameworks—Which One?" *Economic Record* 58(161), pp. 152–68.

Nozick, Robert (1974) *Anarchy, State and Utopia*, New York: Basic Books.

O'Driscoll, Gerald P., Jr. (1977) *Economics as a Coordination Problem: The Contributions of Friedrich A. Hayek*, Kansas City: Sheed, Andrews and McMeel.

—— (1978) "Spontaneous Order and the Coordination of Economic Activities," in Louis M. Spadaro (ed.) (1978), pp. 111–42.

O'Driscoll, Gerald P., Jr. and Rizzo, Mario J. (1985) *The Economics of Time and Ignorance*, Oxford: Basil Blackwell.

Pasour, Ernest C., Jr. (1982) "Economic Efficiency and Inefficient Economics: Another View," *Journal of Post Keynesian Economics* 4(3), pp. 454–9.

Phelan, Christopher (1987) "A Defense of Rational Expectations/General Equilibrium Analysis Against Austrian Objections," *Critical Review* 1(4), pp. 1001–8.

Prychitko, David L. (1993) "Formalism in Austrian-School Welfare Economics: Another Pretense of Knowledge?" *Critical Review* 7(4), pp. 567–92.

Richardson, George B. (1960) *Information and Investment*, London: Oxford University Press.

Ricketts, Martin (1992) "Kirzner's Theory of Entrepreneurship—a Critique," in Bruce J. Caldwell and Stephan Boehm (eds) (1992), pp. 67–84.

Rizzo, Mario J. (1979) "Uncertainty, Subjectivity and the Economic Analysis of Law," in Mario J. Rizzo (ed.) *Time, Uncertainty, and Disequilibrium*, Lexington, MA: Lexington Books, pp. 71–89.

Rothbard, Murray N. (1979) "Comment: The Myth of Efficiency," in Mario J. Rizzo (ed.) *Time, Uncertainty and Disequilibrium*, Lexington, MA: Lexington Books, pp. 90–5.

—— (1994) Book Review (of *Austrian Economics: Tensions and New Directions*), *Southern Economics Journal* Oct., pp. 559–60.

Runde, Jochen H. (1988) "Subjectivism, Psychology, and the Modern Austrians," in Peter E. Earl (ed.) *Psychological Economics: Development, Tensions, Prospects*, Boston/Dordrecht/London: Kluwer, pp. 101–20.

Salerno, Joseph T. (1993) "Mises and Hayek Dehomogenized," *Review of Austrian Economics* 6(2), pp. 113–46.

—— (1994) "Mises and Hayek on Calculation and Knowledge: Reply," *Review of Austrian Economics* 7(2), pp. 111–25.

Schmidtchen, Dieter and Utzig, Siegried (1989) "Die Konjunkturtheorie Hayeks: Episode in Einem Forscherleben Oder Ausdruck Eines Lebenslangen Forschungsprogramms?" *Wirtschaftspolitische Blatter* 36(2), pp. 231–43.

Selgin, George A. (1988) *The Theory of Free Banking: Money Supply under Competitive Note Issue*, Totowa, NJ: Rowman and Littlefield.

Selgin, George A. and White, Lawrence H. (1994) "How Would the Invisible Hand Handle Money?" *Journal of Economic Literature* 32(4), pp. 1718–49.

Shackle, George L.S. (1972) *Epistemics and Economics: A Critique of Economic Doctrines*, Cambridge: Cambridge University Press.

Snowdon, Brian, Vane, Howard and Wynarczyk, Peter (1994) *A Modern Guide to Macroeconomics: An Introduction to Competing Schools of Thought*, Aldershot: Edward Elgar.

de Soto, Jesus Huerta (1992) *Socialismo, Calculo Economico y Funcion Empresarial*, Madrid: Union Editorial.

Sowell, Thomas (1980) *Knowledge and Decisions*, New York: Basic Books.

Spadaro, Louis M. (1978) *New Directions in Austrian Economics*, Kansas City: Sheed, Andrews and McMeel.

Stigler, George J. (1957) "Perfect Competition, Historically Contemplated," *Journal of Political Economy* 65(1), pp. 1–17.

Stiglitz, Joseph E. (1994) *Whither Socialism?*, Cambridge, MA and London: MIT Press.

Streit, Manfred E. and Wegner, Gerhard (1992) "Information, Transactions, and Catallaxy: Reflections on Some Key Concepts of Evolutionary Market Theory," in Ulrich Witt (ed.) *Explaining Process and Change: Approaches to Evolutionary Economics*, Ann Arbor: University of Michigan Press, pp. 125–49.

Sugden, Robert (1992) "Commentary: Austrian Prescriptive Economics," in Bruce J. Caldwell and Stephan Boehm (eds) (1992), pp. 207–14.

Thomsen, Esteban F. (1992) *Prices and Knowledge: A Market Process Perspective*, London and New York: Routledge.

—— (1994) "Prices and Knowledge," in Peter J. Boettke (ed.) (1994), pp. 167–72.

Torr, C.S.W. (1981) "The Role of the Entrepreneur (Review Note)," *South African Journal of Economics* 49(3), pp. 283–8.

Vaughn, Karen I. (1980) "Economic Calculation under Socialism: The Austrian Contribution," *Economic Inquiry* 18(4), pp. 535–54.

—— (1994) *Austrian Economics in America: The Migration of a Tradition*, Cambridge: Cambridge University Press.

Vihanto, Martti (1989) "The Austrian Theory of Price: An Example," *Finnish Economic Papers* 2(1), pp. 82–94.

—— (1994) "Introductory Essay: The Nature and Main Content of Austrian Economics," in *Discovering a Good Society Through Evolution and Design, Studies in Austrian Economics*, Turku: Turku School of Economics, pp. 18–99.

White, Lawrence H. (1984) *Free Banking in Britain: Theory, Experience and Debate, 1800–1845*, Cambridge: Cambridge University Press.

—— (1992) "Afterword: Appraising Austrian Economics: Contentions and Misdirections," in Bruce J. Caldwell and Stephan Boehm (eds) (1992), pp. 257–68.

Wiseman, Jack (1983) "Beyond Positive Economics—Dream and Reality," in Jack Wiseman (ed.) *Beyond Positive Economics*, London: Macmillan, pp. 13–27.
—— (1985) "Lionel Robbins, The Austrian School, and the LSE Tradition," *Research in the History of Economic Thought and Methodology*, 3, pp. 147–59.
—— (1989) *Cost, Choice and Political Economy*, Aldershot: Edward Elgar.

Source: Entrepreneurial Discovery and the Competitive Market Process: An Austrian Approach, *Journal of Economic Literature*, March 1997, XXXV, pp. 60–85.

2

THE SUBJECTIVISM OF AUSTRIAN ECONOMICS

I have chosen subjectivism as my topic for this chapter and surely few will question the appropriateness and importance of this topic. Austrian economics has recently lost one of its great modern masters, Friedrich A. Hayek. It is therefore perhaps particularly fitting to open this chapter with Hayek's often quoted tribute to the role of subjectivism in the growth of economic understanding. It is, he wrote, "probably no exaggeration to say that every important advance in economic theory during the last hundred years was a further step in the constant application of subjectivism" (Hayek, 1955, p. 31). Our thesis will be that the subjectivism that developed out of those pioneering insights of Carl Menger who founded the Austrian school, has come to mean entirely different things to different doctrinal traditions within modern economics—each of which derives substantially or wholly from the Mengerian tradition. In calling for the endorsement of that one variety of subjectivism which informs modern Austrian economics, we shall argue that it is this variety that most faithfully preserves and deepens Menger's own fundamental insights.

THE SUBJECTIVISM OF THE AUSTRIAN SCHOOL

Subjectivism has never, of course, meant any challenge to the possibility of "objective truth" in economics. It has never claimed that "everything is merely a matter of subjective interpretation" by the would-be economist. What the subjectivism of the 1870s challenged was the basic—if unstated—classical tenet that ultimately the only determinant of social-economic phenomena is the objective physical environment. All economic science has endeavored to account for real-world phenomena. The classical economist believed that these phenomena are to be seen as having been inexorably determined by the underlying physical realities. The availability of scarce natural resources, in conjunction with population and its demographics, basically determine the course of human history. What emerges over history is inescapable, it cannot be substantially altered by human will. Economic history emerges as automatically determined by the objective conditions governing and surrounding production. It was against this premise that Menger did revolutionary battle in his 1871 *Grundsätze*—written, we are told, in what he himself described as "a state of morbid excitement" (Hayek, 1981, p. 16).

The central thrust of Menger's book, we argue, was not so much his articulation of a subjective (marginal utility) theory of value, as his vision of the entire economic process of production as expressing the imprint, upon external reality, of the human factor. It was this vision that led him to formulate his theory of goods of various "orders," in which it is the preference of the final consumers that determines the place of each potential resource in the structure of production, and that ultimately assigns market values to all of them. It was this vision that led him (some twenty years earlier than his fellow pioneers in the marginalist revolution, in other schools) to glimpse, at least, the outlines of the theory of marginal productivity within the very formulation of the marginal utility theory of value. What ultimately determines the economic phenomena that we observe in the real world is, in this Mengerian vision, not the physical conditions governing production, but the needs of human beings. It is the latter that determine production methods, and the assignment of market values to goods, and incomes to owners of agents of production. Menger's vision is thus subjective in the fundamental sense that what emerges in real-world economies is the expression of human preferences as exercised against a background of given, passive resource constraints and endowments.

This subjectivist view of Menger differs not only, as already seen, from the classical view. It also differs, at least philosophically, from the Marshallian version of the neoclassical view. In this latter view (which has, largely due to the influence of Knight and his disciples, become the contemporary mainstream view in the United States) economic phenomena are seen as emerging from the interplay of the subjective and objective elements of supply (expressing objective cost conditions) and demand (reflecting consumer preferences). For Menger, as we have seen, the relevant insight is that—while, to be sure, the objective situation has much to do with the specific market outcomes that emerge in the course of the economic process—it is solely the actions of choosing consumers that in fact initiate and drive the process through which these outcomes emerge.

THE INCOMPLETENESS OF MENGER'S SUBJECTIVISM

As we shall see, and as is well known, Menger's subjectivism was incomplete in several respects. But we shall claim that the above kernel of Menger's subjectivist insight remains valid and central for economic understanding. It is this kernel that, during the long and checkered history of twentieth-century (and especially Austrian) economics, sometimes came to be obscured (especially in the early decade of the century). It is the revival of this kernel of subjectivism in the mid- and late twentieth century work of Mises, Hayek and their followers, that constitutes, in this economist's view, the most exciting feature of the resurgence of Austrian economics. And it is, paradoxically, this kernel that has unfortunately become threatened by certain recent developments within Austrian economics itself.

With the benefit of hindsight it is in fact possible to discern within Menger's work precisely those elements in his economic vision that we now see to have been, subjectivistically speaking, profoundly flawed, and relate them to those valid, enduring aspects of his subjectivism that have been, as it were, rediscovered and reaffirmed in modern Austrian economics. And, if we describe these latter, valid elements in Menger's subjectivism as being threatened, paradoxically, by certain developments within Austrian economics itself, the solution to the paradox is perhaps not far to seek. It has been an overenthusiastic tendency on the part of certain Austrian economists in recent years, to escape the legacy of incompleteness in Menger's subjectivism, that seems to have inadvertently led them almost to reject those paramount, valid expressions of Menger's subjectivist vision.

We have seen this vision to consist in the insight that the essential causal determinant shaping economic phenomena is not the physical environment within which economic activity proceeds, but the preference structure of the consumers whose needs inspire that activity. The prime flaw in Menger's vision—as seen from the subjectivist perspective—is his odd belief that this shaping influence exercised by human wants occurs inexorably and automatically, as it were without the intermediation of the human will (Menger, 1981, p. IX). It seems plausible to link this unfortunate view to Menger's apparent (and equally unfortunate) assumption, in his price theory, that values (which he showed to be determined by marginal utilities) occur in the context of complete knowledge. Ignorance, Menger argued, is to be seen as a pathology which should not obscure the underlying economic laws relating to healthy, normal (i.e., omnisciently informed) economic activity (Menger, 1981, p. 200; 1985, p. 56; Kirzner, 1979, ch. 4; 1992, ch. 4).

An example of the baneful influence of Menger's view of the "automatic" translation of consumer needs into the appropriate market values and patterns of resource allocation, occurs in a passage in Schumpeter in which he criticized the Misesian thesis concerning the possibility of rational economic calculation under socialism. And the extent to which post-Mengerian Austrian subjectivism was able to escape these unfortunate influences is expressed in Hayek's sharp reaction to Schumpeter.

Mises has shown how, in the absence of markets for productive resources, socialist planners would simply be unable to plan rationally, because they lack indexes of the relative social importance of the relevant resources. Schumpeter rejected this on what we can see to have been solid Mengerian grounds. The appropriate pattern of resource allocation is implied, for any form of economic society, in the pattern of consumer desires. This follows, for the theorist, Schumpeter (1950, p. 175) argued, "from the elementary proposition that consumers in evaluating ('demanding') consumer goods *ipso facto* also evaluate the means of production which enter into the production of those goods." Clearly Schumpeter (correctly) understood Mengerian theory as implying an automatic, *logical* relationship linking consumer preferences to the correct valuation of productive resources.

And it was this that provoked Hayek to refer to this view of Schumpeter's as "startling." Only for a single mind to which not only the valuation of consumer goods are known but also the conditions governing the supply of the various factors of production, would it be valid to claim such a logical relationship. Schumpeter has simply slid into the (Mengerian) error of disregarding "the unavoidable imperfection of man's knowledge and the consequent need for a process by which knowledge is constantly communicated and acquired" (Hayek, 1949, p. 91).

MENGER'S SUBJECTIVIST HERITAGE: THE DIVERGENT PATHS

We have seen the central subjectivist thrust of Menger's vision. And we have seen the incompleteness of that vision (in its assumption of the normalcy of perfect knowledge.) It appears plausible to see this dominant, but flawed, subjectivism of Menger, as the reason for the divergent paths followed by subsequent generations of economists touched by Menger's influence. We may distinguish three such paths.

(a) *Mainstream economics.* Menger's influence has left a powerful imprint upon twentieth-century mainstream macroeconomics. This influence was introduced, it can be shown, primarily through Lord Robbins' important 1932 book, *The Nature and Significance of Economic Science.* Robbins' work reflected (as made clear in his Preface to the book) the character of Austrian economics to which he had been exposed during the later 1920s. This economics expressed Menger's subjectivism—with all its incompleteness. Austrian economics in the 1920s paid virtually no attention to the problems of ignorance and uncertainty. While Robbins succeeded in shaping modern microeconomics in a subjectivist direction, by making the economizing decision the decisively important analytical unit, he did so while in effect retaining the Mengerian assumption of complete relevant information. In the Robbinsian approach adopted by mainstream microeconomics, as absorbed into the Walrasian context, each market participant is assumed to confront a given and fully known ends–means framework (created symmetrically by the decisions being simultaneously made by the remaining, similarly situated, market participants). Clearly, what we identified as the disturbing flaw in Menger's subjectivism has, in this modern mainstream version of it, become its most central identifying feature.

As an almost natural result of this central feature (the assumption of perfect knowledge), mainstream microeconomics proceeded to extend the Robbinsian framework (in which the individual decision-maker is seen as facing a given, known ends–means complex) to the economy as a whole. The entire economy was seen as somehow facing an economizing problem, as if it was required to allocate given social resources in a pattern calculated to achieve maximum satisfaction of ranked social objectives. Although Robbins himself had assumed perfect relevant knowledge strictly at the level of each individual, the extension of his framework to encompass societal economizing decisions, in effect assumed the possibility of complete, centralized information concerning the entire economy and all its available options, desires and possibilities. With this extension the mainstream view had expanded the flaw in Menger's system to the point where the subjectivist element in Menger's heritage was virtually smothered. It was Hayek's 1945 paper, "The Use of

Knowledge in Society," that decisively rejected this assumption, for any realistic understanding of the operation of the market system.

(b) *Radical subjectivism.* The second path taken by post-Mengerian subjectivists is that which, in the second half of the twentieth century, has been represented most prominently by the work of Shackle and of Lachmann. Although Shackle was a student of Hayek in the 1930s, there is little to suggest that his subjectivism owes much to Menger's specific influence. Lachmann, on the other hand, explicitly drew his subjectivism from Austrian (and especially Mengerian) economics. The Shackle–Lachmann subjectivist path represents the outright rejection of those elements in the mainstream view that we have identified with the flaws in Menger's own subjectivism. But they go much further. Not only do Shackle and Lachmann reject the assumption of perfect knowledge, they tend to emphasize the virtual *impossibility* of relevant accurate knowledge. Decisions refer to courses of action that will have consequences in the future, the future is unknowable; hence even *individual* decisions let alone imaginary societal decisions) must never be seen by economists as being made in the allocative mode central to mainstream microeconomics. The uncertainty of the future must confound and frustrate the (admitted) urge to rationality which humans display. No longer can we see decisions as dictated, in effect, by the given arrays of ends and means relevant to the respective decisions. Decisions are, in this view, made in a manner expressive of the decision-maker's own assessments of what the options are (and what consequences they are expected to generate). These assessments reflect the expectations held at the moment of the decision; they are held, in this view, to be *undetermined* by objective phenomena. This "subjectivism of expectations," to use Lachmann's phrase, undermines traditional microeconomics because it injects an unprecedented degree of subjectivist generated indeterminacy into the economic picture. One can no longer rely, as traditional microeconomics relied, upon equilibrating market forces (driven by rationally maximizing individual decisions) to generate systematic market outcomes. Market outcomes express the decisions made; the decisions made express the expectations that happen to be held at the moment of decision; that is all. This radical subjectivism has thus not only cast away the assumption of perfect knowledge which Menger's incomplete subjectivism had no qualms in making. It has at the same time entirely abandoned those central conclusions of Menger's economics in which, we argued, his subjectivism found expression. In the radical view we can no longer recognize any systematic processes in which consumer preferences come to leave any powerful imprint upon the production decisions governing the uses to which higher-order goods are to be allocated.

The preceding, mainstream "path" had led to the smothering of Mengerian subjectivism as a result of the drastic deepening of the "perfect knowledge" assumption. The radical path has, we have now seen, led to the denial of those central results of economic analysis in which Menger's own subjectivist view of the economic process was reflected. It is against this background that we turn to note the third path taken by economists touched by Menger's subjectivist influence.

(c) *The modern Austrian revival.* This path is that created by the work of Mises and of Hayek. It has brought about, during the past quarter of a century, a significant revival of interest in Austrian, and especially Mengerian, economics. We shall argue that this path preserves what is sound and valid in Menger's subjectivism, steering clear of both the incompleteness in Menger's view (which led to the death of subjectivism in mainstream microeconomics) and the nihilism of the radical subjectivists (which has led to the abandonment of the central subjectivist conclusions of Mengerian economics).

The key elements in this modern extension of Mengerian subjectivism (on this see further Kirzner, 1992, ch. 7) are the role of entrepreneurship in market processes, and the gradual expansion of knowledge generated in the course of the competitive market process. The first of these two key elements we owe to Mises; the second has formed the kernel of Hayekian economics since 1945. Briefly put, the Mises–Hayek theory of the market process sees it as a systematic process of knowledge expansion, the equilibrating character of which is the expression of entrepreneurial discovery. This vision of the market process not only preserves the key element of subjectivism in Menger's theory (i.e. recognition of the primary and dominant role exercised by consumer preferences). It does so without accepting the troubling Mengerian assumption of perfect knowledge. In fact, as we shall see, this modern Austrian view is able to reach Menger's central subjectivist conclusion *only* by introducing the new element of subjectivism needed in order to provide scope for entrepreneurial discovery. Not only are the flaws in Menger's subjectivism no longer necessary for his subjectivist conclusions, it turns out in fact that a new dimension for subjectivism is the necessary link in establishing anew the old Mengerian conclusions. All this deserves more careful attention.

THE MODERN AUSTRIAN SUBJECTIVISM

In this modern Austrian view subjectivist insights reveal two cardinally significant features of economic life. It is these features that make possible the claim (in Mengerian fashion) that markets do systematically tend to express the preferences of consumers. The first of these two features is in fact the direct denial of that feature in Menger earlier described as a flaw in his subjectivism. Whereas Menger's theory of price depended on the assumption of perfect knowledge, the Mises–Hayek understanding of markets emphasizes that, at any moment, markets are pervaded by widespread mutual ignorance on the part of market participants. Markets do *not* at each instant accurately reflect the patterns of consumer preferences of that moment. This recognition of ignorance is the foundation of all subsequent wisdom in regard to the systematic quality of market processes. And it is here that the second of the above two features in the modern Austrian subjectivist view enters our theoretical picture.

This second subjectivist feature recognizes that mutual error on the part of market participants creates opportunities for pure entrepreneurial profits. The emergence of these opportunities offers attractive incentives for entrepreneurial discovery. Subjectivism enters here by way of our appreciation for the way in which such entrepreneurial discoveries are made. The modern Austrian approach emphasizes that it is not sufficient, in order for these opportunities to be grasped (and thus eliminated), that they exist. Unnoticed opportunities are in fact the key feature of the economic world which is entailed by our understanding of market ignorance. For hitherto unnoticed opportunities to be noticed and grasped, they must be discovered; and such discovery requires a special characteristic on the part of potential discoverers, viz. the propensity to be alert. Entrepreneurial alertness is the new subjectivist element implicit, at least, in the work of Mises and Hayek, which is now seen to drive the Mengerian market process through which consumer preferences come to dictate productive decisions. This idea of entrepreneurial alertness was expanded in Kirzner (1973, 1979, 1985, 1989).

So long as unexploited opportunities for pure profit still remain, economic analysis demonstrates that consumer preferences have, in some sense, been defied. A pure profit opportunity expresses the situation where a unit of resource service is currently being assigned to a lower value use than is in fact available elsewhere in the market. This latter unfulfilled value is one through which "more urgent" consumer desires (as measured by money offered) are failing to be served as a result of the current allocation of resources services. The incentive for discovery provided by the available profit opportunity is the element that excites entrepreneurial alertness and thus drives the tendency towards a resource allocation pattern which, in the context of available resources, conforms to consumer preferences (as expressed by their money-backed demand). Modern Austrian subjectivist insights have served to illuminate the validity of Menger's vision of consumer sovereignty in the formulation of allocative decisions.

SCYLLA AND CHARYBDIS AVOIDED

It is instructive to notice how this modern Austrian version of subjectivism avoids the pitfalls inherent in each of the other two varieties of subjectivism we have seen to have derived from the Mengerian heritage. The Robbinsian subjectivism emphasized the allocative choice of market participants. But it did so, it seemed, by tacitly assuming (as in Walrasian theory) that all such allocative choices somehow correctly anticipated one another. There was nothing in the Robbinsian framework that could explain how any pattern of choices that failed so correctly to anticipate each other could systematically generate a more "correct" array of decisions. In other words, the perfect knowledge implicit in the Robbinsian framework (and thus in modern microeconomics) requires us to imagine that market outcomes are automatically dictated (to be sure, via the network of mutually compatible maximizing decisions) by the underlying data (i.e. production possibilities and consumer utility functions) without any human intervention that might be conceived of as arranging that appropriate choices in fact be made. It was this aspect of the Robbinsian system, we saw, that seemed to convert the flaw in Menger's subjectivism into one of its own central features. The modern Austrian subjectivism has avoided this trap both by explicitly rejecting the assumption of perfect knowledge and by introducing a new (subjectivism-friendly) analytical scheme for understanding the equilibrating propensity which markets display.

The Shackle–Lachmann more radical variety of subjectivism, we saw, pointed to the complete denial of systematically equilibrating market tendencies. Whereas Menger's subjectivism was, in Lachmann's terminology, the "expression of human 'disposition,'" modern radical subjectivism argues for subjectivism as "a manifestation of spontaneous action" (Lachmann, 1986, p. 55). In the earlier view choice is the "*result* of the impact of constraints on human dispositions. In the new view choice is not a result of anything, but a *creative act*" (Lachmann, 1986, p. 55). The markets are not to be seen as the systematic result of any set of objective circumstances whatever. Each decision is, in Shackle's phrase, "a new beginning" (Lachmann, 1986, p. 55), in principle wholly disengaged from all previous history. In this radical view, although it is conceded that people's choices are to be seen as rational responses to their perceived circumstances, it is insisted that these perceived circumstances are always, at least in part, the creation of their own mind (and thus by no means necessarily correspond to any actual circumstances). From such a position it is a short distance to the conviction that market outcomes are wholly unlikely ever systematically to manifest any equilibrating tendencies.

The modern Austrian version of subjectivism escapes these nihilistic conclusions by the injection of the entrepreneurial element. This element, although fully consistent with the subjectivist's insights into the autonomy of the human mind, enables us to rescue economic science from the abyss threatened by that radicalism which can discern no systematic continuity whatever in the course of human history.

Although subjectivism indeed affirms the autonomy of the human mind, our awareness of the entrepreneurial element in human action enables us to postulate a systematic linkage which shapes discoveries and actions into patterns that do tend correctly to reflect and anticipate those external phenomena relevant to successful action. In this fashion the modern Austrian version of subjectivism is able to explain and understand equilibrating market tendencies. In fact, as we have seen, it is not merely that this version of subjectivism permits such equilibrating tendencies, it is in fact the pivotal explanatory element which enables us to understand how, in a world without centralized direction, spontaneous social coordination can possibly emerge. This issue separating the modern Austrian version of subjectivism from the radical one deserves further exploration. This is especially the case in the light of some explicit criticisms raised by the radical school, against what we have termed the modern Austrian view.

RADICAL CRITIQUES AND MODERN AUSTRIAN DEFENCES

From the radical perspective the modern Austrian version of subjectivism is so moderate and diluted as to approach incoherence.

Instead of being able to enjoy the best of both worlds (equilibrium theory and subjectivism), modern Austrian economics appears, from the radical perspective, to be shot through with crippling inner inconsistencies.

From the radical perspective, the options facing the social scientist are clear cut. Either one recognizes the autonomy of the human mind—involving the subjectivism, not only of human tastes and preferences, but also of human expectations and human interpretation of current events—or one does not. If human beings are not to be reduced to automatons whose choices are fully determined by existing circumstances (including tastes), then we must recognize the inherent indeterminacy of individual behaviour (and hence of market outcomes). It is all very well, the radical view would argue, to talk of successful entrepreneurial discovery. But the freedom of the human mind requires us, surely, to recognize the ubiquity of human and entrepreneurial error. Such recognition surely snaps, the argument runs, any linkages between initial circumstances and market outcomes, that might render equilibration a plausible possibility. Moreover the inherent unknowability of the future injects, in the radical view, yet an additional element of implausibility into the idea of market outcomes somehow coming into benign coordination with the "underlying realities" (see, for more detail on these radical criticisms of modern Austrian subjectivism, Kirzner, 1992, ch. 1).

After all, the argument runs, the relevant underlying realities presumably mean the future events upon which one wishes one's present decisions to impinge. But such future events are themselves strictly created by current decisions, so, that there is no independent existence at all to any realities to which human activities are to be adjusted. The future that one wishes to anticipate (in the course of one's decision-planning) is created by those selfsame decisions. To believe, as modern Austrian economics (together with mainstream economics) believes, that markets display systematic tendencies in which market outcomes tend correctly to fit in with an independently conceived future, is to surrender (as mainstream economics has surely already surrendered) all claims to consistent subjectivist recognition of the autonomy and freedom of the individual mind.

The modern Austrian version of subjectivism defends itself against these criticisms not by arguing the merits of moderation in subjectivism (as against a more consistent version of it), but by maintaining that a correctly conceived, utterly consistent version of subjectivism does indeed yield the conclusions of modern Austrian economics.

Everyday human experience surely teaches us that human beings do successfully formulate decisions (and even multiperiod plans) in dealing with the vagaries of natural events and the uncertainties inherent in dynamic social intercourse. Neither the admitted unknowability of the future nor the admitted human propensity to err, nor any combination of the two, is able totally to frustrate human efforts to act rationally for the uncertain future. Humankind is not simply a helpless piece of flotsam buffeted by the hydrodynamics of social changes. Markets do display remarkable tendencies towards coordination. Our task as economists is not to explain how mistakes in decision-making may occur, such mistakes offer no mystery challenging our powers of explanation. Our task is to explain the observed tendencies to coordination. Modern Austrian economics, building on the subjectivist tradition from Menger to Mises and Hayek, finds this explanation not, as the radical subjectivists imagine, by compromising our commitment to subjectivist insights, but rather by deepening these insights. In the modern Austrian version of subjectivism, the idea of human entrepreneurial alertness is the analytical device that enables us to see how human creativity is in fact geared towards a tendency pointing to the discovery of opportunities that are in fact "waiting" to be discovered.

It is true that the future is created by current decisions. But it is equally true that that future is, from the perspective of the acting individual, something to be anticipated as if it were a datum of nature. Since each of the current decisions (which together generate the future course of events) is motivated and guided by entrepreneurial alertness, we can confidently assert that such alertness *is* able successfully to tend to link current decisions to the "underlying realities."

SUBJECTIVISM AND THE AUSTRIAN TRADITION

We saw earlier in this paper how Menger's subjectivist perspective enabled him to see how economic phenomena are the expression of consumer valuations operating to govern the prices and uses made of all consumer goods and productive resources. Throughout the history of the Austrian School it is this subjectivism, pioneered by Menger, that has served as the most prominent feature of the school.

This chapter has traced the varied fortunes of the Mengerian subjectivist legacy during the twentieth century. In particular we have argued that the key Mengerian insights find their preservation in that version of subjectivism that has informed and illuminated the modern revival of interest in Austrian economics. It is because alternative versions of the Mengerian subjectivist legacy seemed to have led either to an unacceptable modern neoclassical formalism on the one hand, or to an equally unacceptable radically subjectivist nihilism, on the other, that this modern revival of Austrian economics appears so promising.

REFERENCES

Hayek, F.A. (1949) *Individualism and Economic Order*, London: Routledge and Kegan Paul.

—— (1955) *The Counter-Revolution of Science: Studies on the Abuse of Reason*, Glencoe, IL: Free Press.

—— (1981) "Introduction," in Menger (1981). Originally published as the introduction to *Collected Works of Carl Menger*, London: London School of Economics, 1934.

Kirzner, I.M. (1973) *Competition and Entrepreneurship*, Chicago: University of Chicago Press.

—— (1979) *Perception, Opportunity and Profit*, Chicago: University of Chicago Press.

—— (1985) *Discovery and the Capitalist Process*, Chicago: University of Chicago Press.

—— (1989) *Discovery, Capitalism and Distributive Justice*, Oxford: Basil Blackwell.

—— (1992) *The Meaning of Market Process: Essays in the Development of Modern Austrian Economics*, London and New York: Routledge.

Lachmann, L.M. (1986) *The Market as an Economic Process*, Oxford: Basil Blackwell.

Menger, C. (1981) *Principles of Economics*, New York and London: New York University Press.

—— (1985) *Investigations into the Method of the Social Sciences with Special Reference to Economics*, trans. by F.J. Nock, New York: New York University Press; originally published in German in 1883.

Schumpeter, J.A. (1950) *Capitalism, Socialism and Democracy*, 3rd edn, New York: Harper and Row.

Source: The Subjectivism of Austrian Economics, in G. Meijer (ed.) (1995) *New Perspectives on Austrian Economics*, Routledge.

3

SUBJECTIVISM, FREEDOM AND ECONOMIC LAW

Let me open with some personal observations. I am profoundly grateful for the signal honor of being invited to deliver this inaugural memorial lecture in tribute to the late Professor Ludwig M. Lachmann. I must congratulate the Free Market Foundation and especially Mr Leon Louw, together with the University of the Witwatersrand and my eminent good friend Dean Duncan Reekie, for their admirable vision and initiative in arranging this very special occasion. It is a particular pleasure to greet Mrs Margot Lachmann here today. A distinguished student of human culture who has earned our deepest respect entirely in her own right, Margot is especially entitled to our applause today. It is she who gave Ludwig that lifetime of loyal, devoted support which enabled him to dedicate his own long and productive career to the cause of a more illuminating economic understanding, with such single-minded passion.

But my assignment today is not to eulogize Ludwig Lachmann. My assignment is to share with you some ideas on the foundations of economics—ideas which have emerged out of three decades of discussion and correspondence with Ludwig and which, I dare to hope, have benefited somewhat by my exposure to his utter intellectual honesty and to his luminous, uncompromising subjectivism. Many of you will of course recognize my indebtedness to Ludwig in a good deal of what I shall be arguing today. If at the same time you notice (as you can hardly fail to do) those points in my observations with which Ludwig himself might have expressed spirited disagreement, I feel confident that you will also agree with me, at least, that there could hardly be anything that could please Ludwig more than his being responsible for a lively, no-holds-barred intellectual fight-fest on the fundamentals of economic understanding.

LACHMANN AND THE CENTRALITY OF SUBJECTIVISM

Few will dispute the observation that the unifying thread running through Lachmann's social science was his radical subjectivism. It was radical subjectivism that Ludwig Lachmann deployed in order to deepen our understanding of economic processes. And if one seeks to characterize the intellectual odyssey which made up Lachmann's scholarly career, it seems fair to portray it as a consistent series of deepened, pioneering extensions—the radicalization, if you will—of his own subjectivism. And, we shall see, it is certain characteristic features of Lachmann's subjectivism which raise the problems with which we wish to grapple in this lecture.

Lachmann was entirely unsatisfied by what he called "subjectivism as the expression of human 'disposition'" (Lachmann, 1986, p. 55). It is simply not enough to recognize that decisions made by consumers express the structures of their preferences. Such recognition for the role of subjective tastes would be entirely compatible with the statement of Pareto—a statement cited by Lachmann with disagreement so obviously profound as to border on disbelief (Lachmann, 1977, pp. 56–248)—to the effect that once the consumer has left us a picture of his indifference map, we no longer need him at all (Pareto, 1927, p. 170), since, we then already know exactly what he will decide to do. For Lachmann subjectivism represents, most importantly, "a manifestation of spontaneous action" (Lachmann, 1986). By this way of putting it, Lachmann meant to draw attention to the power of the active human mind to frustrate any pretensions by Paretian—or other—economists to predict, simply on the basis of given scarcity constraints impinging on given preferences, what action will in fact be taken.

Physical realities and constraints have, of course, enormously important consequences for economic outcomes. But the subjectivist must insist that economic outcomes are not determined by any objective physical phenomena whatever. All the powerful influences exercised upon human affairs by external phenomena are exercised strictly through the intermediation of active human minds. Because of this process of intermediation, outcomes are simply not uniquely implied by external phenomena. What people do—the prices they offer to pay, the goods they buy—depends on what they know, believe, and expect, i.e. on what Lachmann (somewhat boldly, perhaps) chose to call "mental acts" (Lachmann, 1977, p. 56). External phenomena certainly do promote discoveries, they do shape expectations, and they do condition knowledge. But they do so only in conjunction with the independent entrepreneurial conjectures of active human minds. What people believe, expect and know is not determined by outside phenomena. What they do is therefore, indeed likely to have been significantly affected by, even influenced by, physical phenomena, but is never determined by them. It may seem to the econometrician that demand for umbrellas is a function of rainfall. The subjectivist economist understands that the full interpretation of such econometric data must take into account the manner in which current rainfall affects people's expectations concerning future rainfall. For many purposes such a full interpretation may not contribute much that makes a difference; but for the most important objectives of economics such an interpretation matters a great deal indeed. So runs the subjectivist's statement of fundamental conviction.

It emerges, then, that a cardinal component of the subjectivist's position is the freedom which, he insists, characterizes human behavior. It is in this freedom that we see most starkly the difference between the subjectivist's view of the world and that of his mainstream economist colleagues. For the latter the decisions of market participants are not free (in the sense used here) they are determined by the data of the situation (including preferences). As Anthony de Jasay has recently remarked: "Choice 'caused' by the chooser's dispositions or preferences is the base hypothesis in all rational-choice theory. The hypothesis is used with particular rigour in economics" (de Jasay, 1991, p. 18). For the subjectivist, human action is, in this sense, "uncaused"; it is not determined by circumstances (even by the agent's own preferences). Heavy rainfall does not inexorably drive the consumer to buy an umbrella—although it may inspire him freely to choose to do so. Human behavior—and the economic phenomena which express this behavior—are, in the most important sense, disengaged from objective, physical, phenomena. There is no inexorable causal nexus running from the latter to the former. It is this freedom[1] (an expression of what Lachmann called "the autonomy of the human mind") which, at first glance, seems to raise the most serious difficulties for the very notion of economic regularities, let alone economic law (Lachmann, 1977, p. 248).

THE DIFFICULTIES RAISED BY SUBJECTIVIST FREEDOM

Economic science emerged as an attempt to understand what appeared to be the unmistakable regularities which are displayed by economic phenomena. For example, the observed tendency of costs and prices to approach each other, was an important point of departure for classical economic theory. The entire history of economic thought can be seen as a series of endeavours more adequately and more satisfyingly to understand the economic laws which appear to govern the economic universe. Yet the subjectivism which has, ever since 1871, seemed so promising for the improvement of economic understanding, seems now to be pointing to the utter impossibility of economic law! Let us not forget that the "external phenomena" relevant to human action are largely made up of the actions of others (and of their consequences). Subjectivist freedom thus implies that, while my decision to buy an umbrella from you may well be inspired by your decision to offer to sell me one for a low price, my decision is nonetheless free, it is not the inevitable outcome of your decision. My decision incorporates my own expectations of future rainfall, and my own expectations concerning the possibility of a better bargain around the corner. These expectations are an expression of what I know (or think that I know) about my environment and, as Lachmann used to insist, "knowledge cannot be regarded as a function of anything else."[2] But if each individual decision is made under such conditions of freedom (of determining influence exercised by the decisions of others), how can we accept the very idea of economic regularities?

There is an irony here. Hayek's tribute to the contribution of subjectivism to economic science is well-known and often quoted: ". . . it is probably no exaggeration to say that every important advance in economic theory during the last hundred years was a further step in the consistent application of subjectivism" (Hayek, 1955, p. 31). But here we appear to have arrived at an almost diametrically opposed conclusion: the most consistent application of the notion of subjectivist freedom appears to sabotage every attempt by economic science to understand observed economic regularities.

The classical economists founded the notion of economic law squarely upon physical, even biological, regularities. The marginalist revolution (and particularly the work of Carl Menger) enabled economists to see how a recognition of the paramountcy of consumer demand pointed the way to a more satisfactory understanding of the coordination achieved by the market economy. Lionel Robbins took these Austrian subjectivist insights and, in his 1932 *Nature and Significance of Economic Science,* introduced them to shape most decisively the development of mainstream microeconomics during the second half of this century. But we now find ourselves confronted with the difficulty that the most consistent application of subjectivism appears to dissolve the very notion of economic law; each decision is made independently, not only of the physical environment, but of the decisions of others. How can one salvage the possibility of economic regularities?

In what follows I shall attempt to show that subjectivist freedom of the decision is not only not fatal for the possibility of economic regularities but, in fact, is the indispensable ingredient necessary for attaining understanding of such regularities. Hayek's tribute to subjectivism can, we shall submit, be seen to be fully applicable to subjectivist freedom, after all. Let us first examine how mainstream microeconomics has, along Robbinsian lines, ostensibly reconciled a systematic theory of price with the freedom of individual decision making. We shall find that the inadequacies in this ostensible reconciliation point to the possibilities offered by a more consistent application of subjectivist insights.

MAINSTREAM MICROECONOMICS

Determinate market outcomes are achieved by mainstream microeconomics by means of two key devices. For simplicity we consider the pure exchange market, without production, consisting only of consumers exchanging given commodities at equilibrium prices. First, each consumer decision is seen as fully determined (within the constraining framework of resource limitations and given market prices) by that consumer's own preferences. The consumer freely exercises his own preferences. Second, all decisions are assumed to have somehow been (as Shackle has put it) pre-reconciled. Each and every decision is already somehow fully adjusted to the opportunities and constraints marked out by all other decisions in the system. It is seen as the central function of markets to ensure, somehow, such full mutual adjustment among decisions. So that determinate final market outcomes, viz. equilibrium market price and the consequent reshuffling of title to the initial endowments, emerge without having inflicted evident violence upon individual freedom. Each consumer has, after all, freely exercised his own preferences.

But even the briefest examination of this theoretical framework must convince us that it rests entirely upon the implicit denial of that freedom—that "manifestation of spontaneous action"—which we found central to Ludwig Lachmann's radical subjectivism. The first of the two devices (referred to in the preceding paragraph) is, of course, simply the Paretian device of accounting for market outcomes, not by reference to the consumer's own "mental acts," but instead by reference to the consumer's indifference map. Any freedom of the consumer to choose a market basket in a way that might permit him to err, to exercise imagination concerning, say future price changes, has been carefully eliminated. What the consumer is to buy is fully determined, independently of any subjective process of choice, by the circumstances (including, certainly, the consumer's own preference structure).

And the second of the above two devices is, of course, even more inconsistent with subjectivist freedom. The assumed pre-reconciliation of decisions postulates a set of supremely potent constraints, exercised by each decision over all others. Such a picture of the market seems, despite all the pre-reconciliation in the world, to be unable to be reconciled with the notion of each decision being free of determining influences exercised by other decisions. It is clear that mainstream microeconomics has achieved its theoretical account of the determination of market outcomes only by completely squeezing out subjectivist freedom from its field of vision.

It is true that mainstream microeconomics has not denied the consumer the prerogative of governing his decision by his own set of preferences. This is, indeed, the subjective element in the theory. But it is a strictly limited subjectivism, a subjectivism of "human disposition," not the Lachmannian subjectivism of active minds.

It is worth noticing that mainstream microeconomics has achieved determinate outcomes only by restricting its subjectivism to that level of explanation which precedes economic analysis itself. Consumer decisions are determined by (admittedly subjective) preferences. Once subjectivism has, à la Pareto, supplied us with the consumer's subjectively derived indifference map, the economic analysis then takes over in completely determinate fashion. There is nothing, in the explanation of the way an individual's decision is (given his subjective preferences) arrived at, that provides scope for human error, or human imagination (or, for that matter, any other subjectivist element). And the manner in which decisions are pre-reconciled in markets offers no scope for any human element whatever; pre-reconciliation is achieved simply by arbitrary assumption. An iron law is postulated that assures the simultaneous solution of all the Walrasian equations; pre-reconciliation is achieved by mathematics, not by human interaction. Neoclassical market equilibrium accounts for market regularities (a) by entirely eliminating the subjectivism of active minds, and (b) by admitting into consideration only that element of subjectivism (the subjectivism of human disposition) which can be excluded from the economic analysis itself.

We shall argue in what follows that an adequate understanding of how market regularities can occur, requires us to pay close attention to the subjectivism of active minds and, precisely for that reason, requires us to incorporate that subjectivism into the body, of our economic explanations. The systematic processes of the market are decisively shaped by the essentially human character, not only of the preferences to which consumer decisions are designed to cater, but also of those acts of the mind which form and inspire the component decision-steps in those processes. It be useful to remind ourselves of what we mean when referring to the human character of action.

THE NATURE OF HUMAN ACTION

As Shackle has pointed out again and again, the decisions which constitute the analytical units in mainstream microeconomics are artificially structured in such a manner as to extrude from them virtually all those features which we associate with human choice. Economic theory has reduced "human action to such terms as could equally well apply to the behavior of inanimate objects" (Shackle, 1972, p. 443). The relevant objectives are presumed to be already given to the decision maker in a clear and definite ranking; there is no scope for agonizing over which of two options is to be valued more highly. The sacrifices needed to be made in order to achieve each given possible objective are presumed fully known; there is no scope for agonizing over what one is giving up in achieving any one objective. The decision has been boiled down to a strictly mathematical exercise; the solution to the constrained maximization problem to which decision making has been reduced is obtainable, given the information assumed to be already fully possessed, in purely mechanical fashion. What has been squeezed out of this picture, we have already seen, is the very possibility of human error, and all recognition of the radical (i.e. Knightian) uncertainty surrounding human choices—that uncertainty which (inevitably entailed by the future-oriented character of human action in an unpredictable world) is the circumstance switching on human resourcefulness and initiative, human dreams, hunches, human imagination and vision. If we are to reintroduce into economic analysis the essentially human character of choice, we must permit choice to be made under those conditions of radical uncertainty which defy any possibility of its effective elimination through the deployment of statistical probability theory. But it is here that we are confronted by the dilemma outlined earlier in this chapter. Surely the indeterminacy surrounding human choice thus seen in its full richness and complexity, the "freedom" which thus insulates human choice from any determining influence that might be exercised over it by external phenomena, renders human choice totally unfit to serve as a building block in the edifice of supra-individual, market regularities.

Human choice seen as embedded in the flux of radical uncertainty appears to be essentially open-ended. There simply are no constraints governing human imagination and human expectations. If a person is marooned on a small island surrounded by shark-infested, unnavigable waters, we know exactly where he will always be able to be found. But if part of those waters were suddenly to dry up, linking the island with the mainland, we have lost all basis for guessing his whereabouts: he could be anywhere. Uncertainty-bred removal of the constraints which circumscribe the decision in mainstream microeconomics, seems to unchain choice to the point where action is entirely unexplained and in fact totally unexplainable. Or so it might seem upon initial reflection.

Careful consideration of the notion of human action as developed especially by Ludwig von Mises, will perhaps convince us that the situation is rather more benignly complex. The situation confronting us is not, we shall argue, one in which human decisions are either fully determined (leaving no scope for the autonomy of the human mind) or totally unexplainable (leaving us with no hope for the understanding of market regularities). There is a third possibility, one which does recognize the autonomy of the human mind, the subjectivist freedom of the human decision, but which is nonetheless able to see how it is precisely the autonomous character of the human mind that can ensure a tendency towards actions which, in a special, subtle sense, do bear the imprint of the external circumstances. For Mises, human action is sparked by an inner autonomous motor which inspires appropriate regard to external circumstances. The external circumstances do not themselves constrain action, but action does nonetheless, and precisely because of the autonomous acts of the mind which inspire action, take external circumstances into account. The key to the matter lies in the notion of purposefulness which suffuses human action.

To say that human action is purposeful[3] is to say far more than (in fact, it may often be more accurate to insist that it is to say something quite different from the assertion) that each decision aims at the maximum fulfilment of given objectives, the greatest possible attainment of given ends. To say that human action is purposeful is to refer to the distinctively human attitude which pervades all wakeful, alert human existence. The purposefulness of human action refers to the circumstance that man is continually alive to changing conditions that may affect his prospects; it refers to man's continuous alertness to newly-noticed possibilities for removing what he believes to be unsatisfactory aspects of his situation. It refers indeed to the drive with which he pursues already-designated objectives; but it also refers to his readiness to recognize new objectives worthy of being adopted. It may indeed refer to the attitude which initiates the deliberate search for the information he knows that he will need for the attainment of his already-designated objectives; but it also refers to the attitude which inspires him to notice items of information the availability of which or the usefulness of which, had hitherto not been known to him (or, at any rate, kept in mind by him). To say that action is purposeful is to say that it is inspired by that restless activity of the human mind, that ceaseless exercise of the human imagination, that continual peering of the mind's eye into the foggy future—which are the characteristic watermarks of man's attitude to his human condition.

It is only through appreciation of this sense of the notion of human purposefulness that we can make sense of Mises's remarks linking action with the uncertainty which pervades the human condition. "That man acts and that the future is uncertain are by no means two independent matters. They are only two different modes of establishing one thing . . . If man knew the future, he would not have to choose and would not act. He would be like an automaton, reacting to stimuli without any will of his own."[4] To anyone trained in modern microeconomics, these remarks must sound strange indeed. In mainstream microeconomics man is seen as being able to choose precisely because he is assumed to know the relevant future; Mises sees choice as possible only because the future is unknown. The explanation, of course, lies in the two quite different notions of choice that are being referred to. Mainstream microeconomics deals with choice strictly in the sense in which a well-programmed computer can "choose" the optimum route through which to travel to a given destination. Mises is referring to genuinely human choice, for which human purposefulness (in the sense described in the preceding paragraph) is a necessary ingredient. It is of course obvious that in a world of complete certainty there can be no scope for that purposeful, alert, attitude which in our world informs and suffuses choice. The very notion of action implies, therefore, that uncertainty which indeed characterizes our world. The very notion of the uncertainty of the future assures us that in such a world human beings will not be able to engage in the mechanical "choice" suitable to automata; they will perforce, because they are human beings, act. Elsewhere I have suggested (Kirzner, 1973, pp. 32–5) that the essential element present in Misesian human action which has been carefully excluded in mainstream microeconomics, should be recognized as the entrepreneurial element in human action. Just as Mises insisted on the uncertainty context of human action, so he insisted on the uncertainty context of entrepreneurship "The term entrepreneur . . . means: acting man exclusively seen from the aspect of uncertainty inherent in every action" (Mises, 1949, p. 254). As we shall see, it is this entrepreneurial element in every action—that element which transforms mechanical decisions into human actions—which enables us to eat our cake and have it, to maintain the subjectivist freedom of the individual decision and yet understand the emergence of those powerful regularities which economic science has, for two hundred years and more, made it its business to explain.

OPEN-ENDEDNESS AND THE OVERCOMING OF UNCERTAINTY

It is the uncertainty which pervades our world which is responsible for that open-endedness of human action which sets it so sharply apart from the mechanical optimization which makes up the decision in mainstream microeconomics. The given ends-means framework which is the setting for the maximization exercises of mainstream microeconomics precludes the possibility of genuine choice because that very framework makes genuine choice unnecessary. The assumptions fed into the model ensure only one exit; these assumptions effectively close off any conceivable alternative exit. Lifting these constraints, relaxing these assumptions, therefore converts a closed model into an open-ended situation. But lifting these constraints does much more, it at once permits us to see the agent as a purposeful human being; we are at once permitted to introduce into our reasoning an element of explanation (reflecting a primordially important feature of human action) which the mainstream model of decision making prohibited us from deploying. That element of explanation is the theory of entrepreneurship, and the feature of human action to which this element of explanation relates is the human propensity—an "entrepreneurial" propensity to discover opportunities to improve one's situation. So that the step from the closed models of mainstream microeconomics to the open-ended world of subjectivist economics is not at all one which does no more than erase the only economic basis for accounting for market regularities. That step, while it indeed unavoidably entails profound scepticism for the determinacy purportedly achieved by those closed models, introduces, at the same time, a powerful new explanatory element into the scientific picture, precisely because that step permits consideration of a critically important element shaping real world events, viz. the element of entrepreneurial purposefulness. Hasty readers of Mises may, I have argued elsewhere, misunderstand his references to the uncertainty in which he insists that human action (and, especially, entrepreneurship) is embedded (Kirzner, 1982, ch. 12). They may conclude that, for Mises, what is important about uncertainty is that it obscures human vision and obstructs the way to efficient choice. They may therefore interpret Mises's emphasis on this uncertainty as an affirmation of the omnipresence of human entrepreneurial error. They may find it puzzling therefore that it should ever be argued that entrepreneurial behavior be seen as equilibrative. Surely that uncertainty which, for Mises is the essential element for entrepreneurial action, implies the inevitability of entrepreneurial error. With such error seen as an essential feature of entrepreneurial activity, how can we rest our explanation for an asserted universal equilibrating tendency upon the activity, of the entrepreneur? (Cf. also Loasby, 1989, pp. 161ff.)

But our observations in the preceding section on the meaning of the purposefulness which Mises sees as central to the human action concept, should help us see the fallacy in such a reading of Mises, and in such a line of questioning. What Mises meant to emphasize, in his insistence on the uncertainty context of human action in general, and of entrepreneurship in particular, was not the inevitability of error. Rather Mises wished to emphasize the distinctive character of that environment which calls forth the entrepreneurial element in each and every human agent. No one need deny that the uncertainty in which human action is embedded renders man prone to error. What Mises was underscoring, however, was that man's success in overcoming error—a success it would surely be a mistake totally to deny—arises out of his propensity to act, i.e. to act in a way which expresses his propensity to discover the existence of opportunities *despite* the acknowledged uncertainty of the future.

From this way of seeing matters it emerges that open-endedness does not at all mean that outcomes are simply random. Open-endedness means that man is free to choose for himself, that is, to determine for himself what he believes the relevant framework for decision to be. Precisely because he is so free to choose, in an environment in which virtually nothing is certain, we can be sure that his choices will be guided, informed and inspired by his purposefulness—by his entrepreneurial propensity to discern, amid the swirling fogs of the future, the outlines of the opportunities which in fact he faces.

SELF-INTEREST, RATIONALITY AND PURPOSEFULNESS: A BRIEF DIGRESSION

To drive home the important insight of the preceding section, it is worthwhile to digress briefly on the various assumptions introduced by different generations of economists in order to "nail down" human decisions in a way that permits us to account for market regularities. Critics of economic theory have traditionally focused on these assumptions as the targets of their ire. They have again and again challenged the conclusions of economics on the grounds of the alleged unrealism of these assumptions. The insight developed in the preceding section requires and permits a different—and, we suggest, a more convincing—line of defence for economic theory.

During much of the nineteenth century economics proceeded on the basis of a strict self-interest assumption. Economic theory was the domain of homo economicus (and his behavior was reliably predictable because the materialistic conception of economics was sufficiently dominant in the nineteenth century to permit the economist to know exactly where the economic interest of the agent lay). Economics has never quite shaken off the stigma of its early fling as the science of materialistic selfishness, and contemporary critics of economics still purport to find ammunition for their attacks in the selfishness charge.

Neoclassical economics distanced itself from the self-interest assumption by drawing attention to the notion of rationality, of efficient allocation of scarce resources, of constrained maximization—in regard to the attainment of whatever objectives one chose to postulate, altruistic as well as selfish. Critics of mainstream neoclassical economics must now focus their criticisms on the alleged unrealism of the assumed propensity of man to remain the cool, careful calculator, unswayed by passion, habit, impulse and error.

Thus the critics of economics (that is, those who indeed challenge the correctness of the view of economics ascribing powerful regularities to market systems) have focused on those various assumptions which economists have used to "pin down" what economic agents in fact decide to do. The insights of the preceding section offer a fresh foundation for understanding market regularities (that is, for drastically narrowing down the range of randomness governing individual behavior). The traditional criticisms of economics would seem, it may be suggested, to have far less relevance for economic theory so conceived (Kirzner, 1992, ch. 12). For we have seen that economic theory may be grounded, not in any assumed tropism pulling decision making unerringly toward the satisfaction of narrowly selfish goals, nor in any assumed model of constrained maximization assumed to govern behavior, but in the simple, universal propensity of man to be wakeful, alert and purposefully oriented towards the uncertainties of the future. The tendency of market outcomes to reflect, at least to some extent, the realities which surround the society of men, derives from the propensity of men shrewdly to size up these uncertainties and to act purposefully to discover and overcome error. That much research needs to be focused on understanding the scope and limits of this propensity need not be denied. That this propensity is indeed sufficient to support much of traditional microeconomic theory must, however, be emphatically affirmed. Let us turn to a brief statement of how this last claim can seriously be made.

ENTREPRENEURSHIP AND THE POSSIBILITY OF SYSTEMATIC MARKET FORCES

We have drawn attention to the role of Misesian purposefulness in systematically overcoming uncertainty. Brief reflection should remind us that, indeed it is precisely upon the power of such purposefulness, that the central theorems of economics have, consciously or otherwise, traditionally depended. Consider the simple theorem that predicts a market tendency towards achieving a single price for a given good in a given market (usually associated with Jevons's Law of Indifference). This tendency obviously rests upon the economist's confidence in the speed and success with which entrepreneurs will pounce upon the pure profit opportunity created by any price discrepancies (which might initially be violating Jevons's Law).

Now, a little reflection must surely convince us that economists' confidence in this powerful tendency supports not only their understanding of this tendency itself, but also their confidence in the tendency of costs and prices to converge, and their confidence in equilibrating tendencies in general, both in the context of the Marshallian single market and in that of the Walrasian system of interlinked markets. Economists typically spend very little time justifying their confidence in this basic tendency for pure profit opportunities to be competed away through arbitrage. And the reason for this is that, within the neoclassical paradigm, the possibility of pure profit itself is something of an embarrassing paradox. The neoclassical assumption of perfect knowledge is, as is well known (certainly ever since Knight's *Risk, Uncertainty and Profit*) simply inconsistent with the possibility of pure profit. So that neoclassical economists must either be hard-boiled about it and insist that their models simply preclude such possibilities (that is, they insist on equilibrium theory while explicitly refusing, on positivist methodological grounds, to see the need for justifying the equilibrium assumption at all), or they must attribute pure profit to sudden unexpected changes in underlying conditions and postulate (without too much elaboration) that "of course" the profit possibilities so generated will rapidly lead to their own equilibrating destruction.

But the rapid self-elimination of opportunities for pure profit is not at all something to be taken for granted as obvious. After all, if an opportunity that exists at a given moment in time has not yet been perceived (and its very existence proves that to have been the case, because to perceive an opportunity for pure profit must be assumed immediately to inspire a move to grasp it), then it is not obvious at all how that opportunity will come to be spontaneously perceived at any subsequent moment in time. After all, if the opportunity has indeed been totally unperceived that means that market participants have been unaware of the worthwhileness of opportunities to search for the pure profit possibilities we are discussing. Clearly our universal reliance on the powerful market forces which tend to eliminate pure profit opportunities, rests on our confidence in the entrepreneurial propensities of market participants. Such entrepreneurial propensities are precisely those which Mises associated with the general purposefulness of human action in the face of uncertainty.

MARKET PROCESSES AND THE SPREAD OF KNOWLEDGE

The central thrust of the preceding sections can be driven home by a restatement in terms of processes of change in knowledge. Subjectivists of all stripes will agree that changes in economic outcomes must express changes in human knowledge. It is only as they systematically modify the knowledge (including expectations regarding the future) possessed by market participants, that we can understand how exogenous changes in physical circumstances (for example) can generate systematic changes in market prices, allocation of resources, and so forth.

Yet it is not at all obvious how such changes in knowledge and expectations can be systematically generated—or, rather, it ceases to be obvious as soon as we abandon the implicit assumption that changes in external circumstances are somehow instantaneously and automatically mapped by corresponding changes in man's knowledge. (Once again, deliberate search activity cannot be relied upon to explain such changes in knowledge—because the relevant question is how do men know what different items of information they must now search for, and how can they know that different ways of searching are now worthwhile, and so on. After all, yesterday's deliberate plans for search was based on an obsolete outline-picture of the world. Today we should, in the light of objectively changed conditions, see that outline-picture quite differently. But how do the changed conditions in fact achieve this changed outline-picture in men's minds?)

We are inevitably driven to the insight that it is man's entrepreneurial propensity upon which we must rely for our reasonable confidence that changes in external circumstances do tend, sooner or later, to come to be noticed by entrepreneurial market participants. And, as pointed out, it is upon this tendency for systematic changes in human knowledge to occur, that economic theory necessarily relies for its most basic, and its most far-reaching conclusions.

SUBJECTIVIST FREEDOM ONCE AGAIN

This chapter began with a discussion of what we have called "subjectivist freedom." We saw how a consistent subjectivist perspective requires us to see human action as undetermined by objective external circumstances (including the circumstances consisting of the actions of other market participants). That statement led us to articulate a serious problem, that of reconciling recognition of subjectivist freedom with the very possibility of understanding economic regularities.

Our discussion has permitted us to find the solution to this problem. Not only have we seen how an open-ended perspective on human decision making—one which sees such decision making as not constrained by the contours of single-exit models—can be consistent with economic regularities. We have in fact seen how it is only by reference to such open-ended concepts of decision making, concepts which offer full scope to subjectivist freedom, that we can begin to appreciate the power and the reach of the entrepreneurial element in individual human action and in market entrepreneurship. Hayek's remarks concerning the contributions of subjectivism to advances in economic understanding, turn out to be fully applicable also to the contribution offered by recognition of subjectivist freedom.

SUBJECTIVIST FREEDOM AND FREE MARKETS

We have emphasized the special meaning we have assigned to the term subjectivist freedom. Subjectivist freedom refers not to any institutional arrangements permitting substantive liberties to the individual market participant, but strictly to the absence of determining control over human behavior exercised by external circumstances. Yet it would be disingenuous for us to fail to note certain important points of contact between the kind of freedom referred to in the concept of free markets, and the subjectivist freedom which we have been discussing. It turns out that the extent to which we can rely on the purposefulness unleashed by subjectivist freedom is not unrelated to the scope for substantive liberties permitted by the institutional context.

Subjectivist freedom inspires purposefulness. But purposefulness can inspire human action to discern the outline of available opportunities only where there is the prospect of an actual opportunity to achieve a desired objective. Where the desired objectives (which an "opportunity" indicates to be in principle available) may not in fact be achieved (even though their availability may have been noticed) due to some externally imposed institutional constraint (for example, a law restricting price increases, or an excess profit tax, or a law prohibiting the production of some specific product)—then we have no grounds for assuming that any kind of "purposefulness" can be depended upon to generate relevant discovery. An uncertain world is a world in which profitable opportunities (as yet unperceived) are likely to exist; it is a world in which as yet unidentified opportunities provide scope for open-ended variety of decision-making, a scope which we have identified as subjectivist freedom; and it is, finally, a world in which the institutional freedom to enjoy discovered opportunities can in fact spark the discovery potential which we have identified as entrepreneurship. As we have seen, it is the latter circumstance which justifies the confidence which economists have in the tendencies of markets to identify—and thus eliminate—opportunities for pure profits.

It is the circumstance that entrepreneurial purposefulness cannot be relied upon unless pure profits are permitted to be enjoyed, that underlay the Austrian critique of the possibility of socialist economic calculation. Government officials whose status, by definition, precludes their being able personally to profit from their commercial discoveries, cannot be depended upon to achieve through planning, or through bureaucratically setting nonmarket "prices" to stimulate effective market activities, those discoveries the generation of which constitutes the real contribution of free markets.

THE ECONOMICS OF SUBJECTIVISM: CRITICISM FROM TWO DIRECTIONS

We can now appreciate why it is that subjectivist economics (as it has emerged, for example, as a result of the Austrian tradition in economic thought) faces attacks from two opposite directions.[5] On the one hand mainstream neoclassical critics are likely to wonder why we have to go through all this subjectivist talk concerning the asserted "freedom" of human action. If, when we come down to the bottom-line entrepreneurship (or whatever) can be relied upon to move markets towards equilibrium, then why may we not, for modelling purposes, operate with equilibrium models exclusively—that is, why may we not use models which behave as if external phenomena independently constrain economic behavior and thus generate economic regularities?

At one level of discussion the subjectivist may be prepared to concede a certain validity to this criticism. For certain purposes it is indeed not necessary to explore the manner in which outcomes emerge as a result of the spontaneous, free choices of market participants; it is sufficient to focus on our degree of confidence that those choices will tend to discover the best relevant options in fact available. But at the deeper level of discussion no such concessions need be made by the subjectivist. At this deeper level the proper response to this kind of mainstream criticism lies in the area of economic methodology; it rests upon an approach to economics which seeks, not replicable predictions, not econometric "explanation" in terms of statistical correlation, but essentialist understanding of actual social phenomena in the manner in which they occur.[6] For this latter approach equilibrium models offer no help at all. They simply assert the outcome; they offer no explanation for its plausible attainment.

But there is a line of criticism of the subjectivist economics which we have outlined in this paper, which proceeds from the diametrically opposite methodological direction (from that of mainstream economics). Such ultra-subjectivist criticism objects, not to our emphasis upon the subjectivist freedom of individual decision making, but to our insistence that such freedom is entirely consistent with (in fact necessary for) the emergence of systematic microeconomic forces. The position taken by these critics is likely to emphasize the possibilities for entrepreneurial error and, in particular, the possibility that interacting entrepreneurial errors may magnify the scope for and likelihood of entrepreneurial errors. (This, for example, is what Keynes was referring to in his comparing the stock market to a casino.)

The proper response to this kind of criticism must lie in further clarifying and articulating the arguments in this paper which have supported the notion of a systematic, all-pervasive human propensity to discover those errors of others which manifest themselves in pure profit opportunities. We must never permit our understanding of human freedom—the subjectivist variety—to obscure our understanding of how freedom inspires human purposefulness.

Markets do work. They work so obviously well that our scientific curiosity is aroused to seek understanding of the counter-intuitive phenomenon of this success. What we have argued here is that the achievement of a deepened appreciation for the nature and implications of subjectivism—an objective which Ludwig Lachmann himself pursued with such steadfast tenacity and with such sparkling brilliance—can here, as elsewhere, offer a most illuminating contribution towards enhanced economic understanding.

NOTES

This chapter was presented as a paper at the University of the Witwatersrand on August 19, 1991 as the inaugural Ludwig Lachmann Memorial Lecture, sponsored jointly by the University of the Witwatersrand and the Free Market Foundation of Southern Africa. Research support by the Sarah Scaife Foundation is gratefully acknowledged. The author is also grateful to Professor Mario Rizzo for helpful discussion during the preparation of the paper, and to members of the Austrian Economics Colloquium at New York University for useful comments on an earlier draft. Only the author is responsible for errors in the chapter.

1. It should be obvious that the term *freedom* used here does not relate to philosophical issues having to do with free will and the like. The term here refers strictly to the absence of any determining influence upon human behavior that might be exercised by external phenomena. The subjectivist's foe is not so much philosophical determinism as psychological behaviorism.
2. Lachmann (1977, p. 92). Although Lachmann never, to my knowledge, made reference to it, it must have given him great pleasure indeed that Shackle—whom Lachmann admired as the master-subjectivist—chose this sentence (together with several others from the same review by Lachmann of a book of Shackle's) to be placed at the head of Shackle's *magnum opus*, *Epistemics and Economics* (1972).
3. As is well known, Mises used the term "rational" as synonymous with "purposeful." On this see Fraser (1937, p. 37); Robbins (1935, p. 93). For an extensive discussion of Misesian human action and its "purposefulness," see Kirzner (1960, ch. 7).
4. Mises (1949, p. 105). Compare also the famous observation by Knight (1921, p. 294): "Consciousness would never have developed if the environment of living organisms were perfectly uniform and monotonous, conformable to mechanical laws. In such a world organisms would be automata."
5. For further discussion of some of the issues raised in this section see also Kirzner (1985, ch. 1; 1992, ch. 1).
6. For further discussion on this issue see Mäki (1990).

REFERENCES

Fraser, L.M. (1937) *Economic Thought and Language. A Critique of Some Fundamental Economic Concepts*, London: A. & C. Black.

Hayek, F.A. (1955) *The Counter-Revolution of Science*, Glencoe, IL: The Free Press.

de Jasay, A. (1991) *Choice, Contract, Consent: A Restatement of Liberalism*, London: Institute of Economic Affairs.

Kirzner, I.M. (1960) *The Economic Point of View*, Princeton, NJ: Van Nostrand.

—— (1973) *Competition and Entrepreneurship*, Chicago: University of Chicago Press.

—— (1982) *Method, Process and Austrian Economics, Essays in Honor of Ludwig von Mises*, Lexington, MA: D.C. Heath.

—— (1985) *Discovery and the Capitalist Process*, Chicago: University of Chicago Press.

—— (1992) *The Meaning of Market Process. Essays in the Development of Modern Austrian Economics*, London and New York: Routledge.

Knight, F.H. (1921) *Risk, Uncertainty and Profit*, Boston, MA: Houghton Mifflin.

Lachmann, L.M. (1986) *The Market as an Economic Process*, Oxford: Basil Blackwell.

—— (1977) *Capital, Expectation, and the Market Process*, Kansas City: Sheed, Andrews and McMeel.

Loasby, B.J. (1989) *The Mind and Method of the Economist. A Critical Appraisal of Major Economists in the Twentieth Century*, Aldershot: Edward Elgar.

Mäki, U. (1990) "Mengerian economics in realist perspective," in B. Caldwell (ed.) *Carl Menger and his Legacy in Economics*, Durham, NC: Duke University Press.

Mises, L. von (1949) *Human Action. A Treatise on Economics*, London: William Hodge & Co. Ltd.

Pareto, V. (1927) *Manuel d'Economie Politique*, 2nd edn, Paris.

Robbins, L. (1935) *The Nature and Significance of Economic Science*, 2nd edn, London: Macmillan.

Shackle, G.L.S. (1972) *Epistemics and Economics*, Cambridge: Cambridge University Press.

Source: Subjectivism, Freedom and Economic Law, *South African Journal of Economics*, 1992, 60(1).

Part II

THE MARKET PROCESS

Some normative perspectives

4

THE LIMITS OF THE MARKET

The real and the imagined

Conventional wisdom asserts the existence of important limits to the operation of markets. Even economists who generally champion the efficiency properties of the market readily concede that significant and widespread cases of market failure provide a valid rationale for government policies suspending or modifying the operation of the market. Our thesis in this chapter, building on insights developed in modern Austrian economics, is that if the nature and functions of the market are properly understood, it must be acknowledged that the market never fails to fulfill those functions. In this sense, the asserted "limits of the market" do not in fact exist. We shall, for reasons which will become obvious, refer to these limits (which we are denying) as, "inner limits." We hasten to add that, as we shall see, this denial of the existence of any "inner" limits to the market does not, by itself destroy the possibility of economically justified active governmental policies. But acceptance of our thesis will, nonetheless, alert us to the searching and challenging questions which must be asked before such policies can in fact be justified on strictly economic grounds.

While this chapter will thus sharply criticize what is generally understood by the term "limits of the market," we will at the same time emphasize a different, valid, and indeed insufficiently appreciated—sense of the term. In this different sense, the term "limits of the market" do not refer at all to any kind of market failure. Instead the notion refers to the institutional pre-requisites for the very existence of the market. We shall refer to such limits as the "outer" limits of the market. We wish to emphasize the insight that, for its very emergence and existence, the market must rely on the presence of extramarket institutions, without which the idea of a market process must be a mere dream. These genuine limits to the market, because they do not refer to market failure, cannot provide any rationale for governmental suspension of markets. But they certainly do point our thinking concerning markets towards the extramarket ethics or legal principles which may, practically speaking, be the necessary basis for those institutions upon which the market itself must rest. Our quarrel with economists concerning this latter point relates to a certain tendency within modern economics to understand the establishment of private property—that bedrock institution required for the very idea of markets—as somehow historically and conceptually independent of ethics. Such "economic" theories of property rights, explaining these rights in terms of blind, amoral, economic forces acting in the prehistory of market societies, in effect deny the existence, or at least the relevance, of "outer" limits to the market.

To sum up our argument in this chapter, then, we will be concerned (a) to deny those "inner limits" to the market which economists affirm in the doctrine of market failure; and (b) to insist upon the importance of those "outer limits" to the market which economists in effect deny in the economic theories of property rights. Proper appreciation for the true ("outer") limits to the market, and recognition for the utter absence of "inner limits" to the operation of the market are both important for understanding the appropriate economic role for government in the market society, and the appropriate limitations for that role. But we shall argue further that it is our very appreciation for the reality of the market's "outer limits" which conduces to our understanding of how imaginary are those alleged "inner limits" implied by the theory of market failure.

Section I of this chapter will present our definition of the market and what we consider to be its central function. Section II will apply these insights to the elucidation of the impossibility of market failure, once the true function of the market is properly understood. Section III will elaborate our thesis concerning the very real outer limits of the market, in terms of its institutional prerequisites, and will apply the thesis to refer critically to the economic theory of property rights. Finally, Section IV will develop our assertion that the mistaken notion of "inner limits" to the market may, at least in part, be attributed to insufficient appreciation for the reality of the market's outer limits.

I

A market economy is a societal arrangement in which the ultimate decisions concerning the disposition of individually held rights to goods and services are exercised by the relevant individuals themselves. In such a pure market economy all the economic outcomes, exchanges, allocation of resources, prices of productive factor services and of consumer goods and services, outputs, methods of production and modes of organization and the structure of production, are all determined by the interplay of voluntary decisions of property owners.

In neoclassical economics the textbook statements concerning the function of the market refer routinely to the achievement of an efficient allocation of society's resources. (It is with reference to this criterion of efficient societal resource allocation that market failure theorists find the market wanting.) Following upon Hayek's 1945 critique of the very notion of societal efficiency in a world of dispersed information, (and mindful of the traditional Austrian rejection of notions of global welfare) modern Austrian economics has dismissed the idea that the function of the market is to allocate resources efficiently. Since information is in fact scattered, it is hardly relevant to apply as a yardstick a notion of global efficiency which could have meaning only for an omniscient mind possessing global control over all economic activity. Instead, the function of the market has been seen as one of *coordinating* the plans of independently acting market participants.[1] In particular, this function has been interpreted as that of promoting the mutual discovery by market participants of the availability of and needs for exchangeable goods and services (Hayek, 1978; Kirzner, 1985, chs 1, 2 and 3; Kirzner, 1989, ch. 4).

It should be noticed that while this view of the functions of the market rejects—on methodologically individualist grounds—holistic treatment of society as faced by the Robbinsian challenge of efficiency in resource allocation,[2] it certainly does recognize a supra-individual function for the market. Successful achievement by the market of this "social" function requires that it spur those discoveries that will promote those sets of individual decisions which will best enable individuals severally to fulfill their respective objectives, in light of their own endowments and in conjunction with the opportunities implicit in the endowments and objectives of others.[3] What it is important to emphasize is that this coordination function, promoting the exploitation by individuals of the potential for mutually gainful exchanges amongst them, can be defined only against the background of given individual rights to endowments. *If* individual A possesses money and is hungry, while individual B possesses a surplus of food but lacks money, *then* we can appraise social mechanisms in regard to their effectiveness in promoting the coordinating mutual discovery by A and by B of the gains to be achieved by exchange. It would have been idle to speculate concerning "coordination" (in regard to the distribution of food and money between A and B) in the absence of some initial given position (reflecting the given initial endowments). If it were possible to talk sensibly of the total utility to A and B (corresponding to alternative distribution of food and money between them) then, of course, (as in neoclassical welfare theory in its many variants), one might imagine being able to assess outcomes in terms of a global optimality criterion. Then, as in mainstream economic discourse, the market might be seen as having the function of computing the solution to that set of simultaneous equations marking out the relevant optimal pattern of allocation. The market might be assessed in terms of its success in regard to this function. But the Hayekian point is that such assessments must, given the impossibility of centralized access to all available, dispersed bits of information, remain entirely imaginary. Instead, the modern Austrian approach argues, we can recognize that markets encourage the identification and exploitation by individuals of hitherto unnoticed opportunities for mutually gainful exchange or cooperation. It is this tendency towards supra-individual coordination which constitutes the discovery function of the market. This function is to alert market participants to possibilities for gain that may, without being yet known to anyone, be inherent in the current pattern of ownership and of preference. This function is, to use modern Austrian terminology, to overcome the "knowledge problem."

II

Market failure theorists focus attention on situations where (as, for example, in the presence of externalities), individual self-interested decision-making produces a globally suboptimal outcome. Individual self-interested decisions pay attention only to private gains and private costs. Where, however, externalities exist, an activity may, for example, generate costs to others, such that what appears to the individual as an optimal choice, affording him significant net gain, may in fact be causing damage to others which outweighs, in some social sense, the gain to himself. Such cases are held to be examples of "market failure."[4] While the economic literature following on Ronald Coase's seminal paper (1960) valuably drew attention to the market's own potential for the private internalization of externalities,[5] this literature yet left ample scope for what appeared to be market failure. Where transaction costs render private internalization unfeasible, markets generate suboptimal outcomes. Cases such as "prisoner-dilemma" situations, situations involving so-called "public goods" (in which "free-riding" is feasible and tempting), provide models of market failure. and thus call for governmental suspension of the market. By limiting the freedom of individuals to act without regard to the social consequences of their actions, governments may hope to improve the allocation of resources (over what would have occurred as a result of market failure).[6]

What we wish to argue in this section is that none of these situations (in which self-interested individual decisions generate what are held to be socially suboptimal outcomes) constitutes valid examples of what could properly be called market failure—in the context of the understanding of the function of the market as developed in the preceding section. In none of these situations has the market failed to tend to coordinate individual decisions in the light of the relevant property right endowments.

Standard theory pronounces these situations to be cases of market failure because that theory, blandly assuming a perspective of imagined omniscience (and skillfully side-stepping the problems of interpersonal comparisons of utility) believes it possible to identify the resulting market outcomes as socially inferior to patterns of resource allocation attainable through government intervention. From this perspective the market must, in such situations, fail to achieve that which is its assigned function to achieve, viz. a socially optimal pattern of resource allocation. But, from the perspective outlined in the preceding section, matters appear quite differently.

From this latter ("Austrian") perspective, the function of the market is to overcome the knowledge problem, i.e. to promote the coordination among individual decisions so as to enable market participants to take advantage of available opportunities for mutually gainful exchange. But, as noted, such coordination can be defined only in the context of a given pattern of individual rights. Within such a context it is the function of the market to promote mutual discovery and, thus, coordination. In situations characterized in mainstream theory as cases of market failure, the pattern of rights is such as to create unsustainably high costs of internalizing troubling externalities. In the light of such costs the resulting market outcomes—no matter how "suboptimal" they may appear from the perspective of omniscience—do tend to promote discovery of relevant information, encouraging fullest exploitation of all available opportunities for mutually gainful exchange. We must, after all, remember that the concept "all available opportunities for mutually gainful exchange" can be spelled out only after taking due account of (a) initial endowments, and (b) of relevant transaction costs. So that, given the high costs of internalizing externalities, the *de facto* distribution of rights (allowing, say, a manufacturer to pollute a river without having to pay for so doing) constrains the discovery procedure of the market faithfully to tend to reflect the given rights framework (by tending to disseminate information concerning the relevant realities to all market participants).

To say that the market process works successfully in the context of externalities is certainly not to pronounce the market outcome socially optimal (if only because we have questioned the meaning of social optimality in a world of dispersed information). Nor is it, in and of itself, to declare governmental attempts compulsorily to internalize externalities, to be a definite error (since, after all, governmental policy may seek to reflect citizens' preferences as these are understood in moral or political terms, rather than in the narrow, austerely "scientific" terms within which economic science is confined). But to recognize that the market process of mutual discovery works in the presence of externalities no less effectively than it does in their absence, should alert us to one serious potential for harm in such governmental policies. To the extent that such policies suspend or inhibit the market process, they are obstructing a process of discovery without offering any substitute for it. Let us not forget that the market process has the function of alerting market participants to opportunities which nobody has expected. To initiate governmental policies to grapple with externalities is, in effect, to pretend knowledge which no one can, in principle, honestly claim to possess.

Where cooperation is of real or imagined mutual benefit to a group of individuals, the market will of course provide scope for such cooperation. The market does, as has often been recognized,[7] make it possible for groups within it to organize themselves in communes or other organizations on strictly socialist principles, if they choose. (This, let us not forget, is how capitalist firms come into existence.) But the market will do more than simply *permit* cooperation. It will offer the incentives for members of such groups *to discover* the fact that cooperation would be mutually gainful. Where the structure of property rights is such as to make it economically feasible for private internalization of external effects to occur, the market will generate the incentives sufficient *to alert* market participants to the benefits so to be gained. The market process has no "inner limits" (in the sense that it fails to encourage necessary cooperation among individuals to form firms or organizations of a size best able to participate in the open-ended competitive process of the market). It is true that the market will not inspire cooperation where the transactions costs of so doing are prohibitive (even though such co-operation may appear highly desirable from a perspective which sees these transactions costs as in principle avoidable—say, through government compulsion). But this does not exemplify market failure or the existence of limits to the effectiveness of the market in alerting participants to opportunities inherent in the given set of rights—with all the benefits and costs that such a set of rights implies. Let us turn now to take note of the real limits to the market—limits which many economists have tended to ignore.

III

These limits on the market are imposed by its institutional pre-requisites. Without these institutional prerequisites—primarily, private property rights and freedom and enforceability of contract—the market cannot operate. It follows that those institutions cannot be created by the market itself. The institutions upon which the market must depend must have been created or have evolved through processes different from those spontaneous co-ordinative processes which we have seen to constitute the essence of the market's operation. It can in fact be shown[8] not only that, of course, we cannot, without a market, rely on spontaneous market processes of coordination to establish the institutions needed for the market to operate, but also that we cannot rely upon *any* spontaneous social forces to foster those institutions. So that these institutional requirements for the market constitute what we have termed the "outer limits" to the market. They mark out the boundaries beyond which any coordinative processes (such as those generating the sets of mutually reinforcing expectations which constitute the system of property rights) must necessarily be of a non-market character.

Emphasis on the nature of these outer limits is important in that it can assist in winning proper recognition for the role of shared ethical principles in the emergence of societal institutions. Surely the principal historical basis for the institution of private property rights or for the institution of enforceability of contract has been man's moral convictions concerning the simple justice of owning what one has produced with one's own effort, or has discovered through one's own alertness, and the injustice of appropriating (through violence or dishonesty) what another has produced, discovered, or otherwise justly acquired. Such shared moral convictions may certainly have evolved over time, and have been partly shaped by economic conditions. But we cannot fail to acknowledge the sharp difference which separates what occurs as a result of spontaneous economic processes *within* market societies, from the complex webs of historical experience which come to be crystallized in the shared moral intuitions which support the institutions which frame market societies. The former processes are themselves intrinsically amoral, they tend to express, faithfully and neutrally, the preferences and values of market participants. The latter crystallization of shared moral intuitions consists, at each moment in history, of sets of explicit or tacit ethical convictions nourishing people's evaluation of and expectations concerning the acts of others. No understanding of the market can afford to ignore the fundamental insight that its institutional foundations are to be sought directly, not in economic considerations but in ethical ones.[9]

The thrust of these observations of ours concerning the outer limits of the market must be to question the perspective insisted upon in the literature seeking to develop the "economic analysis of rights."[10] That literature tends to dissolve the sharp difference we have asserted separating the character of market processes from the character of the processes leading up to the crystallization of the institutions upon which markets must rest for their very existence. That literature would, if carried to the extreme, entirely deny the relevance of outer limits to the market. It would, in this extreme form, recognize both inside and outside the market, only the impersonal, amoral force of costs and benefits. This "economic" force would be seen as operating uniformly within the relevant constraints, whether these be those of secure property rights (as within the market society), or of brute force and fear (as in the Hobbesian jungle). A consequence (of this denial of the relevance of the outer limits to the market) must surely be to weaken the perceived moral basis for the assignment of rights. As a critic of the economic analysis of rights has pointed out, that analysis "offers plenty of good reasons for those assignments of rights which seem intuitively clear to us, but the reasons have nothing to do with the inherent 'rightness' . . . or the 'wickedness' [of the positions of victims of civil wrongs and of those of the wrongdoers]" (Fried, 1978, p. 98). Our purpose in this section is not only to deplore this "sundering of ethical decisions from decisions about rights" (Fried, 1978, p. 96), but to insist (albeit without working out here the proof[11]) that we can*not*, in order to arrive at the market institutions of a free and civilized society, in fact rely upon impersonal economic forces to transform a Hobbesian jungle into a stable and ordered system of law. There *are* outer limits to the market, and to the benignly coordinative properties of the spontaneous economic forces which operate within it. These forces can only be relied upon provided a widely shared ethic already exists which firmly recognizes the "rightness" of the property rights system and the corresponding "wrongness" of theft and fraud.

IV

We have argued in this chapter against the existence of the inner limits to the market asserted by market failure theorists, and in affirmation of the existence of the outer limits to the market (in effect denied by the economic analysis of rights). Our denial of inner limits to the market should alert us to the potential dangers in government suspension of or interference with markets. Our affirmation of outer limits to markets should drive home the need for society-wide acceptance of shared ethical perspectives (and, most likely, for governmental, extra-market enforcement of the rights system implied in such shared ethical perspectives). But it seems important also to emphasize the existence of the market's outer limits in order to appreciate the impossibility of inner limits to its effectiveness.

As noted in Sections I and II, the function of the market process can be defined only with respect to some given initial set of endowments. Only after we can assume some such given initial set, can one define the task of achieving coordination among market participants (so that the opportunities for mutually gainful exchange implicit in the endowment set, together with the preferences of the participants, can be discovered and exploited). It was this insight which led us to recognize that such phenomena as externalities do not generate market failure (at least in the framework of the market's essential function as we explained it to be).

What we wish to point out is that this recognition rests upon an understanding of the importance of the rights framework of the market. For economists who fail to appreciate this importance, welfare conclusions are sought which refer hardly at all to the initial pattern of ownership. For them welfare conclusions are sought relevant to the resources available to society as a whole (as well, of course, as the preferences of individual members of society). For us, on the other hand, who see the function of the market as consisting in the coordination of decisions among holders of rights, the pattern of initial distribution of such rights looms into a position of pivotal importance. If market outcomes, resulting from externalities, are deemed somehow unfortunate, this is seen immediately as attributable, not to the failure of the market to coordinate with respect to the given rights system, but to the pattern of rights which the system has, rightly or wrongly, taken as its initial framework. As we have noted there is significant merit in being able to distinguish sharply between a possibly faulty functioning of the market (a possibility we have denied) and a possibly erroneous initial distribution of rights (a possibility we must certainly recognize[12]).

Towards the attainment of such a more insightful understanding of markets and their function, we suggest that our emphasis on the nature and importance of the outer limits to the market can make a useful contribution. The uniquely valuable character of the spontaneous forces of the market process rests entirely on nonmarket-generated institutions which frame the market. Seeing the outer limits of the market with clarity can help economists avoid the analytical fog which has led so many to see inner limits to the effectiveness of the market where no such limits in fact exist.

NOTES

1. On this see Kirzner (1973, ch. 6), O'Driscoll (1977), Cordato (1992).
2. Robbins (1935, ch. 1).
3. On this point see Buchanan (1964).
4. Bator (1958). See also Schotter (1990, ch. 4).
5. An example of this literature is Buchanan and Stubblebine (1962).
6. Of course, public choice theory has pointed out the fallacy of ignoring the very real possibilities for "government failure"—but that is not our topic in this chapter.
7. See Nozick (1974, pp. 250f.). See also Coase (1937).
8. For such a demonstration, see Kirzner (1992, ch. 10).
9. For a vigorous presentation of this point see North (1992).
10. A classic in this literature was Demsetz (1967). Note that the criticism in the text does not contradict the substance of Demsetz's most interesting analysis—only the suggestion it conveys that rights have evolved historically in a moral vacuum.
11. On this, see above, note 8.
12. For a detailed discussion of the relationship between the problems of externalities and possible flaws in the legal system establishing and protecting property rights, see von Mises (1966, pp. 654–61).

REFERENCES

Bator, Francis (1958) "The Anatomy of Market Failure," *Quarterly Journal of Economics* August.

Buchanan, James M. (1964) "What Should Economists Do?," *Southern Economic Journal* 30(January).

Buchanan, James M. and Stubblebine, William Craig (1962) "Externality," *Economica* xxxi, pp. 371–84.

Coase, Ronald H. (1937) "The Nature of the Firm," *Economica* n.s. 4, pp. 386–405.

—— (1960) "The Problem of Social Cost," *Journal of Law and Economics* 3, pp. 1–40.

Cordato, Roy E. (1992) *Welfare Economics and Externalities in an Open Ended Universe: A Modern Austrian Perspective*, Boston, MA: Kluwer Academic Publishers.

Demsetz, Harold (1967) "Toward a Theory of Property Rights," *American Economic Review* LVII(May), pp. 347–59.

Fried, Charles (1978) *Right and Wrong*, Cambridge, MA: Harvard University Press.

Hayek, Friedrich A. (1945) "The Use of Knowledge in Society," *American Economic Review* 35, pp. 519–30; reprinted in *Individualism and Economic Order*, Chicago: University of Chicago Press, 1948.

—— (1978) "Competition as a Discovery Procedure," in *New Studies in Philosophy, Politics, Economics and the History of Ideas*, Chicago: University of Chicago Press.

Kirzner, Israel M. (1973) *Competition and Entrepreneurship*, Chicago: University of Chicago Press.

—— (1985) *Discovery and the Capitalist Process*, Chicago: University of Chicago Press.

—— (1989) *Discovery, Capitalism acid Distributive Justice*, Oxford: Basil Blackwell.

—— (1992) *The Meaning of Market Process: Essays in the Development of Modern Austrian Economics*, London: Routledge.

Mises, Ludwig von (1966) *Human Action, A Treatise on Economics*, 3rd edn, Chicago: Henry Regnery.

North, Gary (1992) *The Coase Theorem, A Study in Economic Epistemology*, Tyler, TX: Institute for Christian Economics.

Nozick, Robert (1974) *Anarchy, State and Utopia*, New York: Basic Books.

O'Driscoll, Gerald P., Jr. (1977) *Economics as a Coordination Problem: The Contributions of Friedrich A. Hayek*, Kansas City: Sheed, Andrews and McMeel.

Robbins, Lionel (1935) *An Essay on the Nature and Significance of Economic Science*, 2nd edn, London: Macmillan.

Schotter, Andrew (1990) *Free Market Economics: A Critical Appraisal*, 2nd edn, Oxford: Basil Blackwell.

Source: The Limits of the Market: The Real and the Imagined, in W. Möschel, M.E. Streit and U. Witt (eds) (1994) *Marktwirtschaft und Rechtsordnung*, Nomos.

5

THE ETHICS OF COMPETITION

The title of this chapter is, of course, the same as that of the celebrated paper which Frank Knight published over 70 years ago, in which he set forth what is probably the most powerful and profound ethical critique of the market economy ever written.[1] Certain central elements in that critique have succeeded in establishing themselves as part of this century's conventional wisdom concerning capitalism: they have come to be routinely restated in and absorbed from today's principles textbooks in economics.[2] The circumstance that a number of Knight's most eminent students have, in the latter half of this century, come to be identified as the most prominent defenders of capitalism has not, in the mainstream perspective, suggested serious questioning of the validity of Knight's criticisms. Rather this perspective seems to conclude that convincing defenses of capitalism can be achieved only by confining analysis within a narrow economic frame of reference (permitting one to ignore, at least, Knight's ethical worries), or by remembering that Knight himself was careful not to imply that his critique requires us to deny significant merit to capitalism nor to suggest that his critique in and of itself established the ethical inferiority of capitalism to other possible systems of economic organization.

The thesis of this chapter will, on the contrary to mainstream acceptance of Knight's criticisms, be that Knight's ethical objections to the market economy are in fact in large part (though certainly not completely) based on a flawed understanding of how that economy works and what it achieves. It follows that a good deal of conventional textbook wisdom on these matters is similarly flawed. Our concern here is not primarily with Knight's own views as they matured over his extraordinarily distinguished career; this is certainly not the place to examine the evolution of Knight's thinking concerning the ethics of capitalism during the half century following the publication of his 1923 paper. We take Knight's 1923 paper as a point of departure only because of the originality and trenchancy of its critique, because of its seminal influence on mainstream twentieth-century thinking about capitalism, and because it exemplifies the source of what we see as the central fallacy in that mainstream thinking—viz. a flawed conception of the nature and function of competition in the market economy.

Although we shall, on these grounds, seek to refute many of Knight's ethical criticisms of capitalism, we certainly do not wish to claim that such refutation unequivocally establishes the invulnerability of that system to all ethical criticisms. For example, a number of Knight's profound observations raising possibly disturbing questions about the less immediate consequences of the system's operation will be seen to be entirely unaffected by our claims in this chapter. "While men are 'playing the game' of business, they are also moulding their own and other personalities, and creating a civilization whose worthiness to endure cannot be a matter of indifference" (Knight, 1935, p. 47). Our claim here is simply that what we claim to be the invalidities in Knight's critique can also not be matters of ethical indifference.

It will be noted that our disagreements with the mainstream ethical criticisms of the market economy do not derive from disagreements concerning ethics itself. (Knight himself, by the way, is careful to avoid resting his criticisms on any specific ethical foundations; instead he is mainly content to point to aspects of capitalism which would appear to raise as-yet-unresolved ethical questions.) Our disagreements will be seen to derive from divergent ways of understanding the functions and the operation of the market economy. Central to these disagreements are the ambiguities surrounding the nature and role of competition in the capitalist system.

THE MEANING OF COMPETITION

For Knight (and for mainstream economic thought throughout the century) competition means the state of affairs spelled out in the model of perfect competition (Knight 1923, p. 47 fn. and p. 50). The ethics of competition, for Knight, boils down to an ethical analysis of the ethics of the perfectly competitive world, and of the extent to which real world markets approximate that model. It was, after all, Knight himself who had in his *Risk, Uncertainty and Profit* (Knight, 1921, pp. 76–86) definitively articulated the conditions necessary for such a state of affairs. As his eminent student

George Stigler has made clear (Stigler, 1957), it was this articulation by Knight which finally crystallized what modern economists have understood by the term "competition." And it was to be Knight who led the Chicago School's insistence[3] that the model of perfect competition was able to serve economists adequately in their search for theoretical understanding of real world varieties of market competition.

From this Knightian perspective the real world market system can be understood by reference to the model of perfect competition. Although, to be sure, the real world does not fulfill all the conditions required by the model, nonetheless it is that model which enables us to understand whatever systematic market forces real world capitalism reveals. Although a part of Knight's ethical critique of capitalism relates to the divergences between real world capitalism and the "ideal" model of perfect competition, the bulk of his critique refers to the (ethically) less-than-ideal outcomes to be expected from a hypothetically perfectly competitive world itself. It is this perspective which modern textbooks have adopted. And it is to this perspective that we shall, in this chapter, attribute the flawed understanding of the market which we blame for the errors in the Knightian (and contemporary mainstream) ethical critique of the market economy.

We shall—on well established "Austrian" lines—claim that real world competition is to be understood, not by reference to an "ideal" model of perfect competition; but strictly in terms of dynamic ("entrepreneurial") forces—precisely the forces which are explicitly banished from the perfectly competitive model. At issue here is not whether the perfectly competitive model affords us a realistic picture of market economy (few mainstream economists claim that it does), but whether it captures the essence of how the competitive market economy works. Mainstream ("Knightian") theory maintains that the competitive market economy displays systematic regularities only to the extent that it can be reasonably fitted into the perfectly competitive mold. Subsequent generations of Chicago theorists would maintain that as a matter of fact the real world competitive market economy can so be fitted.

Austrian critics of mainstream theory maintain on the other hand, that the systematic regularities displayed by the market economy can be explained only by recognizing that the economy is, at any given point in time, significantly subject to active entrepreneurial forces for which the model of perfect competition can, by definition, find no place. The active competition which is so obvious a feature of real world capitalism is, in this Austrian view, to be understood as exemplifying these dynamic, entrepreneurial forces (rather than an approximation of the conditions established in the model of perfect competition).

THE OPEN-ENDEDNESS OF THE MARKET ECONOMY

Perhaps the most important implication of this disagreement concerning the nature and role of real world competition is that the Austrian view of competition portrays the market economy as "open-ended" (in a sense very shortly to be explained), while the mainstream view sees it as "closed-ended." In the mainstream view the "data" (i.e. tastes, resource endowments, technological possibilities) are, because they are data, seen as "given." They mark out the possibilities for improved allocation in the short run, and for growth in the long run. Optimal available courses of action are implicit in the data. These courses of action set out the boundaries for economic improvement. The economic process is judged in terms of its ability successfully to exhaust these possibilities—but it is out of the question for these possibilities to be transcended. Except as a possibly accidental change in the data, there is no room here for surprise or for discovery—only for efficient or inefficient performance in regard to the system's functions. In this sense the system is a closed one, strictly circumscribed by its data. In the mainstream view the data are given not only in the simple sense of the term, but also in the sense that they are, in principle, known. While many relevant items of information may not in fact be known, at least it is assumed that the costs required to obtain relevant knowledge *are* known. What renders the world closed-ended is, in the final analysis, the assumed completeness of knowledge which this mainstream view expresses. To seek to understand the market economy in terms of the perfectly competitive model is to portray that closed-ended economy as fulfilling its functions by confronting each of its participants with a similarly closed-ended choice situation. Prices and opportunities are arranged to permit (and ensure) those interlocking decisions which constitute the details of the system's fulfillment of its functions. Each situation confronting the individual, and rigorously entailing the relevant optimizing decision, is a closed-ended situation: it consists of a fully specified (i.e. fully known) choice context providing scope for only one ("single-exit") solution.

By contrast, the Austrian view of the world sees it as open-ended, not merely in the sense that realities necessarily diverge from the conditions of the abstract model of the economic theorist, but, more fundamentally, in the sense that what makes the system work is precisely its open-endedness—an open-endedness created by sheer ignorance of relevant possibilities. For the Austrian view competition consists of series of discovery steps,[4] revealing possibilities which were no part of any set of "data." These steps of entrepreneurial discovery are seen as inspired by the pure profit possibilities inherent in the sheer ignorance which pervades the open-ended economy. The function of competition, in this open-ended world of sheer ignorance, is to achieve those discoveries which change the position of the frontiers separating knowledge from ignorance. It is dynamic competition which expands the domain of what is known, continually shifting the location of profitable opportunities and thus continually inspiring yet further discoveries expanding the domain of what is known. These discoveries include not only discoveries of new goods to be produced, new methods of production to be utilized, and new sources of available natural resources, but also discoveries of new needs and desires deemed worthy of fulfillment. The economic process and the essence of its social function is not primarily one of achieving efficiency, but one of revealing knowledge the very availability of which has up until now not been suspected. Let us examine this proposition somewhat more carefully.

THE FUNCTION OF THE MARKET

For the mainstream view (underlying the Knightian ethical critique of the market economy) the function of the market is to efficiently allocate social resources among the multiple competing relevant social goals. Successful fulfillment of this function would occur where "every productive resource [has been placed] in that position in the productive system where it can make the greatest possible addition to the total social dividend as measured in price terms," and rewards have been assigned to "every participant in production by giving it the increase in the social dividend which its co-operation makes possible" (Knight, 1923, p. 48). Knight's critique proceeds to argue that successful fulfillment of this function does not constitute the fulfillment "of a sound ethical social ideal, the specification for a utopia" (ibid.). Much of what we shall have to say in the following pages stems from an entirely different view of what constitutes the social function of the market economy. Our disagreement with

Knight's ethical critique of capitalism rests primarily on a refusal to accept successful fulfillment of the mainstream allocative-efficiency function, as the relevant yardstick with which to measure the ethical achievement of the market system.

For us the function of the market system is to inspire those acts of discovery through which potentially discoverable possibilities can be identified and brought into view. In particular, this function has been described as a "coordinative" function, in that the sheer ignorance which pervades the market economy at a given instant, is likely to be generating sets of decisions which are failing to exploit all available opportunities for mutually gainful exchange among market participants. These decisions are thus "uncoordinated"; a well-functioning market would tend most effectively to stimulate those mutual discoveries which will bring decisions into coordination, permitting fullest exploitation of the potential for mutually gainful exchanges.

It should be clear that this difference in the perceived function of the market economy can make all the difference in the world in one's assessment of the ethical significance of a "successfully functioning" market economy. Much of our quarrel with Knight, depends upon his taking it for granted that the most one can expect from the market system is an efficient allocation of social resources.

SHEER IGNORANCE AND KNIGHTIAN UNCERTAINTY

At first glance it may seem puzzling that we have attributed to Knight a view of the market and of its function which assumes, in principle, the completeness of knowledge concerning relevant information (such as the costs of obtaining needed knowledge). Surely it was Knight who had in his celebrated *Risk, Uncertainty and Profit* emphasized that what separated the real world from the economist's model of perfect competition is precisely that the real world is characterized by uninsurable uncertainty (as contrasted with risk). Surely the essence of Knightian uncertainty is the inescapable open-endedness of real world ignorance which the notion of uncertainty seeks to capture. How then can we charge Knight with the error of assuming complete knowledge?

This is not the place to attempt a full elucidation of this paradox. We certainly do not wish to deny the paradoxical quality of our criticism of Knight; but we must emphatically point out that this paradox is not one of our own making. The insistence on the part of the Chicago School on the centrality of the perfectly competitive model in explaining real world capitalism is of course well known; this insistence has in fact ample basis in Knight's own teaching. The key to solving the puzzle (concerning Knight's attitude to uncertainty) appears to lie in Knight's view[5] that uncertainty cannot be overcome or escaped, that there is nothing in the market process that can systematically narrow the range of uncertainty introduced by the brute fact of the unknowable future. The Knightian entrepreneur is subject to uncertainty, but possesses no capacity to overcome that uncertainty. It follows that for Knight what occurs systematically in real world markets cannot be explained in terms of any systematic market elimination of uncertainty. There *is* no way, with or without a market, to grapple with uncertainty. (Knight was in fact convinced that, on balance, entrepreneurial losses are likely to outweigh entrepreneurial profit (Knight, 1921, p. 347).) What occurs systematically in real world markets can, therefore, be accounted for only by postulating that, for all the uncertainty which characterizes the real world, it is the model of perfect competition which nonetheless successfully captures the systematic elements in the real world. To understand the real world as a *system,* it is necessary to view it as somehow more or less precisely portrayed in the perfectly competitive model from which all uncertainty has been carefully removed. Uncertainty introduces an inescapable fuzziness into the picture; but the picture itself is that marked out by the perfectly competitive model.

It appears, then, that to treat uncertainty as utterly inescapable can lead to precisely similar ways of understanding the real world economy as are sustained by the assumption that the economy is characterized by the complete absence of uncertainty. What permits the Austrian view of the competitive world to understand it as an open-ended system within which a systematic "discovery procedure" is able to occur, is not so much recognition of sheer ignorance, as the recognition of the vincibility of that ignorance. For the Austrian view, the market process is systematic only insofar as that view understands how ignorance generates market opportunities which inspire discovery. A refusal to recognize any such discovery procedure compels a choice between two alternatives: either to abandon any notions of systematic market processes, or to perceive such systematic market processes as arising in spite of inescapable ignorance and uncertainty. The latter alternative is equivalent to the assertion that ignorance and uncertainty can—for the purposes of the relevant explanatory theory—be imagined simply not to exist.

Let us return to our main theme: the claim that an Austrian view of the market as a process of competitive discovery can undermine much of the mainstream ethical case against the market economy. It will be useful to review Knight's classic criticisms. The criticisms that we are concerned with fall into two groups: (a) contentions that real world divergences from the conditions of the perfectly competitive model mean that the market economy must fall short of the efficiency standard which that model represents; (b) contentions that the efficiency attained under the conditions of perfect competition can itself be challenged from the ethical perspective.

THE REAL WORLD AND THE PERFECTLY COMPETITIVE MODEL

Mainstream writers, following Knight, routinely point out that, however useful the model of perfectly competitive equilibrium may be as an explanatory framework for the real world, the latter world in fact displays many features that are utterly inconsistent with the model. So that real world capitalism must, to a greater or lesser extent, invariably fail to achieve the allocative efficiency associated with that model. Under this heading Knight (1923, pp. 50–2) lists: imperfect divisibility and mobility of goods and services; imperfect market knowledge and costly communication between traders (leaving "wide margins for 'bargaining power'" (ibid., p. 50)); imperfect knowledge by potential buyers of the precise usefulness of what they may buy; monopolistic combinations that may arise in "free" markets. Each of these features of the real world violates one or more of the conditions for the perfectly competitive model. Outcomes must, therefore, be expected to diverge from those benign results predicted by the model.

Our reaction to these valid positive observations is that they represent valid normative criticisms of free markets only to the extent that one has accepted the perfectly competitive model as the relevant normative ideal. If one sees the function of the market as that of achieving an efficient allocation of social resources (i.e. that allocation achieved in the perfectly competitive model) then it is reasonable to see these features of the real world (that Knight has identified) as inevitable sources of inadequate market performance of its assigned function. We have seen that for Knight (and for the subsequent twentieth century mainstream) efficient resource allocation is indeed seen as the market's function. For Chicago School economists, indeed, the virtues of the market consist precisely in the market's assumed approximation to the outcomes of the perfectly competitive model. So that imperfect divisibility, imperfect knowledge, and so forth do seem to cast serious shadow on claims for market success.

But, as explained, we wish to escape such a view of the market's function. Recognition of the uncertainty inherent in an open-ended world, recognition of the human propensity for entrepreneurial discovery and innovation, permit us to recognize a social function played by the market economy for which there is no counterpart in the perfectly competitive model. This social function, we have seen, is to stimulate and inspire those discoveries—of the abilities and plans of others, of the availability of resources, of one's own potential needs and desires, and of hitherto unsuspected technological possibilities—which can enhance mutual coordination among the plans made by market participants and the exploitation of unnoticed production possibilities inherent in existing economic circumstances. While the model of perfect competition is, for this perspective on markets, a highly interesting construction, it does not and cannot serve as the relevant normative ideal for the economic problems of the real world. These problems are, as Hayek pointed out in his celebrated 1945 paper (Hayek, 1945), not those of securing optimum social efficiency in resource allocation, but those of mobilizing scattered information—and, we may add, those of inspiring the discovery of entirely new bits of information—in order to enhance the usefulness of decisions made.

From this perspective, it is clear, many of the mainstream criticisms of the market economy (adumbrated by Knight in the above cited passages) melt away as wholly beside the point. Not only does it turn out that these perceived "imperfections" of the market have been so identified only by setting up an inappropriate criterion as the ideal, in fact it can be shown that the alleged imperfections are likely to be positive advantages to the market in its fulfillment of (what we maintain to be) its true social function. As has often been pointed out by Austrians as diverse in their views as Schumpeter and Mises, the dynamic market process is one which is able to proceed only because the conditions for perfectly competitive equilibrium are absent. Imperfect divisibility, imperfect knowledge, and sizes of firms rendering industries oligopolistic rather than perfectly competitive, are important prerequisites for the creation of those entrepreneurial acts of discovery which enable the market to fulfill its true function. It is not, of course, that imperfect divisibility, imperfect knowledge, and the like are to be seen as in themselves evidence or expressions of market success. Imperfect knowledge is not a goal of Austrian economics! Instead it is simply to be noted that to wish away these features of the real world is, given the relevant economic problems we face, to wish away the very "frictions" which are indispensable prerequisites for taking steps towards the solution of these problems.

It may be worth noting that our perspective on the mainstream (Knightian) criticisms of the market are not quite the same as the valuable critique of those criticisms which Demsetz offered many years ago by characterizing those criticisms as representing a "nirvana approach." In Demsetz's words, "The view which now pervades much public policy economics implicitly presents the relevant choice as between an ideal norm and an existing 'imperfect' institutional arrangement" (Demsetz, 1969, p. 1). Demsetz cogently points out that such an imagined choice imagines away the possibly high cost of making the transition between a given "imperfect" arrangement and an ideal one. When such transition costs are taken into account, the "imperfect" arrangement may turn out to be the best attainable one, after all.

The critique offered by Demsetz is able to accept the mainstream identification of the perfectly competitive model as the societal ideal. It is thus able to agree with the mainstream identification of features of the real world as being, in principle, "imperfections" (as compared with the ideal). It simply (and most valuably) points out, however, that recognizing the costs of transition from an actual to an "ideal," may render that "ideal" no longer so ideal after all. Certainly Demsetz's perceptive critique is (within the scope of the mainstream perspective) entirely and importantly valid. But our own disagreement with the mainstream criticisms is more radical in our rejection of the perfectly competitive model either as the relevant normative ideal or as a useful positive explanatory tool.[6]

THE ETHICS OF COMPETITION AND THE ETHICS OF DISTRIBUTION

The second group of Knightian criticisms of the ethics of competition arise mainly out of his dissatisfaction with the distributional outcomes of the perfectly competitive model itself. Knight argues the ethical inadequacy of this distributional outcome on a number of grounds, including the following: (a) the ethical character of this outcome can be no stronger than the principle "that productive contribution is an ethical measure of desert" (Knight, 1923, p. 54)—a principle which Knight rejects; (b) "productive contribution" is measured in terms of price which "does not correspond closely with ethical value or human significance" (ibid., p. 55), (c) market distribution is based on resource ownership, with the ethical justification for such ownership being, in Knight's view, highly questionable (ibid., p. 56). (Knight's criticisms of the distributive outcome of the market also reflect ethical convictions which, while perhaps questionable in themselves, do not depend on the centrality of the perfectly competitive model. For example Knight seems to dismiss outright any possibility of inheritance providing an ethically valid basis for ownership. In general Knight recognizes only "effort" as providing an ethically valid claim to ownership rights. He seems not to be prepared to recognize that inferior competence should be a barrier against being able to demand, on ethical grounds, an income that might have been earned with greater competence (since, after all, society does recognize an ethical obligation to support the entirely helpless). For the purposes of this chapter we are not concerned with this aspect of Knight's dissatisfaction with capitalist distribution.)

Our quarrel with the above Knightian criticisms of capitalist distribution (criticisms echoed in many subsequent mainstream textbooks) arises entirely from the extent to which these criticisms fail to recognize any discovery dimensions in the competitive market process. Knight's criticism's apply, in principle, to a perfectly competitive world in which incomes are distributed strictly in terms of J.B. Clark's theory of marginal productivity. It is in the context of such a world that it may be in order to question, on ethical grounds, the appropriateness of reward according to the market value of productive contribution derived from initially assumed patterns of resource ownership. Our claim is that distribution in the real world market economy characterized by dynamic, entrepreneurial competition, introduces a dimension of possible ethical worthiness which has nothing to do with "productive contribution" (however valued) and in no way depends upon (ethically valid or invalid) resource ownership rights.

This newly introduced dimension of possible ethical worthiness concerns just title to what one has discovered. It is not possible to provide here a full-length analysis of what discovery means and how it may introduce distinctive ethical considerations into discussions of distributive justice.[7] A few brief observations are however in order.

We distinguish sharply between acts of production (including the production of knowledge in acts of deliberate search) and acts of discovery. The former are the subject matter of mainstream microeconomics; they are deliberate transformations of resource services into outputs. The resources services, being sufficient to generate the outputs, are, in a certain sense, already, that output. To possess the inputs is potentially already to possess—or at any rate, to have within one's grasp—the outputs. If ownership rights in inputs are recognized as valid, this recognition itself implies the validity of the ownership of the corresponding outputs. Conversely, in order to establish ethically valid ownership of output, it is necessary to show that (somewhere along the line of legitimate transfers of ownership rights which have led up to the present) output ownership grew directly out of input ownership. Challenges to the legitimacy of output ownership may fairly be grounded in challenges to the legitimacy of input ownership. Acts of discovery are quite different.

Acts of discovery are non-deliberate. They involve alert individuals becoming aware of resources, or possibilities of deploying resources, to which no one else has established any claim. So to discover a resource, or a new way of using a resource is in effect to create that resource, or its new use. Such creation is in no way to be seen as the planned conversion of input into output. It is to be seen as the creation of something entirely new, *ex nihilo*. Legitimacy of ownership in regard to what has been discovered cannot derive from ownership of any inputs, since the discovery is not attributed to any inputs. A discovery occurs *ex nihilo*. One may wish to argue that a discovery is to be attributed to the human-capital quality of alertness possessed by the discoverer. However, as argued elsewhere (Kirzner, 1979, pp. 186–9), following Schumpeter, such alertness cannot be treated as an economic input. An input is a resource (of which its owner is already aware) deliberately deployed in a planful act. Alertness may indeed be deserving of credit for a discovery; but alertness is not deliberately deployed in discovery. As noted in passing earlier, deliberate search (in which alertness may certainly be deployed) is an act of production of knowledge, not one of discovery.

It may at first glance appear that, if acts of discovery are not the outcome of deliberate plans, then the fortunate consequences of discovery must be ascribed to sheer good luck—sharply eroding, in the eyes of many, the ethical claim of the discoverer to what has been discovered. We must insist that this is not the case. To declare an outcome not to have emerged as a result of a planned act, is not necessarily to pronounce that outcome to be ascribable only to sheer luck. There is a category of gain which is neither the planned consequence of an act of production, nor the wholly fortuitous outcome of a blind stroke of luck. This category refers to gains which have been noticed. To notice something worth acquiring is (while we can certainly recognize the element of luck in the circumstance that something was there "waiting" to be noticed) to bring something into existence that was hitherto, for all intents and purposes, non-existent. While the act of noticing (unlike the outcome of a successful search) was not deliberately undertaken, yet the discovered gain is not something which random good luck has thrust into the hands of a sleeping beneficiary. To notice an opportunity worth grasping is to have created something. Only she (or he) who has noticed the opportunity and has grasped it, and no one else, is responsible for and is to be credited with the discovery.

Such discovery is not to be credited to effort, but is nonetheless to be credited to a quality of the discoverer. To say that, because the discovery was not the result of the deployment by the discoverer, of *his* inputs, it therefore belongs to society in general, is to deny that the discovery was made by him (or her) and no one else. Elsewhere this writer has argued that our insights concerning discovered gain appear to coincide with those rather widely shared moral intuitions which are sometimes expressed in the principle of "finders, keepers."

Our point in this paper is not to insist on the moral right of the discoverer. Rather we wish to simply draw definitive attention to an aspect of real world capitalism which appears to bring into one's moral field of vision dimensions of possible ethical significance which are, and must be, entirely absent from the world of perfect competition at which Knight's ethical misgivings were addressed (and to which subsequent mainstream ethical comment has been directed). In the real capitalist economy incomes of all kinds are embedded in an open-ended world of uncertainty in which discoveries are continually being made. The standard theoretical categories of income, such as wages, rents, and interest, are categories taken from the Clarkian perfectly competitive world (in which marginal productivity is the sole operative determinant of income) but are not to be found, in their pure form, in the real world. In this real world incomes invariably partake, to a greater or lesser degree, of the character of pure entrepreneurial profit. To the extent that the Knightian ethical misgivings concerning capitalist distribution derive from exclusive concentration on the marginal-productivity slicing up of the pie produced under perfectly competitive conditions, they must be pronounced irrelevant for a capitalism in which entrepreneurial discovery plays a significant role in income distribution.

CONCLUDING REMARKS

Our thesis has not been to promote any particular ethical perspective upon capitalism. Instead we have merely asked that ethical evaluation of capitalism should proceed from an adequate and full understanding of its operation. An evaluation undertaken from an Austrian perspective recognizing the dynamic entrepreneurial dimension to real world competition will, we believe, show the fallacies in or irrelevance of many of the ethical criticisms of capitalism that have become central to the twentieth century conventional wisdom.

NOTES

Many of the ideas expressed in this chapter were first put forward in earlier versions. See in particular Kirzner (1973, ch. 6; 1985, chs 2, 4, 6; 1989).

1. Knight (1923), all reference here will be to the republished version of that paper in Knight (1935, ch. 2).
2. For a typical and careful example, see Baumol and Blinder (1991, ch. 29).
3. On this see Chamberlin (1957, ch. 15). See also Stigler (1952) and Friedman (1953, p. 38).
4. On this point see particularly Hayek (1978).
5. On this point see Knight (1921), and the discussion in Kirzner (1973, pp. 82 ff.).
6. For discussion of some overlap between Demsetz's position and my own, see Kirzner (1973, pp. 231 ff.).
7. For such a more detailed analysis see Kirzner (1989).

REFERENCES

Baumol, W.J. and Blinder, A.S. (1991) *Economics, Principles and Policy*, San Diego: Harcourt Brace Jovanovich.

Chamberlin, E. (1957) *Toward a More General Theory of Value*, London: Oxford University Press.

Demsetz, H. (1969) "Information and Efficiency: Another Viewpoint," *Journal of Law and Economics* 12, pp. 1–22.

Friedman, M. (1953) *Essays in Positive Economics*, Chicago: University of Chicago Press.

Hayek, F.A. (1945) "The Use of Knowledge in Society," *American Economic Review* 35, pp. 519–30.

—— (1978) "Competition as a Discovery Procedure," in F.A. Hayek (ed.) *New Studies in Philosophy, Politics, Economics and the History of Ideas*, Chicago: University of Chicago Press, pp. 179–90.

Kirzner, I.M. (1973) *Competition and Entrepreneurship*, Chicago: University of Chicago Press.

—— (1979) *Perception, Opportunity and Profit*, Chicago: University of Chicago Press.

—— (1985) *Discovery and the Capitalist Process*, Chicago: University of Chicago Press.

—— (1989) *Discovery, Capitalism and Distributive Justice*, Oxford: Basil Blackwell.

Knight, Frank H. (1921) *Risk, Uncertainty and Profit*, Boston, MA: Houghton Mifflin.

—— (1923) "The Ethics of Competition," *Quarterly Journal of Economics* 37, pp. 579–624.

—— (1935) *The Ethics of Competition and Other Essays*, New York: Harper.

Stigler, G.J. (1952) *Five Lectures on Economic Problems*, lecture 2, London: Macmillan, pp. 12–24.

—— (1957) "Perfect Competition, Historically Contemplated," *Journal of Political Economy* 65, pp. 1–17. Reprinted in G.J. Stigler (1965) *Essays in the History of Economics*, Chicago: University of Chicago Press, ch. 8.

Source: The Ethics of Competition, in H. Siebert (ed.) (1994) *The Ethical Foundations of the Market Economy*, J.C.B. Mohr.

6

THE NATURE OF PROFITS

Some economic insights and their ethical implications

In everyday business terminology, the term "profit" has a fairly well-understood meaning (constructed, in the main, out of accounting categories). In considering the ethical acceptability of business profits, however, it is necessary for the economist first to disentangle the various analytically separate elements that together comprise such business profits. As is well understood in elementary economic theory, most of these separate elements turn out to be identical, in their economic significance, to nonprofit elements. The owner of a business may work long hours; at least part of his business profits must be seen as the equivalent of the wages he could have earned by working for another firm. The owner of a business may have his own funds invested in his firm; part of his business profits must be seen as the equivalent of the market interest income, he could have obtained by investing at the market rate of return in, say, corporate bonds. It is plausible, therefore, to assume that ethical acceptability of such nonprofit elements of accounting profit raises no new questions beyond those generally relevant to nonprofit incomes in capitalist society. The sense in which business profits pose a special challenge for an ethical appraisal of capitalist distribution, therefore, arises strictly from the residual "pure economic profit" element contained in business profits. After filtering out, from accounting profit, all elements that can be construed as market return on capital owned, or implicit wages of management, there remains the possibility of a residual category that cannot be imputed to any factor owner; it appears to be related to the role of the entrepreneur in a way that does not permit it to be treated as his wage, or as market return on his investment. In the last analysis, the ethical evaluation of business profits thus revolves around the nature of "pure economic profit"—both in regard to its economic function and its economic causes. As we shall see, understanding the economic nature of pure entrepreneurial profit may well open up fresh insights concerning the ethical acceptability of business profits as broadly understood in everyday discourse.

ETHICS AND ECONOMICS INTERTWINED

Much of what we shall argue here depends on recognizing the ethical implications of economic insights. We shall not, that is, attempt to offer any innovations in ethical theory. We shall not attempt to persuade the reader to modify any ethical principles to which he subscribes. Instead, we shall proceed to suggest to the reader that the application of these ethical principles to the evaluation of pure profit demands, as a prerequisite, an appreciation for the true economic nature of entrepreneurial profit, along lines that may appear novel and even strange. Once the economic insights necessary for this appreciation have been accepted, we believe, the appropriate ethical evaluation—different though this may turn out to be from that reached conventionally—follows entirely without strain.

It is because of this that the "nature of profit" becomes so central to the task of its ethical evaluation. As we shall see, it is only as a result of careful attention to the economic nature of pure profit that we find ourselves forced to reject standard defenses of the ethics of pure profit. And it will turn out to be the case that from still more careful attention to the economic nature of pure profit there will emerge an understanding of it which opens up fresh dimensions of ethical relevance. It is toward this latter understanding, and a perception of these fresh dimensions of economic relevance, that this chapter sets its aim.

The beginning of wisdom in regard to pure profit is a full appreciation of how difficult it is to understand profit—or, at least, to understand profit in the way we are accustomed to understand the economics and the ethics of other kinds of incomes under capitalism.

THE ECONOMIC AND ETHICAL PROBLEMS OF PURE PROFIT

Let us begin with two commonplace observations. The first observation is that many of us regard as justly earned those receipts which can be attributed to the efforts of the recipient. To the extent that a person's sweat is solely responsible for a particular output, we tend to regard it as unjust for that particular output to be appropriated by anyone else. The second commonplace observation is that many of us regard the fruit of a tree justly to belong to the legitimate owner of that tree. If a justly owned asset spontaneously yields a return, without the effort of any human being, we tend to regard it as entirely acceptable for that return to accrue to the owner of that asset. We do not need, for present purposes, to delve into the philosophical underpinnings supporting these two widespread convictions.[1] They are together sufficient to highlight the problem—at once ethical and economic—raised by pure profit. The economic problem raised by pure profit is that it seems to be uncaused. We can neither trace it to anyone's effort, nor to the spontaneous fruitfulness of any productive source. This is so, as we shall emphasize, simply as a matter of sheer definition. To the extent that a receipt can be attributed to the effort of the recipient, it qualifies immediately as a wage (implicit or explicit). To the extent that the receipt can be seen as attributable to the pure spontaneous fruitfulness of an owned asset, it qualifies immediately as a property-income component of accounting profit. It is only after all such elements have been filtered out, as we have seen, that we arrive at pure profit. This pure profit then appears to present an economic puzzle: if it was not created by any human effort, nor emerged as the fruit of any kind of "tree," how could it possibly have come about?

But at the same time this very difficulty presents a strictly ethical aspect. Whoever grasps this pure profit can lay claim to it on the basis of neither of the two intuitive convictions referred to earlier. He has not expended effort in its creation or acquisition, nor is he the owner of any asset from which it spontaneously emerged. The economic dilemma thus turns out to be matched by a mirror-image ethical difficulty.[2] If this pure profit, economically uncaused as it appears at first glance, must be attributed to pure chance, or to the exploitation of buyer ignorance, this very circumstance appears to render its grasping by an individual seriously vulnerable to ethical challenge. Exploitation of consumer ignorance, of course, raised issues of fraud. And even the beneficiary of pure good fortune does not at all enjoy that intuitive ethical approval of his fortunate situation which, for many of us, attaches to the recipient of that produced by the sweat of his brow, or to the owner of the fruit-bearing tree. We can no longer appeal to a widely shared notion of simple justice to support his grasping of profit. Let us return to ponder on the apparently "uncaused" character of pure economic profit.

If we begin with an institutional framework which recognizes private self-ownership rights and the possibility of acquiring ownership rights in productive resources, we have no difficulty in accounting for the emergence of factor incomes. The worker is able to command a wage for his labor because that labor produces an item for which a consumer (and hence an entrepreneur intending to sell to the consumer) is prepared to pay. Because labor services are scarce, market competition ensures a positive wage to productive labor. The owner of a fruit tree is able to command a price for the fruit of his tree because, given his ownership of the scarce fruit, consumers are, in competition with one another, prepared to pay positive prices to acquire that fruit. Given widespread preference for earlier rather than later receipts, the market for loanable funds yields interest income to lenders, because the borrowers find it worthwhile to offer interest, and scarcity of loanable funds makes it necessary for them to do so. But there seems, on the face of it, to be no earthly reason why, when a consumer buys an item, he should pay a price for it which is more than sufficiently high to cover all costs of resource services (including the borrowing of necessary capital funds) needed to deliver that item to his doorstep at the time he wishes to buy it. The portion of this purchase price which accrues as pure profit is paid, it appears, for nothing at all. It does not pay for the performance of any productive service rendered. It does not pay for the use of capital funds. It cannot be rationalized as being paid in return for the provision by the seller of necessary information—because, to the extent that this *is* the reason why this payment is being made, it follows that it is payment for a service rendered and thus not pure profit after all. It seems that the pure profit portion of the purchase price can emerge only as the result of a fluke, an aberration, and/or of virtual fraud on the part of the seller (who somehow, as the result of consumer ignorance, extracts a price higher than that strictly necessary to provide the consumer that which he is buying). And it is here that the ethical side of the problem of profit comes clearly into focus. It follows from the very circumstance that there appears no economic justification (in the sense of "valid explanation") for the payment of pure profit, that the grasping of such profits must necessarily fail to meet both of the two commonly held criteria for deservedness mentioned earlier. A payment is economically justified if the relevant conditions of supply and demand mark out a positive market clearing price. The circumstance that such justification is absent in the case of pure profit leaves pure profit in an ethical limbo. One is simply unable to point to any *quid pro quo* (such as effort, or the fruit of an owned tree) corresponding to the grasped profit. The ethical problem of profit emerges directly from the economic nature of pure profit.

PURE PROFIT AND THE ENTREPRENEURIAL ROLE

The problematic nature of pure profit is mirrored, of course, in the problematic nature of the entrepreneurial function itself. From the perspective of conventional economic theory this function is a notoriously elusive one. The entrepreneur assembles all the productive services needed to produce a product. He assumes the cost represented by the market values of all these services and receives the market value of the produced output. He retains whatever surplus remains, as pure entrepreneurial profit (or, if the residual is negative, he suffers entrepreneurial loss). But in stipulating that he assumes the costs embodied in the market value of *all* productive services needed for the product, we of course mean to include also all those services provided by the entrepreneur himself which could, in principle, have been hired in the marketplace. His labor services and the services of the assets he owns could have been provided from the outside. In identifying the peculiarly entrepreneurial character of his role, we must certainly not obscure this role by failing to distinguish it analytically from the provision of these nonentrepreneurial services with which the entrepreneurial role is often in real life packaged together. The computation of residual pure profit, as we saw previously, requires that we net out, from the gross revenue obtained from the sale of output, not only out-of-pocket expenditures made by the entrepreneur to command the productive services he buys in the market, but also the market values of the nonentrepreneurial services the entrepreneur himself provides. The pure profit residual accrues to the pure entrepreneurial role played by the entrepreneur. But of what does this role consist? What does the entrepreneur, qua entrepreneur, contribute to the emergence of the product? After all, the productive services he assembles (including his own nonentrepreneurially contributed services) are, by stipulation, together *fully* sufficient for the production of the product and its delivery to the purchaser. The list of assembled services must be a complete one. Inputs produce output; the entrepreneur assembles all the inputs needed for the output. With *all* the needed inputs in hand, what else could possibly be needed? It appears, at first glance, as if the purely entrepreneurial function disintegrates into nothingness as soon as we attempt to grasp hold of it.

Pure profit accrues to the entrepreneur. But we cannot seem to perceive what it is that the entrepreneur does. And, as seen previously, we seem to be unable to understand why the prices paid by purchasers are high enough to leave a residual pure profit. We don't know what the function of the entrepreneur is, and we don't understand how and why he is ever able to retain his residual pure profit. The ethical problem we found to surround pure profit thus parallels our mystification concerning the function and role of the entrepreneur. Much of what follows here is concerned with the explication of the entrepreneurial function.

SOME LEADING THEORIES OF ENTREPRENEURIAL PROFIT

It will be useful, both for its own sake and as preliminary to our own theory of profit, to provide a brief review of the principal economic theories of entrepreneurial profit developed during the heyday of entrepreneurial theorizing (1890–1920).[3] The several major approaches we shall identify attest to the intense interest displayed by the early neoclassical economists in the pure profit concept and in the entrepreneurial role. This contrasts sharply with the virtual silence on these matters which characterized the subsequent half-century of economic thought. We shall identify what we believe to be weaknesses in these approaches but also point out the valuable insights contained in them. Wherever possible, we shall take note of the possible implications which these theories hold for the ethical evaluation of pure profit.

J.B. Clark

Clark's observations on profit occur peripherally to his exhaustive analysis of distribution under conditions of static equilibrium.[4] Under static conditions there is no profit. All incomes are marginal productivity incomes. "Profit has to place in such static conditions. The two incomes that are permanent and independent of dynamic changes are the products, respectively, of labor and of capital. Each of them is directly determined by the final productivity law . . ."[5] Profit emerges only as a result of dynamic change. Suppose a new invention improves the methods of production. This may result in permanently higher wages. "Wages now tend to equal what labor can now produce, and this is more than it could formerly produce."[6] However, as a result of "economic friction," wages may be temporarily lower than their new, higher, static level, leaving a profit margin between output value and production costs, which the entrepreneur is able to grasp.

> The interval between actual wages and the static standard is the result of friction; for, if competition works without let or hindrance, pure business profit would be annihilated as fast as it could be created—entrepreneurs, as such, could never get and keep any income . . . Dynamic theory has to account for the whole of that friction on which *entrepreneurs'* shares depend; while static law determines what wages will be, when the friction shall have been completely overcome, and what they would be at this instant, if friction were immediately to vanish.[7]

Clark is apparently satisfied with the justice of such entrepreneurially grasped profit—despite the circumstance that it does not fit into his own marginal productivity ethic (which, declares wages, for example, to be justly earned only because they correspond to what labor has contributed to the total output). Clark notes that were it not for the friction which permits a temporary profit to entrepreneurs, the latter

> would have no incentive in self-interest to make any improvements, and it is clear that additions which are difficult and costly would be in danger of not being made. Profit is the lure that insures improvement . . . To secure progress, this lure must be sufficient to make men overcome obstructions and take risks.[8]

Yet it is not clear how this renders the grasping of these profits ethically acceptable for Clark. Clark does not appear to recognize any productive service to have been rendered by the entrepreneur, even when he has introduced improvements in productive methods. After all, all that is produced through the new methods is produced by the input services being used. So we do not quite understand how Clark's productivity criteria for distributive justice have been met by the entrepreneur, permitting him to enjoy (the admittedly temporary) profits made possible by economic friction.

On the other hand, Clark *has* provided a solution to the problem of what causes profit to exist at all. Profits are not uncaused; they are caused by economic frictions which prevent the immediate disappearance (through competitive activity) of the profits initially generated by dynamic change. Clark has, importantly, identified pure profit as a disequilibrium phenomenon, and has at least given a name to the source responsible for the temporary persistence of disequilibrium: "economic frictions."

F.B. Hawley

Hawley was an important (but now almost forgotten) U.S. profit theorist at the turn of the century. He is prominently cited by Frank Knight in his survey of profit theories, and Hawley's theory, while sharply criticized by Knight, is recognized by him to contain a valuable element of what Knight believes to be a correct theory.[9] Hawley's work had a profound influence on subsequent U.S. textbook treatments of profit, an influence continuing well after World War II.[10]

Hawley identifies the "distinguishing function of the entrepreneur" as the "assumption of risk," and saw pure profit as "the economic reward for services rendered by the assumption of industrial risk."[11] Were no one to be prepared to assume this industrial risk, it would not be possible for production to occur. Profit provides a reward for this entrepreneurially provided service, and thus also an inducement persuading the entrepreneur to provide this service. It is important, Hawley contends, not to confuse this reward and inducement with the amount an unwilling risk bearer pays in order to insure himself against the risk of loss. This latter payment, "a sum sufficient to cover the actuarial or average losses incidental to the various risks of all kinds necessarily assumed by the entrepreneur and his insurers," is already included among the costs of production.[12] Hawley maintains that production will not occur unless the entrepreneur can be induced to assume risk, through the prospect of a surplus over and above all costs, including the cost of insurance. This is so, Hawley argues, because there is an "irksomeness of uncertainty" attached to each *particular* business project, even where the businessman has confidence in the validity of his actuarial judgment over the long run (during which time losses and gains will tend to offset each other).[13] It is because of this that Hawley asserts that "industrial risks will not be assumed without the expectation of a compensation in excess of the actuarial value of the risk."[14]

It will be observed that Hawley's theory of profit does, within its own framework, adequately address the economic (and, by implication, also the ethical) problem surrounding profit and the entrepreneurial role. The entrepreneur does provide a service, a service that is both essential for the emergence of output and not able to be purchased on the market. Profit is not uncaused, it is caused by the need, if product is to be forthcoming, for the (inescapable) risk of business to be assumed. The consumers are forced to pay prices high enough to permit profits, or else they would not find the products they wish to buy. Hawley does not appear to have much concerned himself with the ethics of profit. He wished to teach economists how correctly to characterize the phenomenon of profit. Yet we can see for ourselves how an ethical defense might be constructed on the basis of Hawley's theory. The entrepreneur provides a special service, one irksome for him to provide; he may be deemed entitled to the reward the market provides as an inducement to him for so providing this needed service.

Yet the framework that Hawley has offered seems unredeemably flawed. Knight put his finger on its central weakness. Hawley assumes "that the 'actuarial value' of the risks taken is known to the entrepreneur."[15] Knight was himself to emphasize, however, that there is a fundamental difference between risk and uncertainty. For Knight "uncertainty" is a term reserved for that which is, as a consequence of the utter unpredictability of future events, inherently indeterminate and immeasurable. So long as Hawley provides no room, in his analytical scheme, for such open-ended, uninsurable uncertainty, he has not rendered plausible the nature of the peculiarly entrepreneurial function. As Knight pointed out,

> [A] little consideration will show that there can be no considerable "irksomeness" attached to exposure to an insurable risk, for if there is it will be insured; hence there can be no peculiar income arising out of this alleged indisposition.[16]

Frank H. Knight

Knight constructed his own uncertainty theory of profit out of elements he found in Clark and Hawley. Clark was right in associating profit with dynamic change; Hawley was right in associating the entrepreneurial function with the residual bearing of uncertainty. But it was left for Knight to forge out of these ideas what he believed to be the correct theory of profit and of the entrepreneurial role. Clarkian dynamic change is, by itself, not enough to generate profit, because it is possible for change to be anticipated.[17] If an increase in the productivity of labor can be generally anticipated, competition among prospective employers will immediately force wages up to the new, higher level. It is only to the extent that change is responsible for ignorance of the future that it can be associated with the phenomenon of profit. And this insight leads Knight to locate the source of profit not in dynamic change itself but in the open-ended uncertainty of the future for which such change is responsible. For Knight it is this inescapable difference between what has been anticipated and what actually occurs, which is responsible for entrepreneurial profit (and loss). So that profits are not forthcoming because an inducement must be offered to overcome some irksomeness of uncertainty bearing; profits and losses are forthcoming because the uncertainty of life continually generates unexpected gains or unexpected losses. The entrepreneur has (certainly as a result of the inducement offered by the prospect of possible profit) placed himself in the position of residual claimant. Knight goes into considerable detail concerning the qualities required for the entrepreneurial function, involving, as it thus does, both responsibility for and control of an enterprise in an uncertain world.[18] But for an understanding of Knight's view of the nature of entrepreneurial profit it is sufficient to focus on the extent to which entrepreneurial judgment (which for Knight appears to refer to the judgment required for the successful carrying out of routine managerial tasks in an uncertain world) and pure luck are inevitably intertwined in the generation of residual profit.[19] Because the entrepreneur exposes himself to residual uncertainty the element of luck plays a decisive part in determining whether the residual left, after paying all contractual income, will be positive or negative.

So that, for Knight, pure profit is not exactly uncaused. It is an implication of the need to operate in a world of uncertainty. In such a world somebody, or everybody, must be left exposed to the vagaries of pure luck. Entrepreneurs choose to occupy such exposed positions; their luck may be good or bad—profits may be positive or negative. Consumers do not deliberately pay a price higher than necessary to cover all costs of production; if they pay such higher prices this is because the course of events happens to have been such as to force the current output price up higher than had been anticipated when the contractual income payments for factor services were agreed upon. Profit emerges because a world of uncertainty is necessarily one in which "a condition of perfect equilibrium is no longer possible."[20] A world of continuous disequilibrium is one in which residual incomes are continually being subjected to unanticipated shocks and readjustments. It is not correct to characterize profits as "having to be paid" in order to induce entrepreneurs to enter (although the possibility of such profits may indeed provide such inducement); in fact, Knight believed rather strongly that, on balance, losses outweigh profits. Profits (or losses) emerge simply because, in an uncertain world, matters never do turn out to be exactly what the best judgment anticipated as being likely to happen.

What Knight has given us, then, is a theory of profit which sees it as caused by uncertainty-bred conditions of market disequilibrium. It should be noted that while this certainly does explain how the phenomenon of profit arises, it does so in a way which does not see profit as the market value offered in exchange for the fulfillment by the entrepreneur of any valuable social function. To be sure, profit and loss are inseparably associated with the entrepreneurial role, and, to be sure, Knight sees a most important place for this role in the capitalist process of production.[21] But the nature of these associations is such that even where profits, rather than losses, have been achieved, these can hardly be seen as payment for the entrepreneurial services rendered. We would rather have to say, according to Knight, that the provision of entrepreneurial services is inseparable from consequent exposure to the possibility of loss and the possibility of profit. Since, on balance, there never may be net profits won by the entrepreneurs in the economy, these net profits cannot, even if they occur, be seen as market generated payments made for, and necessary to induce the provision of, the services of entrepreneurs.

In other words, Knight has, in his own way, solved the purely economic problem of pure profit without being concerned with, and without offering any clues to the solution of, the ethical problems we identified earlier. Where an entrepreneur has won profits there still seems no way of subsuming these profits under the category of justly received incomes (according to the everyday consensus mentioned earlier as providing rough criteria for ethical acceptability). Although by focusing upon uninsurable uncertainty (rather than upon insurable risk) Knight has no doubt restored legitimacy to Hawley's "irksomeness of uncertainty," nonetheless Knight's perspective does not, as we have seen, permit profit to be seen as paid for (and thus ethically justified by) the provision of this service of irksome-bearing. While we now understand what Knight wishes us to see the entrepreneur as doing, we are, therefore, still unable to see how this renders the winning of profit legitimate. In fact, it would seem eminently plausible for a critic to argue that the entrepreneur has no inherent right to the lucky profits that came his way. (Knight himself may well have felt that the entrepreneur's vulnerability to the losses generated by bad luck, somehow makes it not unfair for him to be permitted to keep the proceeds of good luck.[22] But this surely depends on the validity of Knight's conviction that, in general, losses more than cancel out profits.)

J.A. Schumpeter

We list Schumpeter's well-known theory of profit not because his theory offered a fundamental insight not already covered in our brief review of the literature but because of the centrality and prominence of his theory, and because of certain important fresh nuances to be noticed in that theory. For Schumpeter profits are created by entrepreneurial innovations. He sees the entrepreneurial function as consisting in the "carrying out of new combinations," which change the methods of production and/or the. products produced.[23] The energy and leadership qualities of the entrepreneur provide him with the initiative and the will needed to break away from the routine activities of everyday business. It is not so much a matter of originality and ingenuity of invention as of power and determination "in getting things done,"[24] of introducing into practice the inventions that others can see as well as he can.[25] These entrepreneurial innovations together make up the "perennial gale of creative destruction" which, for Schumpeter, is an unmistakable characteristic of capitalism.[26]

The profits won by the Schumpeterian entrepreneur are not windfall profits; they have been deliberately created. By innovating a new technique or a new product the entrepreneur creates a profit-surplus of revenues over costs, for as long as it takes the nonentrepreneurial "imitators" to compete away that difference. For Schumpeter risk and uncertainty have nothing to do with profit (although he would not deny that entrepreneurial activity is inseparable from exposure to uncertainty). Schumpeter believed that the risk associated with an entrepreneurial venture is borne by the capitalist, not the entrepreneur. The profits of innovation are not a reward paid by the market but a gain created by jolting the economy out of its routine pattern.

The similarity between Schumpeter's understanding of the nature of pure profit and that perceived by J.B. Clark is obvious. For Clark, too, as seen earlier in this section, profits emerge as the result of the dynamic change associated with industrial progress. Schumpeter was to recognize this similarity. In surveying neoclassical contributions to the theory of enterprise (in his monumental *History of Economic Analysis*), Schumpeter described Clark's contribution as being "the most significant of all: he was the first to strike a novel note by connecting entrepreneurial profits, considered as a surplus over interest (and rent), with the successful introduction into the economic process of technological, commercial, or organizational improvements."[27]

What distinguishes the Schumpeterian view of pure profit from that of Clark seems to be entirely a matter of nuance. Clark does not seem to emphasize as Schumpeter does the *deliberate* character of profit creation; he does emphasize, more than Schumpeter appears to do, the temporary nature of profit, noting (as we have seen) that it is only "economic friction" which somehow prevents its instantaneous disappearance. The lure of profit stimulates the entrepreneur to introduce technological innovations, with the impression somehow being conveyed that the market is already clearly offering these fleeting profit opportunities in exchange for innovation (rather than their being deliberately engineered by the Schumpeterian entrepreneur's leadership and determination). As we saw earlier, Clark's theory solves the problem of what causes profits: profits are caused by economic frictions which prevent the immediate disappearance (through competitive activity) of the profits initially generated by dynamic change. For Schumpeter, it would seem more accurate to describe his theory as solving the causal problem in profits slightly differently: profits are caused by entrepreneurial innovations; they tend to be ground down to zero by the competition of imitators. As we have seen, Clark's theory of profit was not more than a footnote, as it were, to his comprehensive marginal productivity theory of income distribution under static equilibrium conditions. Schumpeter's theory of entrepreneurial innovation, on the other hand, was the central element in his understanding of the capitalist process.

SOME LESSONS LEARNED FROM THE LEADING THEORIES

Consideration of the theories briefly sketched in the preceding section can significantly advance understanding of the phenomenon of pure profit. These theories point unerringly to the disequilibrium character of profit. It turns out that the problem which we encountered, at the outset of this chapter in explaining the economic causes of profit, was a problem only because we were, at least implicitly, seeking for causes that could operate steadily under settled circumstances. We were looking for a service provided steadily by the entrepreneur that could be understood as commanding a settled market price. Inevitably, we found ourselves forced to acknowledge that, to the extent such a steady service and such a settled market price could be identified, we were no longer dealing with the purely entrepreneurial role and with pure profit. The work of Schumpeter and Knight (in whose ideas, as we have seen, we can find echoes of insights present in the work of Clark and Hawley) incisively identifies profit as a gain that has no place at all in the settled scheme of the equilibrium state. Profits appeared to be without cause, because in the settled scheme of things that was the background of our quest, there can in fact be no profit. Real world profits do exist; they have their cause in the circumstances responsible for and which accompany the real world state of disequilibrium. For Schumpeter profits are created through the leadership with which the entrepreneur propels the economy away from its earlier somnolent, state of equilibrium. For Knight profits are caused by the inevitable failure of market participants, in the disequilibrium world of uncertainty, to correctly anticipate subsequent conditions.

Yet these solutions to the economic problem of pure profits have not provided any help in decisively establishing ethical justification for profit. The ethical challenge, we saw, arose out of the circumstance that profit is neither a property income (comparable to the fruit that grows on a tree that is legitimately owned), nor an income paid as compensation for a productive service rendered. It was this that seemed to place pure profit under an ethical cloud. Consideration of the Schumpeterian and Knightian disequilibrium theories of profit appears, at first glance, to suggest that, indeed, even after as economists we understand how profits arise, one might yet conclude that they lack ethical justification. For both Schumpeter and Knight it is still the case that profits cannot be defended as the fruits of any owned tree, nor as the market value of any provided service. It is true that a consistent defender of private property rights could claim that, since no violation of property rights occurs either in the Schumpeterian or the Knightian scheme of things, the resulting ownership patterns cannot be pronounced unjust. (This is, indeed, the central thesis of Nozick's entitlement theory of justice.)[28] But in regard to pure profit it seems safe to say that many people are, at the intuitive level, simply not satisfied by the entitlement theory. (Perhaps their intuitive misgivings about profits are such as to lead them to question the very property system, consistent application of which appears to legitimize these apparently undeserved gains.)

In the Knightian theory of profit, with its emphasis on the consequence of sheer luck, the undeserved nature of profit appears particularly bothersome. It seems, to critics of capitalist distribution, entirely arbitrary to declare one individual to be the just owner of that which came his way only as a result of a chance occurrence in no way attributable to his efforts.[29] (As noted earlier, it is likely that Knight found himself able to defend profits on the grounds that those who stand to win profits are exposed to losses which, on balance, more than offset the profits.)

Schumpeterian profits are certainly not primarily a matter of luck; they are deliberately created by determined entrepreneurs. As such they might seem to be ethically defendable as the outcome achieved by deliberate effort. Yet such a defense presents something of a puzzle. Once the "imitators" will have absorbed and duplicated the innovations pioneered by the entrepreneur, equilibrium will once again have been attained; no portion of output revenue will then revert to the entrepreneur. It must appear puzzling that the contribution made by the entrepreneur is somehow held to cease as imitators copy his trade secrets. If it is eventually obvious that the nonentrepreneurial factor services are by themselves entirely sufficient to generate the new product or the new production technique (so that the full value of the output becomes justly imputed to them alone), this might be held to be equally valid and relevant immediately after introduction of the entrepreneurial innovation. If, on the other hand, it is held that, absent the pioneering effort of the entrepreneur, the new technique might never have come to pass at all, and that this entitles him to a share of the output revenue, then it is not clear why this does not entitle him to a similar share for as long as the revenue stream endures. In a nutshell the Schumpeterian concept of profit does not facilitate its being easily fitted into a productivity-return ethical category. Let us turn to yet another theory of profit, similar in spirit, to a degree, to both the Schumpeterian and Knightian theories, but yet providing a unique twist that can perhaps help us in solving not only the economic problem of profit but also the ethical problem as well.

THE ARBITRAGE THEORY OF PURE PROFIT

This theory of profit is that of the Austrian economist Ludwig von Mises. It seems appropriate to call it the *arbitrage* theory of profit[30] because it focuses on the sense in which profit is simply the price discrepancy between two markets, today's market (in which, say, productive resource services are bought and sold) and tomorrow's market (in which the output of these productive services will be sold). Arbitrage opportunities arise when today's market prices are (after taking interest expense into account) out of line with the true, higher values that will be revealed in tomorrow's market. As Mises said,

> What makes profit emerge is the fact that the entrepreneur who judges the future prices of the products more correctly than other people do buys some or all of the factors of production at prices which, seen from the point of view of the future state of the market, are too low. Thus the total costs of production—including interest on the capital invested—lag behind the prices which the entrepreneur receives for the product. This difference is entrepreneurial profit.[31]

The Misesian theory shares with Schumpeter's theory and with Knight's theory the insight that profit is a disequilibrium phenomenon. (Arbitrage profits are possible only because arbitrage activity has not yet squeezed them out of existence.) But the emphasis in the Misesian discussion is on the ability of the superior entrepreneur to identify, more correctly than others are able to do, where today's market undervalues future output.

> An entrepreneur can make a profit only if he anticipates future conditions more correctly than other entrepreneurs. Then he buys the complementary factors of production at prices the sum of which, including allowance for the time difference, is smaller than the price at which he sells the product.[32]

Schumpeter's emphasis was on the leadership and determination expressed by the entrepreneur in creating new procedures of production. Mises's emphasis is on the superior perception on the part of the entrepreneur as to where resources services are currently undervalued.

Knight's emphasis was on the extent to which luck can benefit the agent who exposes himself to residual uncertainty. Mises's emphasis is on the vision exercised by the superior entrepreneur. Mises does not, of course, underestimate the role of uncertainty in creating opportunities for profit.[33] "The ultimate source from which entrepreneurial profit and loss are derived is the uncertainty of the future constellation of demand and supply. If all entrepreneurs were to anticipate correctly the future state of the market, there would be neither profits nor losses."[34] But for Knight profit appears to arise, *after* the entrepreneur has taken up his exposed position, by a fortunate change which everyone (including, very possibly, this entrepreneur) has failed to foresee. For Mises, on the other hand, the profit-making entrepreneur is he who (while everyone else has failed to see the course of future events) sees the opportunity created by the errors of the other market participants. For Knight luck is a decisive factor generating profit; for Mises superior vision is the decisive factor in the grasping of profits.

We emphasize these nuances of difference between Mises, on the one hand, and Schumpeter and Knight, on the other, because, as we shall try to show, it is these differences which hold important implications for the ethical evaluation of pure profit.

PURE PROFIT AND THE ETHICS OF DISCOVERY: AN OVERVIEW

Once we identify profit as the result of the circumstance that the entrepreneur "anticipates future conditions more correctly than other entrepreneurs,"[35] we have within our grasp the solution to the ethical problem of profit identified earlier in this chapter. The entrepreneur "sees" the future more accurately than others do. Because others see the future inaccurately, there is generated a gap between the present market value of resources and the (discounted) market value of output (as it will, in fact, turn out to be in the future). The entrepreneur, in seeing the future more accurately, in effect sees this gap. (Indeed, it is the very prospect and incentive of gaining from such perceived gaps which concentrate and focus the entrepreneurial vision to more accurately glimpse the future.) What the entrepreneur sees is a prospective increment of value which others, although in no way handicapped as compared with our entrepreneur, have somehow failed to see. (In fact, the increment of value is nothing but the market expression of this failure on their part correctly to see the future.) We argue that profits grasped by the entrepreneur are in the nature of an unowned, unperceived object first discovered by an alert pioneer, who, in the view of many, becomes the legitimate private owner of that which he has discovered, on the basis of the "finders-keepers" ethic.

Up until now our discussion concerning ethics referred to only two criteria on the basis of which general opinion seems prepared to endorse ethical acceptability of gain. These were (a) compensation for productive service rendered, and (b) gain directly derived ("fruit from an owned tree") from private property legitimately possessed. We now wish to recognize a third criterion, a criterion that (although apparently widely accepted in everyday discourse) appears alien to the world scheme of economics but is, we believe, crucially important to the evaluation of outcomes in an uncertain world. It is on the basis of this "finders-keepers" criterion that we shall argue the ethical defensibility of pure entrepreneurial profit. In the following pages we shall develop somewhat more fully (a) the nature of discovery, and (b) the discovered character of pure entrepreneurial profit.

THE MEANING OF DISCOVERY[36]

In the world of standard economics there is a widely employed scheme of classification the assumed exhaustiveness of which we wish to challenge very vigorously. In this scheme it is assumed that economic gains can be understood either as the deliberately achieved goals of human effort, or as windfalls attributable to sheer luck. (In addition, of course, this scheme recognizes the possibility of sequences of events in which luck and effort intertwine.) No other category of cause besides planned result of deliberate activity, and fortunate outcome of sheer good fortune, is recognized. If an outcome was not deliberately aimed at, it must be seen as purely lucky. We wish to insist that a third possible source for economic gain, a source entailing ethical implications of an entirely different character, must be recognized. This source is deliberate human discovery, not to be attributed to unaided luck but (at least in part) to the alert attitude on the part of the discoverer. It is the alertness of human beings that enables them to notice and profit by what they find.

Standard economics understands the meaning of search activity. One decides to search for an object, or for an item of information, in exactly the same way as one decides to engage in every other kind of deliberate productive activity. Such a decision is seen as rigidly determined by the value of the prospective find to the searcher, in conjunction with the relevant costs of search. The determination is, in the economics of search, seen as being made in the context of assumed probabilities governing the techniques of deliberate search.

Deliberate search, however, is not at all the same as spontaneous, alert discovery (although, certainly, the two may occur together). Someone looking up a telephone number in a telephone directory is engaged in deliberate search. Someone who, walking along a city boulevard, notices a public telephone and realizes that this will permit him to make an important telephone call, has made a discovery. (Someone who notices the availability of a telephone directory and is thereby spurred to undertake a search for an important telephone number presents an example of how discovery and deliberate search may be intertwined.)

The special ethical relevance of spontaneous discovery arises precisely from the circumstance that it can be classified neither as a deliberate activity nor as an occurrence strictly attributable to blind chance. If I deliberately produce output using only legitimately acquired productive resource services, commonplace ethical intuition is inclined to recognize my just title to what I and my resources have produced. If I am lucky in the sense that a fortune has fallen from heaven directly in my lap, commonplace ethical intuition is not at all clear on the legitimacy of my claim to sole ownership of this fortune; after all I did not lift a finger in achieving this windfall. Critics are often inclined to argue that such windfalls somehow belong to "all mankind." It is not a simple matter to rebut such a position on the basis of commonplace intuition. What I claim here is that he who alertly grasps an opportunity for gain—an opportunity in principle available to others but which has remained ungrasped because as yet not noticed—occupies a distinct ethical box, neither that labeled "producer of output with legitimately owned resources," nor that labeled "lucky beneficiary of windfall gain." The ethical box occupied by the alert discoverer of an available opportunity might well be labeled "finders-keepers."

The finder (i.e., the discoverer) of this opportunity might lay claim to what he has discovered, not because he deliberately produced it but because he alertly noticed it. He might reject the criticisms of those who denounce private appropriation of lucky windfalls on the grounds that these criticisms are not relevant to his situation. Criticism of ownership based on pure luck cannot apply to the gains won by alert discovery. The lucky winner in a purely chance situation has done nothing to generate this outcome, which is unrelated to his efforts, his actions, his thoughts, and his purposes. The opportunity noticed by the discoverer is the direct creation of that discoverer's alertness, vision, and self-confidence. He was not deterred by the opinions of others; he saw what he saw and grasped it. He did not produce it deliberately; his unique vision brought it into economic existence. In a very real sense, he created what he discovered.

The creative aspect of alert discovery deserves to be emphasized. It seems plausible to attribute the finders-keepers ethic to the insight that the discovered object owes its very existence, as it were, to the discoverer. Had he not discovered it, that object would, for all human intents and purposes, be nonexistent; it would not figure in anyone's plans, purposes, or evaluations. An object produced out of the producer's owned resources is considered the just property of the producer because it *is* those resources, simply in different form; the pie *is* the sum of the ingredients out of which it has been baked. But a discovered object has been created, as it were, *ex nihilo*; its discoverer is considered its owner, not because he owned the inputs from which it has been produced but precisely because it has not been produced out of inputs. The discovered object has been brought into existence from nonexistence, simply through its having been discovered. Its discoverer is, in an ethically relevant sense, its creator.

The person into whose lap falls a valuable object has not created that object (assuming that others notice its fall just as soon as that person himself does). He is simply the location where sheer, blind luck has placed that object. The person who, owning resources, has deliberately employed them to produce output has not created that object out of nothing; he has deliberately fashioned it out of owned inputs. The discoverer of an object, available to but unnoticed by everyone else, has, in the relevant sense, created that object out of nothing, simply by virtue of the alertness of his personality. That alertness links the discovered object indissolubly with his personality; commonplace ethics finds this link sufficiently convincing to place the discovery in an ethical box entirely distinct from that labeled "windfall gain."

THE DISCOVERY CHARACTER OF PURE PROFIT

The arbitrage theory of profit, which we identified earlier with Ludwig von Mises, permits us to see entrepreneurial profit as a wholly discovered gain. Both the economic problem of profit and the ethical problem of profit dissolve once one recognizes the discovered character of pure profit. Profits, we found, cannot conceivably arise in equilibrium conditions; this is because equilibrium is, by construction, a state in which nothing (that is relevant to the analysis) remains to be discovered. Profit arises strictly in disequilibrium precisely because disequilibrium conditions are the directly implied consequences of as yet ungrasped opportunities "waiting," as it were, to be discovered. The appearance of an arbitrage opportunity between two markets is simply the manifestation of the failure of those selling in the low-priced market to be aware of buyers in the other market who are prepared to pay more; of the failure of those buying in the high-priced market to be aware of sellers in the other market who are prepared to sell for less. These failures in mutual awareness constitute an as yet undiscovered opportunity for pure profit. The entrepreneur who notices the price gap is making the relevant discovery. In grasping the profit constituted by this price gap he is, by his superior alertness, bringing into existence and into reality something of which no one was aware. It seems intuitively appealing to see the entrepreneur as the just owner of what he has discovered, not because he has provided a productive service, not because he claims the benefit conferred by pure luck, but because he is the finder, the creator of what he has discovered, and is thus entitled to be its keeper.

Our assertion that discovery-generated profit is not to be understood as the market value of a productive service provided by the entrepreneur perhaps may be challenged as an unnecessary complication. It perhaps may be argued that, even if one grants the crucial role of discovery in generating profit, this need not prevent us from seeing profit as a factor income. So that all that is required in order to understand pure profit within the traditional, Clarkian scheme is to recognize its emergence as due to deployment of a newly identified factor, the entrepreneurial propensity to discover. There is no need, it may be held, to justify pure profit in terms of a finders-keepers (i.e., a creators-keepers) ethic. Pure profit may be justified, surely, as being simply the additional value we can attribute to a factor service furnished by a particular class of factor owners, that is, to the service of discovery provided by entrepreneurs. We believe this argument to be faulty; it is *not* possible, we maintain, to treat entrepreneurial discovery as a productive factor.[37]

The key point is that, by its very nature (following from the sharp distinction drawn above between pure discovery and deliberate search), the pure propensity to make discoveries—or alertness—is not capable of being deliberately deployed. If one focuses on any such deployable propensity, in fact one must not be thinking of pure discovery at all but of a kind of deliberate search. In the market context pure entrepreneurship is not for hire—because if "entrepreneurial" services are, in fact, the object of sellers' offer to sell and buyers' offer to buy, then clearly the true entrepreneurs are those doing the buying—the services they are buying are not the relevant entrepreneurial services at all. It is these buyers' alert discovery (of the worthwhileness of deploying the services they are buying) which constitutes the element of pure discovery in the situation. To put the matter somewhat differently, an entrepreneur never perceives his alertness, his discovery potential, as a valuable, available factor able to command incremental value. Either he already perceives the available incremental value or he does not. (If he perceives the existence of this incremental value but must now search to ascertain the precise route to its realization, what we have is the already perceived opportunity of producing valuable knowledge through search, not a potential pure discovery at all.) If he does not yet perceive the availability of any incremental value, there is nothing, in the range of deliberate actions available to him, which promises any such gain at all. An engineer asked to identify the productive agents "needed for" the production of a product may certainly list, as one of these agents, an intangible such as "knowledge." But he will not list "initiative," or "awareness of the opportunity to produce the product," because the very notion of what is needed in order to produce a product presupposes the prospect (based, obviously, on an already existing initiative, on an already possessed awareness of the productive possibilities) of producing (if the listed necessary productive ingredients are forthcoming).

It is for these reasons that the pure profit perceived and grasped by the successful entrepreneur cannot be justified as simply the market value of a special kind of productive service he was able to provide. The notion of a market value (which presupposes sellers knowing they can provide the service they propose to sell and buyers knowing the service is available for purchase) is simply not applicable to pure discovery (to which we have seen the pure profit must be traced).

FURTHER REFLECTIONS ON THE DISCOVERED NATURE OF PURE PROFIT

This insight into the discovered nature of pure profit is closer to the Schumpeterian than to the Knightian view of profit, but it permits us to see something not so easily seen in the Schumpeterian view. The difference between the Misesian view and that of Knight is a decisive one. Although for both profit is a disequilibrium phenomenon associated strictly with the open-ended uncertainty of an unexpectedly changing world, it emerges quite differently for each of them. For Knight it emerges because the world has changed in a way that was expected by nobody, including the profit-winning entrepreneur; his profit *is* in the nature of a windfall. For Mises, on the other hand, profit is won through the superior vision of the entrepreneur, through his power to transcend the uncertainty which has misled other market participants to undervalue present resources.[38] The relation between Misesian profit and Schumpeterian profit is a more subtle one. For Schumpeter profit is deliberately created as the pioneering, innovating entrepreneur disturbs the somnolent calm of the existing routine. This disequilibrating activity consists in acts of creativity, or at any rate, in introducing into practice the creative novelties thought up by others. (Schumpeter labeled the entrepreneurial process the "perennial gale of creative destruction.")[39] So that one might be tempted to apply a creation ethic to Schumpeterian profits, too. We must not, however, forget that Schumpeter insisted that it is no part of the function of entrepreneurial leadership "to 'find' or to 'create' new possibilities. They are always present, abundantly accumulated by all sorts of people. Often they are also generally known and being discussed by scientific and literary writers. In other cases there is nothing to discover about them because they are quite obvious."[40] Clearly, it would be difficult to apply a finders-keepers ethic to this kind of picture of the entrepreneurial function. On the other hand, the arbitrage view of profit is not inconsistent with the notion of innovative production possibilities. Earlier discussion of this view of profit by the present writer have sometimes been misunderstood in this regard. The emphasis placed on the superior vision of the entrepreneur has been interpreted as denying him genuine creativity, since that which can be seen presumably exists, in some sense, before it has been noticed. For similar reasons, critics often wish to emphasize the inherent unknowability of the future; the future, they insist, is not to be considered as a rolled-up tapestry to be gradually unrolled as time passes but as something that is being continually created out of nothing in the course of the events and decisions which make up the flowing sequence of human history. They are thus unhappy with the arbitrage view on the grounds that it appears to deny this inherent unknowability and inescapable uncertainty of the future. How can we ascribe to the entrepreneur the capacity of seeing into the future when the future is not yet "there" to be seen? If we insist on viewing the entrepreneur as arbitrageur, are we not thereby suppressing the entrepreneur's role as innovator and creator of new products, new techniques, and new ideas?

Our view is that while entrepreneurship may very well (and in the real world certainly very frequently does) manifest itself in acts of innovative and technical creativity, the economic significance of such acts is yet to be seen in the strictly arbitrage aspect of such activity. The innovator is entrepreneurial in that he believes he has discovered a new way of deploying inputs—a way that will reveal the present market as undervaluing these inputs. The creativity we have emphasized in regard to entrepreneurial profit grasping consists not in the concrete innovative creations through which profit opportunities are identified and gasped but in the circumstance through which these innovative creations compel us to recognize how the market has (in regard to these innovative possibilities) undervalued the relevant inputs. It is the discovery of a price gap which others have failed to see which makes up, for the pure theory of entrepreneurial profit, the relevant creative aspect. So long as one is confined (as one is within the Schumpeterian framework) to recognizing entrepreneurial creativity only insofar as it is manifested in changed techniques of production, one's attention is deflected from the pure discovery element contained in every successful entrepreneurial venture.

It is true that the future is not a rolled-up piece of tapestry. Rather it is a tapestry that is being continually woven by the actions of individuals who are able to choose freely. Yet it should be clear that the successful entrepreneur, who located a new store in an area he believes will shortly become rather heavily populated, is in fact "seeing" the future. Although that future must be created by the further choices of many freely choosing persons, the entrepreneur has "seen" it—more correctly than others have. His purchase of the land on which to build his store has taken advantage of the market's failure to value that land at its full value—in terms of the services it can and will provide to this larger future population.

In talking of "more correct" or "less correct" entrepreneurial vision, in referring to noticing opportunities others have failed to notice, we are not, of course, attributing any kind of moral culpability to those who have failed to see the future correctly. If we use the term "error" to describe the failure of others to see what the successful entrepreneur sees, this term is used strictly as a metaphor. No one can be "blamed" for not foreseeing the future course of events correctly. But, on the other hand, we must not deny "credit" to the entrepreneur who does correctly see the future.

He is not simply the lucky beneficiary of a chance turn of events. He really did guess the future correctly, not perhaps with certainty but with sufficient conviction to inspire him to undertake his venture. When that venture turns out to have been a profitable one, we are entitled to describe the successful entrepreneur as having made a discovery; he should, for many of us, be entitled to keep that which he found.

TOWARD A BROADER THEORY OF DISTRIBUTIVE JUSTICE[41]

Although this chapter has focused narrowly on the ethical acceptability of pure profit, its central insights point to a broader issue, that of distributive justice in general. We conclude this chapter by briefly drawing attention to this broader context. The truth is that the traditional approach to distributive justice has suffered, we maintain, by failing to incorporate considerations relating to the ethical status of discovered gains. Once we recognize the nature of discovery, we appreciate that the total "pie" which is being "distributed" is, in fact, a pie the very size of which is being discovered, in fact created, during and through the very process of distribution. By this we do not mean simply that (as is, of course, well recognized in the literature of distributive justice) the size of the total social output, being a function of the incentive system, is itself determined, to some extent, by the distributive pattern adopted. Instead, we are referring to the circumstance that a significant proportion of production activity is inseparably intertwined with the pure discovery engaged in by market participants in their entrepreneurial roles. Real world production is, almost inevitably, partly a matter of entrepreneurial vision in identifying where resources can be obtained, what products are worthwhile producing, what techniques will be most successful and most economical, and so forth. The size of total output and, in particular, the size of the total complex of available resources is something that cannot, even in principle, be thought of in isolation from the system of rewards assigned to entrepreneurial discovery.

There never is a "given pie," or even a given complex of resources (from which to "bake the pie") available to society. So that the notion of "distribution" (and hence "distributive justice"), a notion presuming something "there" to be distributed, is a highly problematic one. The notion of a given pie or given available resources rules out any possible query as to whether, perhaps, any of the output attributable to the resources ought to accrue to him who *created* the resources *ex nihilo*, as it were. After all, the resources are seen as somehow "given," before the issue of distributive justice makes its entry.

It is our position, indeed, that in confining attention to the issue of how given output, or given resources, are to be justly distributed, theorists of economic justice have illegitimately blocked from consideration a most important series of possibilities. These possibilities arise out of the circumstance that, in our real world of open-ended uncertainty, an enormous contribution to the total size of output is made by those whose alertness has brought to society's attention the availability of resources, the availability of techniques, and the desirability to consumers of specific kinds of output. Appropriate rewards (and incentives) for this kind of contribution require that we step outside the framework of a given available set of goodies that must be shared out. We require a perspective which recognizes that, quite apart from the attribution of these goodies to relevant inputs, there is also the primordial issue of how it came to be discovered at all, that these inputs and worthwhile output possibilities were, in fact, available. The theory of pure profit outlined in this chapter finds its place in such a broader-gauged approach to economic justice.

NOTES

1. We take these widespread ethical intuitions for granted, not because we believe they are self-evidently true and correct but because our goal is to understand pure profits in terms of widely held ethical convictions. (This will hold, in particular, also for our use of the finders-keepers ethic later on in this chapter.) It follows, of course, that our arguments will properly be held at least partly irrelevant by those who, in fact, refuse to accept those widely held ethical intuitions.
2. Throughout this chapter we will be referring to the ethical "difficulty" or "problem" associated with pure profit. Of course, no difficulty or problem will exist for one who, indeed, believes that the phenomenon of pure profit is ethically undefendable. Although we will be using the terms "difficulty" and "problem," it is not our intention, in so doing, implicitly to beg the ethical question involved. From the perspective reached by the end of this chapter, suggesting a possible line of ethical justification for pure profit, it seems useful to introduce discussion by focusing on what will eventually be seen, we shall argue, to have been only apparent difficulties and problems.
3. This section draws substantially upon the material in Kirzner (1989, ch. 3). The history of theories of profit and entrepreneurship is a rich one. See in particular Hébert and Link (1988). My brief review makes no attempt at completeness in coverage; instead, it identifies several key approaches, an understanding of which (and of the shortcomings of

which) can, I believe, conduce to an appreciation of the Misesian theory discussed here.

4. Clark (1899).
5. Ibid., p. 201.
6. Ibid., p. 405.
7. Ibid., pp. 410–11.
8. Ibid., p. 411.
9. Knight (1921, pp. 41–8).
10. On this see Bronfenbrenner (1960).
11. Hawley (1900).
12. Hawley (1901).
13. Ibid., p. 604.
14. Hawley (1893).
15. Knight (1921, p. 43).
16. Ibid., p. 46.
17. Ibid., pp. 35–7.
18. Ibid., p. 271.
19. Ibid., pp. 277–83.
20. Ibid., p. 272.
21. In fact, Knight (1921) argued that it is the entrepreneur (who, while himself owning no inputs, assembles them to generate output) who must be considered the real "producer" of capitalist output (p. 271).
22. See Knight's statement: "Both in abstract ethics and from the standpoint of social interest in adequate motivation, a proposal to reduce high profits raises the question of using the proceeds to reduce losses" (Knight, 1949, p. 546.
23. See Schumpeter (1934, pp. 74ff.).
24. Schumpeter (1950, p. 132).
25. Schumpeter (1934, pp. 88–9).
26. Schumpeter (1950, p. 87).
27. Schumpeter (1954, p. 894). See also Schumpeter (1934, pp. 128–9), where Clark's theory is described as the closest to Schumpeter's own.
28. Nozick (1974, ch. 7).
29. Critics of capitalism have, indeed, even challenged the notion of self-ownership on precisely these grounds; see for example Roemer (1988, p. 154).
30. On this see further Kirzner (1973, pp. 85–6); Hébert and Link (1988, p. 152).
31. Mises (1962, p. 190).
32. Mises (1949, p. 291).
33. Rothbard (1985) has argued that this recognition and emphasis by Mises on the role of uncertainty in the generation of pure profit is inconsistent with the interpretation which the present writer has given Mises's theory. For Rothbard, an "alertness" theory of profit must do away with uncertainty. Although I have not been able to follow Rothbard's reasoning on this matter, the reader may wish to explore this issue further. See also Hébert and Link (1988, pp. 132ff.).
34. Mises (1949, p. 291).
35. Ibid.

36. This section draws substantially upon chapter 2 of my *Discovery, Capitalism and Distributive Justice* (1989).
37. For further discussion of this point see Kirzner (1985a, pp. 187–8; 1985b, pp. 27–8).
38. I have sometimes been (justifiably) criticized for making it seem as if the Misesian entrepreneur can win profits but never suffer losses. The superior vision of the entrepreneur sees profit opportunities; this explains profits but does not account for losses. The truth is, of course, that losses arise in exactly the same context as do profits, namely, when entrepreneurs, acting in an uncertain world, act to grasp what they think they see. Those who correctly see what others have not seen make profits. Those who "see" what, in fact, is not there to be seen (so that they buy resources at prices not justified by subsequent output values) suffer entrepreneurial losses. It is because we recognize that entrepreneurs are interested in making profits rather than losses that we are unable to treat losses and profits, as Knight does, as being wholly symmetrical.
39. Schumpeter (1950, p. 87).
40. Schumpeter (1934, p. 88).
41. For an elaboration of the broader agenda appealed for in the text see, in general, my book *Discovery, Capitalism and Distributive Justice* (1989); see especially chapter 7 for certain qualifications to the ideas set forth perhaps too unequivocally in this chapter.
42. For an earlier criticism of the notion of distribution, based on considerations not emphasized hem, see Mises (1949, p. 255).

REFERENCES

Bronfenbrenner, M. (1960) "A Reformulation of Naive Profit Theory," *Southern Economic Journal* April, pp. 300–9.

Clark, J.B. (1899) *The Distribution of Wealth*, New York: Macmillan.

Hawley, F.B. (1893) "The Risk Theory of Profit," *Quarterly Journal of Economics* 7, p. 460.

—— (1900) "Enterprise and Profit," *Quarterly Journal of Economics* 15, p. 75.

—— (1901) "Reply to Final Objection to the Risk Theory of Profit," *Quarterly Journal of Economics* 15, p. 610.

Hebert, R.F. and Link, A.N. (1988) *The Entrepreneur: Mainstream Views and Radical Critiques*, 2nd edn, New York: Praeger.

Kirzner, I.M. (1973) *Competition and Entrepreneurship*, Chicago: University of Chicago Press.

—— (1985a) *Perception, Opportunity, and Profit*, Chicago: University of Chicago Press.

—— (1985b) *Discovery and the Capitalist Process*, Chicago: University of Chicago Press.

—— (1989) *Discovery, Capitalism and Distributive Justice*, Oxford: Basil Blackwell.

Knight, F.H. (1921) *Risk, Uncertainty and Profit*, Boston, MA: Houghton Mifflin.

—— (1949) "Profit," in W. Fellner and B.F. Haley (eds) *Encyclopedia of the Social Sciences* 12, reprinted in *Readings in the Theory of Income Distribution*, Philadelphia: Blakiston.

Mises, L. von (1949) *Human Action*, New Haven, CT: Yale University Press.

—— (1962) *Planning for Freedom and Other Essays and Addresses*, 2nd edn, South Holland, IL: Libertarian Press.

Nozick, R. (1974) *Anarchy, State and Utopia*, New York: Basic Books.

Roemer, J. (1988) *Free to Lose: An Introduction to Marxist Economic Philosophy*, Cambridge, MA: Harvard University Press.

Rothbard, M.N. (1985) "Professor Hébert on Entrepreneurship," *Journal of Libertarian Studies* 3(2), pp. 281–6.

Schumpeter, J.A. (1934) *The Theory of Economic Development*, Cambridge, MA: Harvard University Press.

—— (1950) *Capitalism, Socialism and Democracy*, 3rd edn, New York: Harper and Row.

—— (1954) *History of Economic Analysis*, Oxford: Oxford University Press.

Source: The Nature of Profits: Some Economic Insights and their Ethical Implications, in Robin A. Cowan and Mario J. Rizzo (eds) (1995) *Profits and Morality*, University of Chicago Press.

7

COORDINATION AS A CRITERION FOR ECONOMIC "GOODNESS"

INTRODUCTION[1]

From the very beginnings of economic science, economists (and the public) have been convinced that economic theories can offer impartial guidance for public policy. In other words economic science, it has always been believed, can objectively pronounce some policies to be economically "bad," and other policies to be economically "good." For the age of Adam Smith there was little ambiguity in the phrase "economically good" (or its opposite). That which increased the "wealth of nations" was clearly economically good. And for classical economists what constitutes a nation's wealth seemed reasonably clear.[2] As economics (following on the marginalist revolution) advanced through the era of neoclassicism, the precise nature of the economic criterion came to be developed far more critically and self-consciously. The emergence of the theory of welfare economics during the first half of the now concluding century consisted, to a significant degree, in attempts to grapple ingeniously with conceptual problems raised by the subjective character of utility, as distinct from objective wealth (and thus by the difficulty of aggregating a society's economic well-being). Hayek's mid-century insights concerning the dispersed character of available knowledge in society[3] further challenged the possibility of treating the economic problem facing society, as being that of achieving global efficiency in the allocation of resources. Recent critiques[4] of traditional welfare theory have radically questioned the very possibility of devising an economic criterion that might, independently of particular moral philosophical positions, be deployed in order to pronounce one economic state of affairs (or one economic policy) to be "economically better" than a second.

This chapter, building on certain earlier works,[5] sets forth a clear-cut, objective criterion, *coordination,* which may satisfy the intuitive conviction of economists that their science does objectively demonstrate the economic "goodness" of some economic policies (and the economic "badness" of other policies)—without running into any of the above-mentioned difficulties which have dogged twentieth century welfare economic theory.

WHAT IT IS WE ARE LOOKING FOR

In searching for an objective criterion for service as an index of economic "goodness," we are not seeking to square the circle. Certainly "goodness" of any kind is a normative notion calling for a justification in moral-philosophical terms (which may, at least for the economist, involve subjective convictions rather than objectively established definitive conclusions). But such a criterion may nonetheless be identified in objective terms (i.e., in terms that themselves do not beg the moral-philosophical question of defining "goodness"); that criterion may then (subject to independently adopted moral-philosophical principles) serve as an objective criterion for economic goodness. An illustration from early nineteenth-century economic literature may be helpful on this point.

In 1831, Richard Whately, an Anglican cleric, delivered a course of lectures on political economy at Oxford.[6] In introducing his subject, he apparently found it necessary to defend himself against some who had questioned the propriety of a clergyman's interest in the "science of wealth." Whately's response to his critics was ingenious (and, one suspects, somewhat playful). He pointed out that research into the causes of a phenomenon (such as wealth) does not, by itself, imply any moral approbation of that phenomenon. After all, Whately argued, a medical researcher exploring the causes of a disease does not, one presumes, hope to enhance the incidence of this disease. Scientific research, Whately was arguing, is not by itself an expression of a commitment in favor of (or against) the phenomenon which is the topic of exploration.

Now certainly a policy which reduces the incidence of a disease cannot be described as "good" without additional moral-philosophical insights. But the disease itself can be defined objectively and scientifically; a policy which reduces the incidence of disease may then on the basis of independently established moral principles be pronounced as medically good policy.

What is needed for an objectively-based normative economics, is a criterion which, like the criteria which identify a particular disease, can be unambiguously identified by economic science and which, again as in the case of disease, seems likely to be able to serve as a norm for goodness in the light of independently established, widely shared or otherwise assumed moral principles. For Whately, wealth offered itself as such a criterion (although, as we have seen, he was playfully coy as to whether he envisaged economic goodness to be correlated with its increase or with its decrease). But the subjectivist insights of the Marginalist Revolution rendered "aggregate wealth" unacceptable as a criterion for economic goodness.

STANDARD ATTEMPTS TO IDENTIFY THE CRITERION OF ECONOMIC GOODNESS

Economists during the early and central decades of this century labored hard in order to establish a scientifically defined criterion for economic goodness. These efforts constitute the history of twentieth century welfare economics. From the perspective provided by an understanding of Austrian Economics at the close of the century, these efforts, ingenious and brilliant though they were, largely failed to achieve their objective. They depended either, as in Pigouvian welfare economics, on the futile idea of somehow aggregating utility across the individuals making up society, or, as in the standard interpretations of Paretian welfare economics, on the flawed notion of seeing society as a single decision making entity seeking to achieve global efficiency in its pattern of resource allocation.

From the perspective of the methodological individualism and subjectivism which nourish Austrian Economics, the idea of aggregating utility is simply meaningless (not just wrong)—since utility is seen as essentially nothing more than a degree of importance attached by a decision-making individual to an option, in his comparison of it with other options.[7] Similarly the notion of societal efficiency is viewed by Austrians as less than coherent, since not only does society in fact not make decisions, in any but a metaphorical sense, but as Hayek showed us,[8] the essence of an economic problem facing society consists precisely in the dispersed character of existing knowledge—which dispersed character renders entirely moot the notion of centralized allocative efficiency (for which centralized information must be a necessary prerequisite).

We should point out that these "Austrian" difficulties do not reflect any conceptual difficulty in deploying economic science for policy purposes. There is no difficulty in arguing an "ought"-statement which depends, for its factual basis, on an independently established "is"-statement. These "Austrian" difficulties stem from the conceptual difficulties associated with constructing a coherent notion of what is economically good for society. The Austrian methodological tenets we have referred to seem to invalidate, as science, any global notions of economic goodness that might serve as policy yardsticks. In other words, it seems, the global notions of economic goodness needed in order to evaluate social policies must themselves remain outside science. Economic science cannot, it appears, be deployed for social-normative purposes, only because the criteria we wish to apply in our evaluations cannot be coherently defined except as pure (non-scientific) judgments of value. Positive science may not, without appealing to non-scientific judgments of value, be able to pronounce heart disease desirable or undesirable. But these judgments of value are not needed to identify heart disease (and thus to be able scientifically to identify its causes). The "economic well-being of society," on the other hand—even before one begins to consider whether it is morally worthy of being desired—is a concept which, we have argued, is simply undefined and undefinable, as long as we confine ourselves to positive categories of subjectivist and methodologically individualistic economics. Certainly such economics will, by itself, be unable to identify specific policies as able to enhance the "economic well-being of society."

But all this means that we have reached something of an impasse. Economists have always assumed that their positive findings can be of direct assistance in advising rulers. Economists have always believed that their discipline does teach us about the virtues or vices of free markets. The purism expressed in the proceeding paragraphs seems to have unhelpfully propelled us rapidly toward an intellectual dead-end.

In this chapter we shall argue that we can escape this impasse. The notion of "coordination" fits precisely the specifications we are seeking to apply. It refers to an objective state, which economic science is able to identify and describe and which does, in general, appear to be a matter of moral concern to many thoughtful observers of economic phenomena and economic policies. This notion is not vulnerable to the subjectivist and methodologically individualist objections which we found to challenge standard welfare economics. Economics science is thus, through the coordination notion, able, we shall maintain, to provide an objective criterion in terms of which the economic goodness and badness of economic situations or economic policies, may be judged. We certainly need moral philosophy to help judge the goodness (or badness) of greater degrees of coordinatedness; but we do not need any help from moral philosophy in order to identify the coordination concept and associate specific economic policies with either greater or lesser likelihood of generating coordination. In this way economics may, in principle, be able to provide objective measures of (what independently established moral principles declare to be) economic goodness.

COORDINATION DEFINED

A fully coordinated state of affairs, for our purposes, is one in which each action taken by each individual in a demarcated set of actions, correctly takes into account (a) the actions in fact being taken by everyone else in the set, and (b) the actions which the others might take were one's own actions to be different. An example of what we mean by a state of coordination is presented in the activities of air controllers in charge of flights into and out of a busy airport. It is generally understood that the function of the air controller is to coordinate these flights in order to ensure smooth and safe scheduling of departures and arrivals. It will be useful to consider in precisely what the air controller's coordinative responsibilities consist.

Clearly, were two airplanes to collide, we would say that the actions of their respective pilots were not mutually coordinated. Each pilot failed correctly to take into account what the other pilot was doing. Had Pilot No. 1 known that Pilot No. 2 would place his plane at the particular point and at the time at which the collision occurred, he would not have placed his own plane at that point, at that time; and similarly for Pilot No. 2. What the air controller does in coordinating flight activity is to ensure that no such failure in each pilot's taking into account of the other's actions, should ever occur. But of course the objective of the air controller goes beyond the avoidance of collisions. The objective is also to expedite the smooth movement of aircraft into and out of the airport, so as to minimize the time spent in unneeded waiting. A pilot held in an unnecessarily long holding pattern is, in effect, failing to have his actions coordinated with those of the other pilots—since if he were utterly sure that no other aircraft would be in his vicinity during the immediate future, there would be no reason for him not to proceed to land immediately.

We notice that the coordinative activity of the air controller is deliberately and centrally planned. It is, predominantly, "top-down" coordination. Each pilot coordinates his activity with the actions of the other pilots, in effect, by entrusting decision-making to the air controller. Having confidence in the air controller's expertise, he takes the actions of other pilots into account, not by being himself in direct communication with them, but by agreeing (at the same time as, he is given to understand, the other pilots are similarly agreeing) to obey the instructions of the controller, to whom is assigned the task of explicitly arranging the coordination of the flight patterns.

When we identify coordination as being the criterion for economic "goodness," we are asserting that, from the perspective of those whom economists aspire to serve, the function of an economic system is to coordinate the activities of its participants. For one convinced that a centrally planned economy is the economic system to be preferred, central planning (like the activity of the air controller) is the preferred instrument for the achievement of coordination. For those convinced of the virtue of Adam Smith's "invisible hand" a free market is able to achieve, spontaneously and without central direction, coordination among its primary participants, the consumers and the owners of resources. Certainly one of the tasks of economic theory is to help determine which of these two options is closer to the truth.

FURTHER REFLECTION ON THE MEANING OF COORDINATION

We were concerned, earlier in this chapter, to establish that "coordination" is a state of affairs that can (like a disease) be objectively defined and described, without the need for any value judgments or moral considerations whatever. It was only in order to identify greater degrees of coordination as being "better"—analogously to being able to describe a more effective cure for a disease as being a "better" drug—that moral judgment concerning the desirability of greater coordination—analogous to the judgment that it is morally desirable to eliminate disease—enters the picture.

This earlier emphasis of ours underscores what should by now be obvious,[9] viz. that what is meant by coordination is not the presence of a *pattern of activities* which appears pleasing to the economist, or to anyone else. People do sometimes speak of one color scheme being a better-coordinated one than a second scheme. In making those kinds of statements reference is certainly being made to the pleasing or unpleasing character of the configuration of colors. But that is not at all the way we have defined coordination for purposes of serving as a criterion of economic "goodness." An air collision is an example of imperfect coordination, in our sense of the term, not because of the tragically unfortunate character of the collision, but because of the obvious failure which the collision demonstrates, on the part of each of the two colliding pilots, to have taken adequate account of each other's actions. When we wish to take coordination as our criterion for economic "goodness," we imply, not that a coordinated state is one which reflects the beauty (in the eyes of the morally relevant public) of the particular patterns of decisions which happens to make up that state, but that we understand that morally relevant public to consider the coordinated state (because, and only because, it conforms to our definition of coordination) to be morally desirable. It is not that we define coordination by reference to what is morally beautiful. It is that we believe that moral beauty is widely perceived to inhere in the state of coordination as we have defined it i.e., as a state in which no action would be different than it is, were the agent to have known more accurately what it is that other decision-makers are doing, or what they might be prepared to do under alternative circumstances.

A COMPLICATION IN THE DEFINITION OF COORDINATION: AN IMPORTANT DIGRESSION

It should be carefully noted that the criterion we have selected as an indicator of economic goodness is, while itself entirely objective and value-free, able to be defined only against the background of some initially-given pattern of property rights. Given a pattern of property rights designated, say, as A, we may meaningfully seek to judge a particular piece of legislation or an entirely different pattern of property rights, as to whether it offers greater or lesser coordinative potential than does A. That notion will be made in terms of the notion of coordination as defined from the perspective of rights system A. Without some initially given rights pattern, a notion of coordination cannot be assigned specific meaning. In particular, it will not be possible to judge "absolutely" between two property rights systems (system A and system B) in regard to their comparative coordinative potentials—without any given starting position.

To see this at the most elementary level, imagine that agent alpha prefers a marginal unit of beef over a marginal unit of chicken, while agent beta prefers the chicken over the beef. It will make all the difference in the world, in our judgment of coordination or miscoordination in regard to the distribution of beef and chicken ownership, whether we (i) begin with a situation in which alpha and beta "own" the chicken and beef respectively, or (ii) begin with a situation in which alpha, say, "owns" *both* the beef and the chicken. From the perspective of situation (i), coordination would require that alpha finish up having the beef, and beta having the chicken. But from the perspective of situation (ii), it is that initial situation (in which alpha owns both the beef and the chicken) which is the coordinated situation. From a strictly economic perspective (i.e., from a perspective which is neutral in regard to the relative morality or legality of alternative initial property rights patterns of distribution) one cannot pronounce situation (ii) as economically "bad"—even though that situation would be perceived as uncoordinated, were our initial vantage point to have been a situation in which the beef and chicken were, initially, differently distributed.

It might then seem that the notion of coordination is not entirely objective, after all. What is seen as coordination from the perspective of one particular property rights system, based presumably upon one particular adopted moral framework, may well be seen as discoordination in regard to a second property rights system, based on a different adopted moral framework. So that the coordination criterion appears, contrary to our earlier assertion, to be a morally relative notion.

But recognizing the validity of the insights presented in this section does not contradict our earlier assumptions. It is true that coordination cannot be defined except within a given, adopted moral/legal framework; nonetheless, within that framework, it offers an objective criterion. This criterion is itself admittedly unable to discriminate between the economic goodness of different moral/legal frameworks, unless one of them is taken as the relevant starting point. But this does not render the criterion itself arbitrary. The question, "How far is it to Chicago?" cannot be answered except be reference to some "arbitrarily-given" starting point. Yet the concept of distance is itself entirely objective, not at all arbitrary. As elsewhere argued,[10] the efficacy of the market process is itself not a meaningful notion unless embedded in some exogenously given moral/legal framework. What we see in regard to the coordination norm is exactly the same case.

Moreover, we should remind the reader that the more traditional attempts, in standard welfare economics, to fashion a criterion of economic goodness, were, quite similarly, relative to the initial pattern of rights distribution. As Ezra Mishan showed many years ago,[11] a welfare optimum cannot be defined except within the framework of a given ownership pattern (since the wealth effects arising from alternative ownership patterns will affect the utility schedules or indifference maps from which welfare theory construes its patterns of optimalities). Although the specific sense in which our coordination criterion is definable only relative to a given rights framework is somewhat different from that demonstrated by Mishan in regard to the standard welfare-theoretic apparatus, the essential insight is entirely the same. And while this "relativism" should be carefully noted and respected (and while, in consequence, the scope within which "scientifically objective" welfare theory can be deployed is narrower than one might perhaps have thought), it does not destroy the objectivity of the welfare criterion, properly used. The case with the coordination criterion is entirely similar.

So that when we use the coordination criterion to assess, for example, Mises's arguments in regard to the possibility of socialist economic planning, it offers us insights which must be carefully identified. To take matters at a most simple level, it would be incorrect to assert that Mises proved that the central planners' decisions under socialism are literally uncoordinated. By definition, all the decisions of the central planners, since they are consciously arrived at within a single (attempted) "plan" must—no matter how incoherent and mistaken that plan may be shown to be—have been "coordinated" in the sense that each part of the "plan" is, at least superficially, made with awareness of each part of the "plan." What Mises showed, of course, was that at a deeper level, the central planner cannot create a true plan, since he cannot engage in "economic calculation," i.e., each part of the "plan" is necessarily made without full awareness of its true implications for other parts of the attempted plan. What this means, in terms of our notion of coordination is that the actions called for by the attempted central plan are uncoordinated in the sense that, were the various agents in the socialized economy to have the freedom to make their own decisions (with full awareness of each other's decisions and potential decisions), (i.e., were they to be assigned specific property rights), they would find it mutually beneficial not to follow the pattern of actions in fact dictated by the central plan—even if the central planner's objective was that of fulfilling the preferences of agents, to the greatest socially possible extent. The economic inadequacy of socialist planning is thus to be understood as seen from the hypothetical starting point of some (i.e., any) pattern of private property rights.[12]

COORDINATION AND COORDINATION

There is a certain ambiguity in the word "coordination" which urgently calls for our attention.[13] Sometimes we use the word coordination (as in the phrase "complete coordination") to refer to the fully coordinated state (as defined above). But at other times we use the word coordination to refer to the process in the course of which a state of discoordinatedness gradually comes to be replaced by successive states of greater and greater degrees of coordinatedness.

So that, if an economist asserts that the market "coordinates" the activities of its participants, this may mean one of two possible things. It may mean that that economist is maintaining that the market has achieved that equilibrium state in which all activities are in a state of complete mutual coordinatedness. (In that equilibrium state market exchanges are such that each participant takes into account, in effect, the plans of each other participant. So that, by confronting each market participant with the appropriate price incentives, the market may be said to be coordinating all the decisions being made, i.e., to be arranging those incentives to be operating that are able to achieve this state of complete coordinatedness.) Or that original assertion may have a quite different meaning. It may mean that the economist is maintaining that while, at any moment of time during the course of the market process of equilibration, all activities are *not* fully coordinated, nonetheless that process is tending steadily to reduce the degree of discoordinatedness that initially existed among the activities of the market participants. These two assertions are quite different assertions. Understanding what a particular assertion in fact means, and avoiding confusing that assertion with a second assertion (that may in fact not be being made at all) may be of considerable importance. An example of the importance of such understanding follows.

DYNAMIC COMPETITION AND THE COORDINATING PROCESS

This writer has often drawn attention to the possible equilibrative properties of dynamic entrepreneurial competition.[14] From an initial state of affairs in which productive activities are not taking advantage of existing resource or technological availabilities, entrepreneurial entry, based on innovative recognition of these availabilities, may generate a dynamically competitive process during which the older inefficient producers come to be replaced by more efficient producers. It is clear that, from the consumers' point of view this process is economically "good"; it provides them with products which are cheaper and/or better, as judged by them. I would also argue that this process is "good" in that it better coordinates the preferences of consumers with the availabilities of resources (and thus with the potential actions of resource owners). It is here that critics have rebelled.

Surely, it is again and again objected, this dynamically competitive entrepreneurial entry—no matter how beneficial it may be held to be—cannot be described as coordinative.[15] After all, despite all the undenied benefits of this entry (as judged by consumers), this entry drastically disrupts ("discoordinates") the activities of those older, less efficient producers (and their employees) who are being destroyed by this new competition. Surely this kind of Schumpeterian creative destruction should be recognized as (perhaps valuably) disrupting the coordination which had previously prevailed in the industry. Up until the new innovation, production plans smoothly dovetailed with consumer decisions. As a result of the innovation those earlier plans (and all the plans, say, of potential employees who have been training in preparation for entry into the now obsolete production procedure) have been irrevocably disrupted. Surely this dynamic competition must be recognized as discoordinative! So run the objections. But our earlier discussions should have made clear why these objections are not valid; in the important sense of the term this dynamically competitive entry must be seen as coordinative, not discoordinative.

Certainly this entry disrupts the earlier-made plans of inefficient producers and their employees and suppliers. Based on their earlier, now disappointed expectations, those producers may certainly see themselves as being "hurt" by the new innovations. But those earlier plans of the inefficient producers were in fact part of the network of plans that were being made, which were poorly coordinated with other potential decisions on the part of other owners of resources. The owners of those other resources would have been ready—and, when the innovative competing entrepreneur approached them they were in fact ready—to offer resource services to the market which could have made possible the provision to consumers of better and cheaper products. The consumer who (being unaware of such possibilities) had continued to pay high prices for the inferior products of the older producers, were making decisions that were not appropriately taking into account the potential decisions of other resource owners and other potential producers. The innovative competitor who, entering the industry and pushing out the older firms, is disrupting their earlier plans, is replacing a less coordinated set of market activities, by a better coordinated set. In the "dynamic" sense of the term "coordination" (identified in the preceding section of this paper), this brash, aggressive competition is coordinative. The disruption it causes in the earlier plans of the inefficient producers is the evidence for and manifestation of the earlier state of discoordinatedness which has generated the changes (of which this disruption is a part). The apparent earlier calm which, as a result of the aggressive new competition, has been followed by sudden disruption, was in fact utterly misleading. That calm was a facade expressing the presence of as yet undiscovered (but very real) discoordinatedness; dynamic competition shattered that calm, replacing the earlier uncoordinated sets of activities by a better-coordinated set.

It is true that the disappointment of earlier-made plans of (the inefficient) producers may hit them with a sense of great pain. But, from the perspective of the coordination criterion for goodness, that pain is hardly of relevance. Notice that this assertion reflects no moral judgment of the older, inefficient producers. Their innocence need not be doubted; nor the reality or moral significance of their pain. We simply point out that the coordination criterion is not measuring goodness by any aggregate measure of well-being (because we believe that economic science cannot recognize the validity of such aggregates). In fact, well-being is not referred to in the coordination criterion at all. Moreover, the pain suffered by the older, inefficient producers has arisen only because those inefficient producers had believed (innocently, perhaps, but nonetheless erroneously, and, from the consumers' perspective, harmfully), that they could continue indefinitely to rely on the consumers' failing to take advantage of alternative available opportunities. From the perspective of the coordination criterion this "pain" thus appears to be based upon an illusion, the removal of which has definitely positive merit. What has been taken from the inefficient firms is nothing but the false expectations which their illusions had nourished, that they would be able to continue to rely on consumers' remaining ignorant of better opportunities available to them elsewhere. The coordination criterion (that is, the moral principles which pronounce this criterion to be a useful standard, among other possible standards, of "goodness") refuses to acknowledge the relevance of any pain which accompanies the realization of the falsity of such expectations. We may indeed have compassion for the pained victim of such self-delusion, but such compassion is not part of that moral dimension of social goodness which we seek to isolate by the adjective "economic," a moral dimension which the coordination criterion seems to capture very neatly.

COORDINATION AND PARETO-OPTIMALITY

It will be noticed that the coordination criterion bears a certain formal resemblance to Pareto-optimality. In this section we briefly examine this apparent resemblance, and clarify our reason for rejecting the Paretian criterion in favor of coordination.

A state of full coordinatedness is, of course, Pareto-optimal. If each participant is taking full account of actions (and potential actions) of each other participant, this clearly means that all courses of action which might be preferred by any one participant without hurting anyone else, must already have been successfully pursued. Conversely, if a Pareto-preferred course of action *is* available, this must mean that, to some extent, participants have not taken full account of what others might be prepared to do under all relevant circumstances; Pareto-suboptimality corresponds to imperfect coordination. Yet to use Pareto-optimality as the criterion of economic goodness is not the same as using the coordination criterion; the formal congruence of the two concepts does not at all imply that the philosophical or moral meanings of these two criteria are the same. Pareto-optimality is generally understood to be a concept that ingeniously permits us to talk of the overall well-being of society without having to confront the problems of interpersonal utility comparisons. The coordination criterion does not purport to say anything whatever about aggregate well-being.

The Pareto-optimality concept (because it is generally understood as representing, in a certain limited sense, maximum possible aggregate well-being) is widely used as a criterion relevant to "social efficiency" in the allocation of society's resources (a notion seen as similar to that of individual efficiency in budgeting scarce individual resources among competing individual ends). A Pareto-suboptimal state of affairs is socially inefficient, because somehow that state of affairs reflects a failure to achieve the highest level of aggregate well-being that might have been attained. The coordination criterion implies nothing about any such notion as social efficiency. In fact it emerged as a deliberate attempt to be able to say something about the economic goodness of policies or situations *without* becoming embroiled in the well-known analytical and conceptual difficulties which render the notion of social efficiency unacceptable to Austrian economists.[16]

Because the Pareto-criterion is understood to be concerned with aggregate well-being, its serviceability as a yardstick of economic goodness depends on our willingness to accept aggregate well-being—defined in terms of satisfaction of individual preferences—as a relevant moral norm. Notice that this does not mean that in making judgments based on Pareto-optimality considerations, standard welfare economics has committed itself morally to this norm.[17] It merely means that, in using Pareto-optimality as the criterion for goodness, it is presuming that those to whom welfare economics provides technical advice do share this moral commitment. Nonetheless use of the Paretian-criterion does, somewhere along the line, presume a moral acceptance of the satisfaction of individual preferences as an important element of "goodness." Use of the coordination criterion involves no such moral commitment at all, on anybody's part. Use of the coordination-criterion presumes that those advised by the economist are morally concerned that members of society undertake their actions in a way that does not inevitably spell disappointment and/or regret (such as must ultimately ensue from patterns of action which incorrectly anticipate and depend upon the actions of others in the system.) This moral concern is clearly a different one from that generally understood as implicit in the deployment of the Pareto-criterion.

CONCLUSION

There is no doubt that when the layperson is led to believe that a particular piece of legislation is good economic policy, he understands that to mean that this legislation overwhelmingly tends sooner or later to improve chances for the greater overall prosperity of society, with "prosperity" itself being understood by the layperson to be measurable in fairly definite terms. Economists have struggled mightily to render this vague notion of global economic "goodness" precise and objectively definable. One criterion after another has been proposed, only to have it be rejected on theoretical-consistency grounds. For economists concerned to preserve the sense of economic meaningfulness strictly on methodologically individualistic grounds, and aware of the challenge posed for economic meaningfulness by the circumstance of dispersed knowledge, the difficulty of devising an acceptable criterion for economic goodness has been particularly daunting. In this chapter I have outlined the case for taking "coordination" (particularly in the process sense of this word) as the criterion for which economists have been searching.[18]

NOTES

1. Helpful comments on an earlier draft were gratefully received from members of the Austrian Economics Colloquium at New York University. The author is especially indebted for stimulating and insightful criticisms and suggestions contributed by David Harper and Sanford Ikeda.
2. There were, of course, differences among classical economists concerning the precise definition of wealth. On this see Kirzner (1960, pp. 29–32).
3. See Hayek (1949, 1945).
4. See e.g. Hausman and McPherson (1993).
5. See Kirzner (1963, pp. 33–44, 297–309); (1973, ch. 6); O'Driscoll (1977); Cordato (1992).
6. See Whately (1855, p. 25).
7. For a classic statement of these problems in welfare economics, see Robbins (1935, chs III and VI). Readers of Robbins' book will be aware of the extensive influence of Robbins' ideas upon this chapter.
8. Hayek (1944, 1945).
9. The assertion in the text is contrary to the (surprisingly) opposite interpretation of this writer's position suggested by Daniel Klein (1997, p. 331).
10. See Kirzner (1994).
11. Mishan (1976). I am indebted to Mario J. Rizzo for reference; see also Rizzo (1980).
12. This exposition of Mises's economic calculation demonstration of the impossibility of socialist central planning may, concededly, seem forced. Certainly Mises himself intended to show that, from the perspective of the central planners themselves, their "plan" must necessarily fail to be a true plan, since the planners *cannot* be aware of the full consequences of each part of their plan for each other part. We do not at all question the validity of this assertion, and it is of course the basis of our discussion in the text. However, in order unambiguously to rank the economic "goodness" of the market economy and the centrally planned economy respectively, this assertion may not be sufficient. Conceivably, "unplanned" socialism (i.e., socialism with its fatally-flawed central "plan") might in some sense be judged economically superior to the literally unplanned outcomes of the competitive market. The coordination criterion enables us to translate Mises's own demonstration (of the impossibility of a true central plan) into a coordination-based assessment of the relative economic superiority of the market economy and the centrally planned economy respectively. For such a translation, we have argued in the text, some initial private-property pattern of rights assignment must be assumed, in order for a coordination-based comparison to be able to be rigorously attempted.

13. On this see Kirzner (1992, pp. 190–2).
14. See e.g. Kirzner (1973, p. 81).
15. See e.g. Klein (1997, p. 331 and fn 7).
16. For literature directly or indirectly critical of the notion of social efficiency, see Littlechild (1978, pp. 77–93); Rizzo (1979b) and Rothbard (1979); Egger (1979, pp. 118–22).
17. On this point we must disagree with the position taken by Hausman and McPherson (1993).
18. We must readily grant that even if the arguments in this chapter are accepted, we have not yet firmly established the usefulness of the coordination concept as the criterion for economic goodness. The serviceability of the coordination criterion, as a device with which to rank a series of alternative policies, has yet to be concretely demonstrated. Nevertheless, casual consideration of such welfare issues as the socialist calculation debate, suggests that the coordination criterion can fairly easily be used for at least some evaluative purposes. In addition, the *formal* congruence of this criterion with the Paretian criterion, noticed earlier in the text, suggests further scope for the serviceability of the coordination criterion, along lines traditionally pursued within the standard Paretian welfare economics.

REFERENCES

Cordato, R.E (1992) *Welfare Economics and Externalities in an Open-ended Universe*, Boston, Dordrecht, London: Kluwer.

Egger, J.B. (1979) "Comment: Efficiency is Not a Substitute for Ethics," in M.J. Rizzo (ed.) *Time, Uncertainty, and Disequilibrium*, Lexington, MA: Lexington Books.

Hausman, D.M. and McPherson, M.S. (1993) "Taking Ethics Seriously: Economics and Contemporary Moral Philosophy," *Journal of Economic Literature* 91, pp. 671–731.

Hayek, F.A. (1945) "The Use of Knowledge in Society," *American Economic Review* 35. Reprinted in Hayek (1949).

—— (1949) *Individualism and Economic Order*, London: Kegan Paul.

Kirzner, I.M. (1960) *The Economic Point of View*, Princeton, NJ: Van Nostrand.

—— (1963) *Market Theory and the Price System*, Princeton, NJ: Van Nostrand.

—— (1973) *Competition and Entrepreneurship*, Chicago: University of Chicago Press.

—— (1992) *The Meaning of Market Process, Essays in the Development of Modern Austrian Economics*, London: Routledge.

—— (1994) "The Limits of the Market: the Real and the Imagined," in Möschel *et al.* (1994), republished as chapter 4 in the present volume.

Klein, D. (1997) "Convention, Social Order, and the two Coordinations," *Constitutional Political Economy* 8, p. 331.

Littlechild, S.C. (1978) "The Problem of Social Cost," in Spadaro (1978).

Mishan, E.J. (1976) *Cost-Benefit Analysis*, rev. edn, New York: Praeger.

Möschel, W., Streit, M.E., and Witt, U. (eds) (1994) *Marktwirtschaft und Rechtsordnung*, Baden-Baden: Nomos.

O'Driscoll, G.P., Jr. (1977) *Economics as a Coordination Problem: The Contributions of Friedrich A. Hayek*, Kansas City: Sheed, Andrews and McMeel.

Rizzo, M.J. (ed.) (1979a) *Time, Uncertainty, and Disequilibrium.* Lexington, MA: Lexington Books.

—— (1979b) "Uncertainty, Subjectivity, and the Economic Analysis of Law," in Rizzo (1979a).

—— (1980) "The Mirage of Efficiency," *Hofstra Law Review* 8, pp. 648ff.

Robbins, L.C. (1935) *The Nature and Significance of Economic Science*, 2nd edn, London: Macmillan.

Rothbard, M.N. "Comment: The Myth of Efficiency," in Rizzo (1979a).

Spadaro, L.M. (ed.) (1978) *New Directions in Austrian Economics*, Kansas City: Sheed, Andrews and McMeel.

Whately, R. (1855) *Introductory Lectures on Political Economy, Delivered at Oxford in Easter Term*, 1831, 4th edn, London: John W. Parker.

Source: Coordination as a Criterion for Economic "Goodness," *Constitutional Political Economy*, 1998, 9, pp. 289–301.

Part III

STUDIES IN THE MISES–HAYEK LEGACY

8

REFLECTIONS ON THE MISESIAN LEGACY IN ECONOMICS

This chapter was first published as a paper by the *Review of Austrian Economics* in honor of the memory of Murray N. Rothbard. As I wrote it, my mind went back over 40 years, to the first time that I had met him. It was at the opening session of the Seminar in Economic Theory which Professor Mises conducted in the fall semester of 1954. That occasion was also my first meeting with Ludwig von Mises, and it is etched deeply in my memory. Two statements by Mises at that seminar meeting stand out in my recollection. One statement was his very opening substantive sentence that evening. "The market," Mises began, "is a process." (See also the statement in *Human Action* (1966, p. 257): "The market is not a place, a thing, or a collective entity. The market is a process.")

Coming as I did from a rather spotty undergraduate training in economics (and mainly along Keynesian lines), Mises's statement, I recall, left me completely puzzled. I had thought of the market as a place, an arena for exchanges, as an abstract idea referring to voluntary exchange translations. I could not fathom what on earth could be meant by the observation that the market is a process. I now, in retrospect, consider that all my subsequent training and research in economics, both before and after obtaining my doctorate under Mises, has consisted in learning to appreciate what it was that Mises meant by this assertion.

The second statement by Mises which stands out in my memory from that September 1954 evening, is a reference that Mises made to Murray Rothbard. Murray had, it appeared, recently completed a paper which Mises found to be excellent. He briefly but warmly complimented Murray on that piece of work, and expressed the hope and the prediction that Murray would continue to produce a great deal of future work of similar excellence. The years since 1954 have amply borne out Mises's hope and his prediction.

Murray Rothbard's output during these four decades has been prodigious. The breadth of his reading across so many disciplines has been breathtaking; his sheer energy in producing thousands of pages of published work has been stupendous. It is a privilege to contribute this paper to a memorial issue dedicated to the memory of Murray N. Rothbard.

This chapter will have to do with the first of the two statements made by Mises at that 1954 seminar session. I will be taking issue with a certain tendency, present in a number of recent expositions of Mises's work, to de-emphasize (or even flatly to deny) the centrality of the idea of the market as a process in the Misesian system. I consider clarification concerning the character of the Misesian system to be of critical importance for the future direction of modern Austrian economics, and for its ability to contribute fruitfully to the restoration of economic understanding for the economics profession and for intelligent lay people at large. And this matter is also, of course, of fundamental importance in projecting an accurate overall view of Mises's own contributions. While I shall, in my argument, be taking issue with a number of relevant statements by Rothbard, I trust that the reader will appreciate that the purpose of this paper is simply to further that very Misesian legacy to which Rothbard dedicated his entire life's work as an economist. It is as a memorial to Murray Rothbard's consistency in this regard, and his willingness to bear formidable costs to his professional career in order not to compromise the honesty of his expositions, that this chapter has been written. The purpose of any critical observations in this chapter (whether directed at Rothbard or at others) is certainly not to stir up strife within the Austrian camp; quite the reverse. I am convinced that a clear, shared understanding of Mises's central vision can bring together all those who appreciate the intellectual content of the Misesian legacy. To contribute an attempt in this direction, in honor of the memory of an outstanding exponent of that legacy, is the purpose of this chapter.

THE MISESIAN MARKET PROCESS

My own understanding of what Mises means when he describes the market as a process can be stated simply, as follows.

Mises saw the market process as a continually *corrective* process driven and constituted by active entrepreneurial grasping of pure profits.

> The essential fact is that it is the competition of profit-seeking entrepreneurs that does not tolerate the preservation of *false* prices of the factors of production. The activities of the entrepreneurs are the element that would bring about the unrealizable state of the evenly rotating economy if no further changes were to occur.
>
> (Mises, 1966, pp. 337–8; emphasis in the original)

The market process consists, that is, in the continual correction of false prices that occurs in the course of entrepreneurial competition. If exogenous changes were not to occur, this corrective process would eventually lead to a price structure for factors of production and consumer goods, in which all entrepreneurial profit has been squeezed out. In the real world, at any given moment, factors of production are able to be purchased at false prices, prices which permit entrepreneurs to capture pure entrepreneurial profits. False prices are false in that they incorrectly reflect the relative urgency of consumer demand for the various alternative possible products that can be created with these factors. It is this discoordination between what might be produced and what in fact is being produced, which offers alert entrepreneurs opportunities for pure gain.

> What makes profit emerge is the fact that the entrepreneur who judges the future prices of the products more correctly than other people do buys some or all of the factors of production at prices which, seen from the point of view of the future state of the market, are too low.
>
> (Mises [1951] 1962, p. 109)

Entrepreneurs "are the first to understand that there is a discrepancy between what is done and what could be done." Their activity brings about a systematic adjustment of factor prices. They "bid higher prices for some factors of production and lower the prices of other factors of production by restricting their demand for them." Their activity also generates price adjustments for consumer goods.

> In supplying the market with those consumers' goods in the sale of which the highest profits can be earned, they create a tendency toward a fall in their prices. In restricting the output of those consumers' goods the production of which does not offer chances for reaping profit, they bring about

> a tendency toward a rise in their prices. All these transformations go on ceaselessly and could stop only if the unrealizable conditions of the evenly rotating economy and of static equilibrium were to be attained.
>
> (Mises, 1966, p. 336)

All this ceaseless sequence of corrective price adjustments constitutes Mises's entrepreneurial market process.

This Misesian corrective process from a false set of prices towards a set of fully mutually adjusted prices may be restated in the terms in which Hayek understood the market process to constitute a "discovery procedure" (Hayek [1968] 1978, ch. 12). "False" prices reflect the decisions of entrepreneurs who have not yet understood the correct implications of consumer preferences (present or future) for the relative values of resources today. The way in which entrepreneurial activity tends to correct such false prices is through their realization of the profit possibilities inherent in such false prices. Grasping these profit possibilities is the way in which entrepreneurs express their discoveries concerning the correct valuation of resources (and thus, in effect, concerning better ways in which resources can be deployed in serving the preferences of consumers). The tendency which this entrepreneurial process generates towards equilibration is thus one of gradually enhanced mutual anticipation on the part of market participants. In the theoretical limit, in the hypothetical state of equilibrium in which no entrepreneurs would earn profit or suffer losses, we would be able to say that "all people . . . anticipate correctly the future state of the market" (Mises [1951] 1962, p. 108). Although it was Hayek, rather than Mises, who extensively articulated the nature of the market equilibrating process as one of gradually enhanced mutual knowledge, there can be no doubt that an interpretation of the Misesian process in terms of enhanced mutual knowledge is a valid one. Disequilibrium prices are "false" prices; as entrepreneurial profit taking nudges prices towards their correct levels, entrepreneurs have been led to more accurate anticipations concerning relevant future market configurations.

What makes possible the entrepreneurially driven process of equilibration is active market competition. It is only the possibility of unrestricted entrepreneurial entry which permits more alert entrepreneurs to deploy their superior vision of the future in order to correct the misallocations of resources reflected in the false prices which characterize disequilibrium. It is the continual threat of such entry which tends to keep incumbent entrepreneurs alert and on their toes. The reason that Mises had little patience for the concept of perfect competition (see his approving reference to Hayek's pioneering essay on this matter, "The Meaning of Competition" (Mises, 1966, p. 278n)), was that this concept can relate only to an already attained state of equilibrium. It has nothing to do with, and can throw no light upon, the competitive forces which drive the entrepreneurial market process. In deepening his (and our) understanding of the competitive process as consisting in a discovery procedure, Hayek was articulating insights that are, at the very least, thoroughly consistent with Mises's own understanding of the dynamic entrepreneurial competition which, for Mises, constitutes the heart of this market process.

THE SHARED UNDERSTANDING OF MISES AND HAYEK ON THE MARKET PROCESS

To draw attention, as we have in the preceding paragraphs, to the shared understanding that is apparent in Mises's and Hayek's treatment of the market process, is not to "homogenize" separate systems or "paradigms" of economic thought. Mises and Hayek are, to be sure, distinct thinkers with different views—sometimes fundamentally different views—on many issues in economic theory and method. There is a definite contribution to be made, towards properly understanding each of these two great Austrian economists, by drawing attention to the matters on which they disagree. But, we must insist, (a) the general character of the market process does *not* constitute such an area of disagreement; and (b) this area of shared understanding is so central to the work of both Mises and Hayek, that our awareness of their common position in this matter must definitively dispel any suggestion of the existence of a Misesian "paradigm," in regard to the market process, that is sharply to be distinguished from a Hayekian "paradigm." Yet such claims have recently been made.

MISES AND HAYEK DEHOMOGENIZED?

Professor Salerno has, in a number of recent papers (1990, 1991 1993, 1994), initiated a line of intellectual historiography designed to drive a wedge between Mises's and Hayek's understanding of markets. Murray Rothbard and Jeffrey Herbener (Rothbard 1991, 1992, 1994; Herbener 1991) have hailed Salerno's thesis as providing definitive grounds for the rejection by all "Misesians" of what Salerno, Rothbard, and Herbener see as grave "Hayekian" errors.[1]

The asserted distinctions on the basis of which Salerno declares the existence of two paradigms, a Misesian and a Hayekian, can be summarized as follows: (a) Hayek was trained under Wieser, and this accounts for his failure to have absorbed the Mengerian insights which, through the teachings of Böhm-Bawerk, later matured into the Misesian position (Salerno, 1993, p. 114); (b) Hayek believed that "in order for prices to fulfill their knowledge-disseminating and plan-coordinating functions, the economy must subsist in a state of (what Salerno calls) 'proximal equilibrium,' wherein realized prices are always fairly accurate indicators of future prices" (p. 128); Mises, on the other hand, considered the concept of equilibrium as only a mental tool. It "is impossible to determine and meaningless to suggest that the real economy is closer to the FSR [final state of rest], and therefore manifests a superior coordination of plans and greater allocative efficiency, at one instant of time than it was at a previous instant" (p. 129). The social role fulfilled by prices does not depend on the attainment or near attainment of the FSR. This leads directly to the next point. (c) For Hayek, allocative efficiency consists in plan coordination among market participants. For Mises, on the other hand, the social efficiency achieved by the market consists (and is always perfectly attained) in the *ex ante* "appraisement and allocation of resources [by entrepreneurs] in strict accordance with anticipated consumer preferences" (p. 130). Salerno recognizes that, in regard to *ex post* efficiency, entrepreneurial errors are inevitable in a world of uncertainty and change. However, apparently the only systematic process which Salerno recognizes in Mises as tending to correct such *ex post* inefficiencies, is that in which less astute entrepreneurs come to be weeded out of the system through their repeated speculative failures and resulting losses (pp. 131ff.). (d) For Hayek the essence of the market process and of its social function, is in its overcoming of the "knowledge problem" arising out of dispersed knowledge "among the multitude of individual consumers and producers" (p. 115). It is this property of the market, and its absence in the socialist economy, which identified, for Hayek, the fundamental weakness of socialist planning. For Mises, on the other hand, Salerno and his colleagues claim, even if the socialist planners were miraculously endowed with perfect information, they would nonetheless be unable to "rationally calculate how to combine resources to render efficient production" (Herbener, 1991, p. 43).

It is, indeed, especially the interpretation of Mises's thesis concerning the impossibility of socialist economic calculation that has been perhaps the central focus of Salerno's "two-paradigm" thesis. After a number of pages in which Salerno (quite unsuccessfully, it must surely appear) seeks to refute Leland Yeager's definitive paper (Yeager, 1994) demonstrating that Mises's thesis does, after all, require that we attribute to Mises at least implicit recognition of Hayek's "knowledge problem," Salerno sums up as follows: "Thus market oriented PC [i.e., perfect competition] theorists, such as Hayek and Yeager, and neoclassical socialist GE [i.e., general equilibrium] theorists are brothers under the skin" (Salerno, 1994, p. 119).[2] Let us indeed, then, take up Salerno's treatment of the Misesian thesis; it will, I believe, permit us to confront Salerno's major points of contention. We shall, I further believe, be able in this way to place our finger not only on the source of the two-paradigm fallacy, but (at the same time), also on a significant element in Mises to which Salerno has properly drawn attention. The circumstances that Salerno's recognition of this element in Mises has, in our judgment, unfortunately misled him (and Rothbard) to see fundamental divergence where none exists, should not blind us to the value of this characteristically Misesian insight for Austrian economic understanding.

MISES AND THE CALCULATION PROBLEM

Salerno and Rothbard are fully justified in emphasizing the subtlety of the Misesian concept of economic calculation. With much of what they say in exposition of that concept, this writer is in full agreement. He objects only to the quite unwarranted conclusion which they draw from that exposition to the effect that the Misesian calculation problem has nothing whatever to do with Hayek's knowledge problem. A possible contribution to this unfortunate misunderstanding lies, I believe, in Hayek's earlier ambiguity concerning the nature of his knowledge problem. This writer has for a number of years (see Kirzner [1984] 1992, p. 149), pointed out that Hayek's brilliant 1945 paper, "The Use of Knowledge in Society," was seriously confused in making it appear that the function of prices in communicating knowledge was a function that is filled, in principle, also in the state of equilibrium. Salerno and Rothbard would be on firm ground if they objected, as this writer has objected, to such an equilibrium treatment of the place of knowledge and the communication function of prices. But the truth is (as becomes evident in Hayek's later work, see especially Hayek [1968] 1978) that Hayek's knowledge problem relates fundamentally to those states of affairs in which—precisely because of the knowledge problem—market agents are making plans which do not, in the fullest sense of the term, dovetail with each other.

As Salerno and Rothbard point out, calculation is needed in order to appraise the wisdom of prospective action. Without the tool of genuine money prices, economic agents would be reduced to comparing goods sacrificed and goods received, in the face of their obvious heterogeneity and incommensurability. Such an agent would be called upon, in effect (except in the simplest of Crusoe economies), to make decisions with his eyes closed; he would have no way of knowing whether his outcome represents profit or loss. Market prices provide the indispensable tool needed for calculation. Because the socialist society does not include resource markets, its central planners must operate without known resource values. Their decisions must be made, in effect, with eyes closed.

Under capitalism, entrepreneurs make their plans based on their entrepreneurial awareness of the resource prices they must pay in the more immediate future, and of the product prices they anticipate that they will be able to command in the more remote future. These anticipated prices provide the entrepreneur with cardinal numbers on the basis of which to appraise the profitability (or its absence) of prospective entrepreneurial activities. In the absence of resource prices under socialism, rational central planning is literally impossible, as Mises stated (and as Salerno and Rothbard quite correctly emphasize in their interpretation of Mises).

Where Salerno and Rothbard have (as demonstrated by Yeager) gone astray,[3] is in their refusal to recognize that this impossibility of rational calculation and action under socialism *can* illuminatingly be recognized as arising out of the limitations of the human planning mind—in other words, as consisting in a disastrous knowledge gap which, without market prices for resources, it is impossible to bridge. We may readily concede that Mises did not articulate his calculation problem in terms of knowledge; but this does not in the slightest imply that that problem cannot be seen to consist of a knowledge problem. Reasonable interpreters of Mises may disagree on whether (as this writer emphatically believes to be the case) Mises's calculation problem is indeed seen more clearly when its knowledge implications are made explicit. But there is no basis whatever for claiming that, in exposing these knowledge implications of the Misesian argument, one is distorting or falsifying that argument.

To be unable to calculate the worthwhileness of a prospective action taken in a market society, is, after all, to not know the importance to others of the goods and services one commits to that action, and the importance to others of the goods one will obtain from that action. It is quite true, that Mises pointed out (and Salerno and Rothbard cite this again and again) that the calculation problem would exist even for a socialist planning authority possessing on its desks and in its computer memories, the fullest technological information of the age, full information on available resource availabilities, and full (and somehow, unanimous) information of the social ranking of the importance of ends. This is because, even armed with such "knowledge" (or, perhaps, precisely because the authority would be engulfed by these floods of information), the members of the authority would still not know what they would need to know, in order to calculate. As Leland Yeager has explained, possessing all this information is not the same as having assimilated it, and having been able to deploy it (whether by computing the solution to simultaneous equation systems, or whatever) to discover the relative values of the relevant resources and products. The members of the authority would not know what one needs to know in order to calculate the worthwhileness of prospective decisions.

For Mises (as Salerno and Rothbard correctly point out) prices are not primarily signals economizing on the cost of communicating information.[4] Their social function consists in providing decision makers with meaningful cardinal numbers with which to calculate the worthwhileness of prospective actions. To be "meaningful" we do not require these cardinal numbers to be roughly equal to or close to relevant equilibrium values. We require only that, at each point in time, these cardinal numbers reflect the interplay of the decisions made by the keenest (as well as those less keen) of the entrepreneurial minds in the market economy. In all this, I am in complete agreement with Salerno and Rothbard.

But it is precisely here, I believe, that Salerno and Rothbard have, in properly drawing attention to an underemphasized element in Mises's position on economic calculation, been led into error. The element being here referred to is that, for Mises, even market prices that are very far from their equilibrium values perform a valuable role in enabling entrepreneurs to calculate. Let me emphasize even more starkly the aspect of this element in Mises which appears to have most impressed Salerno and Rothbard: even if we could imagine that the equilibrating market process has not yet succeeded in nudging disequilibrium prices at all towards equilibrium, these prices yet perform their social role in making possible economic calculation. It is apparently this aspect of the Misesian position which has taught Salerno and Rothbard that what makes calculation possible cannot be and is not that knowledge-enhancing process which, for Hayek and other Austrians, constitutes the process of market equilibration. It followed, for these two scholars, that the Misesian calculation problem under socialism cannot and must not be identified with the Hayekian knowledge problem (which tends to become solved during the course of the equilibrating market process). But there is no reason at all to arrive at such an understanding (or, rather, misunderstanding) of Mises's position.

FALSE PRICES AND LESS FALSE PRICES

As cited earlier, Mises certainly did recognize that disequilibrium market prices are, in a sense, "false prices": they reflect erroneous expectations (i.e., erroneous "knowledge") being held by entrepreneurs concerning the true preferences of consumers. It is the equilibrating force generated by the process of entrepreneurial competition, we saw, which for Mises tended to replace false prices by less false prices. We have every reason to believe that, when Mises sees market prices as effective tools for entrepreneurial calculation, his view of prices is, at the very least, rendered even more benign by his understanding of the market process in which earlier false prices have tended to have become replaced by less false prices. (Of course this tendency may be frustrated by entrepreneurial error in an uncertain, changing world. There is no guarantee that today's prices are necessarily less false than yesterday's. But this possibility does not eliminate the existence of a systematic process in which entrepreneurial profit-seeking activity identifies those false prices which promise pure profits, and, by grasping those profits, tends to replace them by prices which more accurately reflect the true values to consumers, of resources and products.)

Salerno and Rothbard are right to emphasize that for Mises the prices which prevail at any time fulfill their function of rendering economic calculation possible. This, we must insist, is not because all prices, at all times, are "market clearing prices," in any sense relevant for our evaluation of the social efficiency of the price system. After all, false prices reflect production plans which are, by definition, at variance with the true preferences of consumers. The Misesian insight that all prices, at all times, render economic calculation possible, arises out of two closely related circumstances: (a) at each instant in time, the price offers and bids, and thus also the realized prices, reflect the expectations of the most canny entrepreneurs in the market (so that what may, a day later, with the wisdom of hindsight, indeed be seen as having been false prices, were nonetheless, in terms of the most perceptive entrepreneurial assessment of the preceding day, at that time expressive of the most judicious readings—the best knowledge—of consumer preferences); (b) at each instant in time, current prices are the outcomes of processes of entrepreneurial profit-seeking corrections of still earlier false prices; at no time, in the real world, can we say that the corrective market process has not yet begun its work. At each instant, therefore, current market prices reflect the best conceivable estimates of relative consumer preferences. The calculations which entrepreneurs make by reference to such prices (and by reference to such expected future prices), are thus informed by the assessment of the shrewdest of entrepreneurs, operating under the powerful incentive of winning pure profits.

What we wish to stress is that the capacity of market prices to inspire calculative economic activity is based solidly on the extent to which prices do express correct assessments of (i.e., the relevant knowledge regarding) both current and future preferences of consumers, and the current and future production plans of other entrepreneurs. As Mises pointed out in his first statements on the calculation problem (see, e.g., Mises [1922] 1936, pp. 115–17), market prices are not perfect tools in this respect: but they are extraordinarily valuable tools nonetheless. Their value surely lies in the expression of the best available entrepreneurial knowledge concerning market conditions.

It is quite true that for Mises this "best available entrepreneurial knowledge" expressed in current market prices would be valuably useful for calculation purposes, even if one could imagine these prices not already to reflect the corrective entrepreneurial market process which tends to replace false prices with prices less false. But the circumstance that in fact current market prices reflect that corrective market process (and our awareness that Mises did indeed emphasize this circumstance in regard to market prices) should convince us that an appreciation of the role of market prices stated in terms of the "Hayekian" knowledge problem is simply a somewhat differently articulated appreciation for the calculative properties Mises taught us to understand to exist in those market prices.

SOME OBSERVATIONS ON THE MISESIAN LEGACY

Mises had a profound and subtle understanding of the market's operation. In that understanding, the character of the market as a process in which mistaken entrepreneurial judgments tend to come to be replaced by more accurate judgments (and thus one in which false prices are replaced by less false prices), was a central feature: Hayek, too, had his own understanding of the market's operation. In certain respects, particularly in its articulation of the role of knowledge and discovery, that understanding can be differentiated from that of Mises. But the centrality of the knowledge-corrective character of the market process for both Mises and Hayek cannot seriously be doubted. Whatever the differences between a Hayekian articulation of the market process and a Misesian articulation, the centrality of the notion of the corrective process for both, is the crucially important circumstance. It is this that should convince us that any talk of a Hayekian "paradigm" which differs fundamentally from the Misesian paradigm should be dismissed as not only reflecting a mistaken doctrinal judgment, but as reflecting a mistaken judgment with potentially catastrophic implications for the future of Austrian economics.

Austrians are a beleaguered minority in the economics profession today. One of the core doctrinal issues separating Austrian economics from the mainstream is that Austrians understand the entrepreneurial character of the market process. We learned this from Mises. From Hayek we learned additional, complementary insights. If we wish to preserve and build upon the Misesian legacy, we must not generate confusion (both among Austrians and their opponents) by exaggerating perceived differences between Mises and Hayek, to the point where the centrally shared insights of both are dangerously obscured.

NOTES

1. Because of Salerno's initiating and prominent role in the "two-paradigm" literature, this section refers primarily to his writings. However, similar statements can typically also be found in the above cited papers of Rothbard and Herbener.
2. The biting sarcasm employed in this assertion is but a relatively mild example of the rhetorical excesses appallingly to be found in the "two-paradigm" literature against such writers as Hayek, Lachmann, and others charged with having diverged from the asserted "Misesian paradigm." I take this opportunity strongly to protest the use of verbal terrorism in

Austrian economics. Even if (which is far from being the case) the asserted criticisms of Hayek, Lachmann, and others were valid, there would be absolutely no justification for the manner in which these great economists have been treated in the literature under discussion. The near-demonization of Hayek and Lachmann for alleged deviations from an asserted Misesian orthodoxy is a most distressing phenomenon. If Austrian economists (and the *Review of Austrian Economics*) are to be able to work constructively in the rough and tumble of the intellectual market place, anything approaching rhetorical brawling must once and for all be rejected.

3. This chapter concentrates critically only upon those aspects of Salerno's and Rothbard's papers which are directly relevant to our placing the market process at the center of Mises's system. We do not take up here any criticism of a number of related assertions contained in these papers (concerning: entrepreneurship, uncertainty, the future, alertness, discovery, and coordination) which this writer finds puzzling, contradictory, or otherwise based on possible misunderstanding.
4. This is the aspect of Hayek's 1945 paper which the mainstream literature (and now Salerno *et al.*) have seen as central to Hayek's position. This writer has long deplored according centrality to such a "communication" role, and has argued that Hayek's later work suggest that he, too, saw beyond such a narrow interpretation of the role of prices (see Kirzner [1984] 1952, ch. 8).

REFERENCES

Hayek, Friedrich A. (1978) "Competition as a Discovery Procedure," in *New Studies in Philosophy, Politics, Economics, and the History of Ideas*, Chicago: University of Chicago Press. This paper was delivered as a lecture in 1968.

Herbener, Jeffrey M. (1991) "Ludwig von Mises and the Austrian School of Economics," *Review of Austrian Economics* 5(2), pp. 33–50.

Kirzner, Israel M. (1984) "Prices, the Communication of Knowledge and the Discovery Process," in Kurt R. Leube and Albert H. Zlabinger (eds) *The Political Economy of Freedom: Essays in Honor of F.A. Hayek*, Vienna: Philosophia Verlag. Reprinted in I.M. Kirzner (1992) *The Meaning of Market Process: Essays in the Development of Modern Austrian Economics*, London and New York: Routledge.

Mises, Ludwig von (1936) *Socialism: An Economic and Sociological Analysis*, trans. J. Kahane, London: Jonathan Cape; German original published in 1922.

—— [1951] (1962) "Profit and Loss," reprinted in *Planning for Freedom*, 2nd edn, South Holland, IL: Libertarian Press.

—— (1966) *Human Action: A Treatise on Economics*, 3rd rev. edn, Chicago: Contemporary Books.

Rothbard, Murray N. (1991) "The End of Socialism and the Calculation Debate Revisited," *Review of Austrian Economics* 5(2), pp. 51–76.

—— (1992) "The Present State of Austrian Economics," Working Paper of the Ludwig von Mises Institute.

—— (1994) Review of Bruce Caldwell and Stephan Boehm (eds) *Austrian Economics: Tensions and New Directions, Southern Economic Journal*, October.

Salerno, Joseph T. (1990) "Ludwig von Mises as Social Rationalist," *Review of Austrian Economics* 4, pp. 26–54.

—— (1991) "Commentary: The Concept of Coordination in Austrian Macroeconomics," in Richard M. Ebeling (ed.) *Austrian Economics, Perspectives on the Past and Prospects for the Future*, Champions of Freedom Series, Vol. 17, Hillsdale, MI: Hillsdale College Press.

—— (1993) "Mises and Hayek Dehomogenized," *Review of Austrian Economics* 6(2), pp. 113–46.

—— (1994) "Reply to Leland B. Yeager on 'Mises and Hayek on Calculation and Knowledge,'" *Review of Austrian Economics* 7(2), pp. 111–25.

Yeager, Leland B. (1994) "Mises and Hayek on Calculation and Knowledge," *Review of Austrian Economics* 7(2), pp. 93–109.

Source: Reflections on the Misesian Legacy in Economics, *Review of Austrian Economics*, 1996, 9(2), pp. 143–54.

9

MISES AND HIS UNDERSTANDING OF THE CAPITALIST SYSTEM

To someone not familiar with Mises's understanding of the market, there would, on the surface of Mises's exposition, appear to be a puzzling tension in that exposition—a tension having to do with some very basic elements of Mises's position. We shall find that the resolution of this tension is, once it has been explained, fairly obvious, but we shall also find that a careful consideration of this resolution can help us more fully appreciate the uniqueness (and the intellectual integrity) of Mises's understanding of the capitalist system.

A TENSION WITHIN MISES'S ECONOMICS?

The apparent tension in Mises to which we refer relates to the nature and significance of the market prices for inputs and outputs which emerge at each moment in the real world. These actual market prices are described by Mises as reflecting an "equilibrium of demand and supply"; they actually equalize "the size of the demand" with "the size of supply"; in the "unhampered market," any "deviation of a market price from the height at which supply and demand are equal is"—apparently instantaneously—"self-liquidating" (Mises, 1966, p. 762). It is on this basis that Mises pronounces any government interference with market prices of commodities, of resource services (including wage rates), (i.e. any requirement that a price at a given date be different from the value which the unhampered market would have generated for that date) as disturbing the "equilibrium of demand and supply" (ibid.), and therefore, in general, as producing results which are (from the perspective of the government itself) worse, not better, than the conditions which the government wished to improve.

Professor Salerno has interpreted this Misesian position to mean that all market prices are "market-clearing prices" (Salerno, 1993, p. 121); he has interpreted this position as asserting that "the constellation of resource prices that emerges on a market unhampered by legal restrictions *always* reflects the circumstance that existing resources are devoted to their most valuable uses as determined by entrepreneurial appraisements of future output prices" (ibid.). The impression conveyed here is that actual market prices are, in the relevant sense, the "correct" prices, the prices that ensure that resources are channelled to their most valuable uses. Interference with these prices necessarily obstructs the efficiency with which the market allocates resources.

And yet, on the other hand, Mises is clearly entirely aware that the market prices at any given date are almost certainly not the "correct" prices. In Salerno's words, market prices are, as a consequence of the unavoidable errors of entrepreneurial judgment under uncertainty, "also disequilibrium prices" (ibid.). In Mises's own words, the market prices at any given date are, in contrast to the imaginary prices that would characterize the imaginary "final state of rest" (Mises, 1966, p. 245), seen as "*false* prices" (ibid., p. 338; emphasis in original). It is the market *process* during which the competition of profit-seeking entrepreneurs modifies these false prices, tending to ensure that they be replaced by prices more closely and "truthfully" reflecting the underlying preferences of the consumers. What stimulates this process is the realization by entrepreneurs that the existing market-generated pattern of resource allocation is *not* the ideal one. There is, in fact, "a discrepancy between what is done and what could be done" (ibid., p. 336).

One can surely sympathize with the beginner-reader of Mises who finds himself puzzled by these statements which seem, when taken together, to claim that actual market prices are the correct, equilibrium, prices, but that they are also false, disequilibrium, prices; that the pattern of resource allocation actually achieved at any given date is optimal, but is, at the same time, not at all as efficient as it might be.

TENSION RESOLVED

A more mature student of the Misesian system is able to reassure such a puzzled beginner. There is no internal tension in Mises's exposition. What needs to be understood is the distinction between what Mises calls "the plain state of rest" (or simply "the state of rest" (Mises, 1966, pp. 244ff.) on the one hand, and what he calls the "final state of rest" (a state not identical with, but closely related to Mises's concept of the "evenly rotating economy"—the Misesian concept which is the closest to standard Walrasian general equilibrium[1]), on the other. It is not our purpose here to elaborate on Mises's "final state of rest" or on his "evenly rotating economy." What we wish to do is to clarify key aspects of Mises's "plain state of rest." For students coming to Mises from a background in standard microeconomic theory, it is easy to misunderstand Mises's "plain state of rest." It is easy to misunderstand it, in particular, as corresponding to the mainstream short-run equilibrium state. This might lead the student to misunderstand Mises's statements concerning the "equilibrium of demand and supply," in a particular market, as corresponding to the conditions prevailing at the intersection of the Marshallian demand and supply curves. But this would be quite mistaken. The Marshallian intersection refers to a state of affairs in which all participants (and all potential participants) in a specific market have somehow become aware of that price which is capable of clearing the market, and have correctly anticipated that that price would indeed prevail in this market. A price that "clears the market" means, in this mainstream sense of the term, one which ensures that all those who might, were they to be informed as to this prevailing price, be prepared to sell (buy), are in fact so informed and are in fact able to find buyers (sellers) willing to accept their offers to sell (buy) at this prevailing price. Mises's "plain state of rest" does not entail any such assumptions concerning the state of information. This plain state of rest "comes to pass," in the real world, "again and again" (Mises, 1966, p. 244). "At any instant all those transactions take place which the parties are ready to enter into at the realizable price." "When the stock market closes, the brokers have carried out all orders which could be executed at the market price." Clearly, such a state of rest (which, as Mises emphasizes, "is not an imaginary construction," but a state achieved again and again in the real world) refers to the completion of transactions between only those who are aware of the existing situation. The "supply and demand" which are continually in equilibrium in Mises's world, do not refer to the supply and demand schedules so basic to mainstream microeconomic theory. They refer simply to the circumstance that, in any situation, those potential transactors who have been aware of available mutually beneficial trade possibilities, will all certainly have moved to take advantage of these opportunities; once these opportunities have been grasped, market activity of course ceases, the plain state of rest has been attained.

To describe the price emerging from these exchange transactions as a "market-clearing price" (Salerno, 1993, p. 121), is therefore misleading. Certainly the price permits all those who stand to gain by exchanging at this price and who are aware of this—to exchange to the point where no known remaining mutually gainful opportunities exist. But the term "market-clearing price" (a term not used by Mises) is used in standard economics to refer to the exhaustion of all mutually gainful exchange opportunities under the hypothetical conditions of (relevant) omniscience. Standard economics indeed notoriously proceeds, in applying supply and demand theory to the real world, to operate as if conditions of relevant omniscience can be taken as given. Mises is certainly not making any such assumption of omniscience. His market prices are certainly not "market clearing prices" (in the usual sense of that term). There is, one is able to reassure the puzzled reader, therefore no contradiction in his exposition. Real world market prices are not the equilibrium prices of standard economic theory. (Real world prices relate to equilibrium only in a very narrow sense, a sense to which no attention at all is given in standard theory.) Real world prices are indeed likely to be "false" prices, setting off entrepreneurial-competitive activity modifying the pattern of resource allocation. The real world pattern of resource allocation at any given moment can be described as optimal only relative to existing information in fact possessed by entrepreneurial market participants. The tension in Mises is quite imaginary; it is perceived—quite understandably and reasonably perceived—only as a result of reading Mises through the spectacles acquired in studying mainstream economics.

But this resolution of the puzzle should itself surely raise a different puzzle of its own. It would appear, if one accepts the above interpretation of Mises, that Mises's references to what is achieved every day in the market must, while certainly true, strike any economist as being merely *trivially* true. The optimality achieved every day in the market is optimality only within the extremely narrow framework relevant to real world conditions. All those aware of the opportunities for mutually gainful exchange that are in fact available, take advantage of these perceived opportunities. To recognize this truth may be an achievement for someone who had not previously understood the significance (and mutual gainfulness) of interpersonal exchange. But this has little to do with the central insight which all economists share, concerning the effectiveness of markets in tending to stimulate the exhaustion of *all possible* opportunities for mutually gainful exchange. For this we must of course proceed, with Mises, to recognize that the market prices at any date are surely "false" prices, prices which generate entrepreneurial activity likely to cause those false prices to change. Certainly Mises clearly understood, and clearly expounded, the competitive entrepreneurial process that continually tends to replace "false" prices by more "truthful" prices. But, then, one can only ask, what is the point of emphasizing the apparently trivial Misesian insights concerning what is actually achieved every day in the "plain state of rest?"

The purpose of this chapter is to argue that, in emphasizing these apparently trivial insights, Mises revealed his unique understanding of what is achieved in the capitalist system. To appreciate this, it will be helpful to go back to the pioneering vision of the founder of the Austrian tradition, to Carl Menger. (It is perhaps worth while recalling that Mises, referring to his first reading, in 1903, of Carl Menger's *Grundsätze*, remarked that "it was the reading of this book that made an 'economist' of me" (Mises, 1978, p. 33).)

THE VISION OF CARL MENGER[2]

Menger is usually recognized as one of the three pioneers of marginal utility economics, offering economists a theory of subjective value. But, in regard to a subjective theory of value, the claims made on behalf of Menger's originality are somewhat clouded. As Professor Streissler has shown (Streissler, 1990), there were German economists of the early nineteenth century, with whose works Menger was unquestionably familiar, whose value theory had incorporated subjective insights long before Menger. Yet Menger certainly believed that his *Grundsätze* was breaking entirely new ground. (Hayek has told us that Menger "is said to have once remarked that he wrote the *Grundsätze* in a state of morbid excitement" (Hayek, 1934).)

What appears to have happened was that Menger glimpsed, at least, a grand perspective on the functioning of the entire market system which contrasted radically with the still dominant Ricardian way of seeing that system. For the Ricardian vision, the size and rate of growth of aggregate output, and the pattern of its distribution among the factor classes which produce it, are inexorably determined, at least in the long run, by objective, physical realities. In the explanation of such determination there is no place for any roles for human resourcefulness, human valuation, human expectations, human discoveries. Menger, on the other hand, glimpsed a way to understand economic history in diametrically opposite terms. For this view, the physical and biological realities recede into the background; it is the impact of the actions of human beings which alone actively determines the course of human events. It was this revolutionary new vision which, we suggest, was responsible for the "morbid excitement" with which Menger wrote his book. And this was a vision that had certainly not been shared by the early nineteenth-century German pioneers in the subjective theory of value, to whom Streissler has referred.

It was Menger, rather than any forerunners, who (already in his 1871 book) recognized how it is the consumer valuation of output which tends to be reflected in the market prices of the relevant inputs—which Menger identified as "higher order goods"—making Menger a pathbreaker in the development of neoclassical marginal productivity theory. It was this insight which drew the attention of the profession to the truth that the importance of the means needed to achieve specific ends is governed entirely by the importance attached to those ends. This is not merely an insight demolishing cost theories of value; it is an insight which introduces a new understanding of economic causality throughout the economic system. Every act of production, every market transaction, is set in motion and wholly governed by consumer preferences. Armed with this radical, and quintessentially "Austrian," vision of Menger, we may return to Mises and his understanding of the capitalist process.

MISES AND THE DOCTRINE OF CONSUMER SOVEREIGNTY

The concept of "consumer sovereignty" entered into economic terminology, it appears, largely as a result of the work of the late William H. Hutt.[3] This concept became central to Mises's understanding of the market economy. We shall argue that, in emphasizing this centrality, Mises was simply pursuing the Mengerian vision which we have briefly discussed in the preceding section.

In *Human Action*, one section of chapter 15 ("The Market") is entitled "The Sovereignty of the Consumers." In that section (a mere two pages, in a 900-page treatise) Mises presented, we believe, his own vision of the capitalist process. Mises explains that while entrepreneur-producers directly control production and "are at the helm and steer the ship," they are not supreme; the "captain is the consumer." "Neither the entrepreneurs nor the farmers nor the capitalists determine what has to be produced. The consumers do that" (Mises, 1966, p. 270). "A wealthy man can preserve his wealth only by continuing to serve the consumers in the most efficient way." So that "the owners of the material factors of production and the entrepreneurs are virtually mandatories or trustees of the consumers" (ibid., p. 271). Mises finds only one instance where the wishes of the consumers can be flouted. We shall, later in this chapter, pay a good deal of attention to this exception to the general rule of consumer sovereignty.

In *Human Action* not much further attention is paid to the idea of consumer sovereignty, but there can be no doubt as to its centrality for Mises's understanding of the market economy. This writer vividly recalls Mises's continually repeating, in his lectures and seminar presentations, the assertion that it is by his decisions to buy or refrain from buying, that the consumer controls the pattern of production. A glance at the index to a volume of Mises's more popular and shorter pieces (Mises, 1990) reveals how frequently the idea of "consumer sovereignty" shaped his thinking, especially in his later years.

Now there is no doubt that, in emphasizing the supremacy of consumers in the market economy, to popular audiences, Mises was often going beyond his role of positive scientist; he was often appealing to widely shared judgments of value. "A free-market economy," Mises was in effect explaining to his audiences, "caters precisely to the people whom you, my audience, wish to endow with power, viz. the consuming public." A society's resources, no matter by whom they are owned, are inevitably placed at the command of those whom Mises's audiences would wish to be placed in command. Mises was certainly entitled to draw normative conclusions from his economics (so long as he refrained from claiming scientific status for the judgments of value on the basis of which those conclusions are drawn). But in fact for Mises the doctrine of consumer sovereignty was much more fundamental and significant than its being a normative application of positive economics. The doctrine of consumer sovereignty was, in its own right, an important part of positive economics; it was a scientific theorem marking the completion of Menger's vision. What happens in markets is, whether one deems this desirable or undesirable, that consumers shape the pattern of resource use, and the assignment of resource rewards, according to their preferences. The pattern of production we observe at any date, the outputs being produced, the methods of production being employed, and the rewards being given to the various owners of productively used resources, are those dictated by consumers.

Entrepreneurs are powerfully motivated to take the most careful heed of consumer preferences, as these are anticipated and imagined by the shrewdest and most alert participants in the market. The consumer is indeed "the captain." This *may* be seen as a desirable feature of the market economy; but whether this is so seen or not, for Mises the significant scientific point is simply that this consumer supremacy does in fact prevail. In free markets it is the consumers whose preferences govern every act of production, and every transaction involving the purchase and sale of a unit of resource service.[4]

CONSUMER SOVEREIGNTY AND THE MUTUAL BENEFITS DERIVED FROM EXCHANGE

In order better to appreciate the meaning and significance of consumer sovereignty, it may be helpful to contrast the doctrine of consumer sovereignty, on the one hand, with the doctrine of mutual benefit derived from exchange, on the other. The market is often hailed as the arena in which all parties to freely made exchanges benefit (in their own *ex ante* best judgment); the market is the social framework permitting and stimulating all possible positive-sum exchange games. The recognition of this achievement of the market in this way, is certainly an important economic insight. It is indeed possible to interpret the entire market process, involving resource markets, processes of production, and product markets, as being simply an elaboration of the central circumstance that all parties to voluntary exchanges are beneficiaries of these exchanges. (There is a solid basis for the conjecture that Walras's more mature expositions of general equilibrium theory including production, emerged simply as the logical extension of his earlier version of general equilibrium in the pure exchange economy.) But the doctrine of consumer sovereignty, taken in conjunction with what we have described as Menger's vision, permits us to see the overall character of the market process from an entirely different angle. What happens in the market economy is not merely that the owners of resource services and those eager to consume the products (able to be produced with these resource services) are, through the intermediation of entrepreneurial producers, led to mutually beneficial exchanges. What happens in the market economy is that the owners of resource services are led to sell those services to those producers whose production plans are best calculated to cater to consumer preferences. The preferences of consumers determine the uses to which resources are assigned. As we have cited from Mises, "the owners of the material factors of production and the entrepreneurs are virtual mandatories or trustees of the consumers." The market may certainly validly be seen as the arena in which the potential benefits from voluntary exchanges are extracted; it is, however, even more fundamentally, the arena in which the value scales of consumers come to govern the disposition of potential factors of production.

THE SIGNIFICANCE OF PRIVATE PROPERTY

For Mises, the doctrine of consumer sovereignty offers an insight into the social role fulfilled by the institution of private property. There is, as a matter of scientific fact, no conflict of interest between the owners of productive resources (whether land or labor power), on the one hand, and the consuming public on the other. The owner of a productive resource can derive economic benefit from his resource only to the extent that he places it at the service of the consuming public. As we have already cited from Mises, a "wealthy man can preserve his wealth only by continuing to serve consumers in the most efficient way." The doctrine of consumer sovereignty demonstrates the harmony of interests existing in a market economy between owners of resources and consumers. Recognizing this harmony of interests is merely another way of sharing Menger's vision. It is the circumstance that consumers dictate the allocation of resources, which in fact creates this harmony of interests. And of course it is the institution of private property which permits and stimulates this harmony of interests.

Because entrepreneurs compete in resource markets, inspired by the hope of winning pure profit by redirecting the deployment of resources in ways more satisfying to consumers, we are able to understand how indeed consumers control and ultimately direct the pattern of production, the organization of industry, and the allocation of resources among competing industries. But Mises pointed out one situation—the case which he called the "monopoly price" case—in which the doctrine of consumer sovereignty does not apply. "Monopoly prices are an infringement of the sway of the consumers" (Mises, 1966, p. 272). For this monopoly price situation, the institution of private property does not spell a harmony of interests between the resource owners and the consuming public. For that situation—and only for that situation—it might indeed be rational for consumers to invoke political power to modify the outcomes forthcoming from the unhampered market. It was Mises's merit (and a reflection of his intellectual integrity) to identify this case and accord it the scientific attention it deserves. Unfortunately, not all Mises's followers have properly appreciated the place which his theory of monopoly price plays in his overall understanding of the capitalist system.

MISES AND THE THEORY OF MONOPOLY PRICE[5]

The nature and place of monopoly theory in Mises's system differs radically from the part which monopoly theory plays in standard microeconomics. For standard economics a monopolistic market for a produced commodity differs from a (perfectly) competitive market primarily in that the monopolist producer faces a downward-sloping demand curve, so that the profit-maximizing decision by the monopolist producer permits him to charge a price which is higher than the marginal cost of his output. Monopoly theory is then a theory exploring the peculiarities of decision making by a *producer*; the consequences of monopoly decision making are assessed primarily in terms of the way such decision making may be held responsible for resource misallocation, in regard to the economy as a whole. For the Misesian theory of monopoly price, matters are quite different.

For Mises, monopoly is identified *at the level of resource ownership*—not, except as a derivative, at the level of the decisions made by producers. For Mises, the possible case of resource monopoly (where the entire supply of a scarce resource is controlled by a single resource owner) is of scientific and normative interest not in terms of possible "misallocation of resources" (a concept which is not clearly identified in the Misesian system). The case of a resource monopoly is of interest insofar as it may affect incentives in a manner *at variance with the doctrine of consumer sovereignty*. Depending upon the degree of elasticity of demand for the monopolized resource, it may be the case that its owner may extract greater revenue from the market by withholding (or even destroying) part of the resource stock which he owns than he could extract by placing all of it at the service of consumers. He might then charge a "monopoly price" which would enable him to gain by thus withholding part of his resource stock. If this is indeed the case, then we have an exception to the general rule of consumer sovereignty. We have an exception to the general rule that private ownership of resources results in a harmony of owners' interests with those of the consuming public. We have a case where it is in the interest of property owners, in effect, to deny consumers the productive capacity of the resources they own. For Mises, the austere, *wertfrei* scientist, such a case is not, by itself, "bad" or "inefficient." It is simply a case which, unlike any other possible situation, pits the interests of consumers against those of a property owner. It would not be irrational, in such a case, for consumers to explore political avenues through which to modify the outcomes that would emerge from the unhampered market.

Given the availability of substitute resources (i.e. given the likelihood that the demand curve for the resource may be sufficiently elastic to make it impossible to gain by withholding part of the resource supply from production), given the incentives for entrepreneurial innovations likely either to increase the supply of this resource, or to reduce the uniqueness of any particular monopolized resource, Mises did not believe that the case of monopoly price is an empirically important case.[6] But it remains an intriguing theoretical possibility. It is intriguing for Mises, one feels quite certain, primarily in its unique property of permitting production to be conducted in a pattern which no longer faithfully reflects the preferences of consumers. It represents the theoretical possibility that, as a result of an accident of the pattern of resource ownership, Menger's vision may be partly inaccurate; economic phenomena may, in an unhampered market, *not* be shaped exclusively and entirely by consumer demand; sovereignty over production may not reside entirely in the preferences of the consuming public, but in the ownership rights of one or more resource owners.

As with many theoretical exceptions to generally prevailing patterns, the case of monopoly price seems of importance, for the Misesian system, not so much in the intriguing possibility which it itself represents, as in the light which it throws on the more general pattern—that to which Menger's vision and the doctrine of consumer sovereignty do apply. Indeed, now that we understand the sweeping generality of the doctrine of consumer sovereignty, we can perhaps better understand certain aspects of Mises's system which, at the outset of this chapter, we found mystifying.

MISES, MARKET PRICES, AND CONSUMER SOVEREIGNTY

It will be recalled that Mises had made certain assertions concerning the actual market prices that prevail in real world markets, which we found puzzling. Those assertions attributed apparent optimality properties to these prices, and to the transactions to which they give rise. We were able to establish, certainly, that Mises emphatically understood that the market prices on any given date are likely to be false prices, generating corrective entrepreneurial-competitive production activity. But we were left mystified regarding the sense in which the everyday market prices (and the transactions to which they give rise) can be pronounced the "correct" prices, prices consistent with an "equilibrium of demand and supply." Surely, we asked, the simple insight that in any market, exchanges benefit all parties to them (in their own best estimation)—and the related insight that, to the extent that potential beneficiaries are aware of the possible opportunities arising from exchange, they can surely be relied upon to take advantage of them—is too simple, almost too trivial, and too limited, to permit Mises to denounce any governmental interference as counterproductive. Perhaps the insights we have gained in the preceding sections of this chapter can help demystify Mises's position.

Once we have understood the central position of the doctrine of consumer sovereignty in Mises's overall system, we can surely sense and appreciate the deep respect Mises felt for the *actual* market prices of productive resources. Certainly these prices are likely to be "false" prices, in that they necessarily imperfectly anticipate the true future valuations of consumers for the various possible potential products (at the times when these products might conceivably be made available to consumers). Nonetheless these prices, and the transactions in which they emerge, are wholly governed—of course, ignoring now the special exception of the monopoly price case—by the preferences of consumers; these prices and these transactions fulfill Menger's vision, they express consumer sovereignty. Mises would of course not deny that, in the absence of omniscience, actual prices and actual plans for production, may only imperfectly reflect the patterns of intensity of consumers' preferences. But "sovereignty" need not imply that the wishes of the sovereign are instantaneously, successfully, carried out; it may surely mean that each act of those directly or indirectly acknowledging that sovereignty, is motivated by the incentive of fulfilling those wishes as far as human effort and human will can succeed in doing. Even the mistakes which may occur under pressure of this incentive, must also be attributed to the supremacy of the sovereign. Surely this was Mises's profound insight into the character of the capitalist market process: at every moment the decisions made by entrepreneur-producers and resource owners, are directly or indirectly made under the powerful incentive to cater to the true pattern of consumer preferences. Each market price for a resource directly reflects the judgments of competing entrepreneurs as to the most valuable use—valuable as judged by anticipated consumer willingness to pay—to which that resource can be assigned. Each production plan that is initiated at any given moment expresses the judgments of competing entrepreneurs (acting in the light of the resource market prices of the moment, and in the light of their anticipations of the market prices for future products) as to the most effective ways of deploying productive resources in the service of satisfying consumer preferences.

The circumstance that, in the face of the utter uncertainty of the future (and in the face of the similarly imperfectly informed state of market participants concerning present economic conditions)—the production plans initiated at any given date are inevitably flawed, does not in the slightest qualify the assertions made at the conclusion of the preceding paragraph. The near-certainty that hindsight will reveal the "falsity" of present prices, and the "inefficiency" of present production plans, does not in the slightest degree cast a shadow on the validity of Menger's vision, or upon the reality of consumer supremacy, at all times. The truth remains that, at any given time, the market is effectively deploying the best current information commanded by market participants, and the most accurate and shrewdest entrepreneurial judgments concerning future market conditions. What drives and motivates such deployment, economic analysis reveals, is the incentive to win pure profit, through improving the faithfulness with which consumer preferences are respected in the patterns of production.

So that when Mises declares any intervention by government which might alter market prices (or other decisions that might have been made in an unhampered market) to be harmful, he does not imply that the prices (or other decisions) which would have emerged in an unhampered market on any given date are optimal (in the sense that they accurately reflect all the considerations which an omniscient observer would wish to have taken into account). What he means is that the existing conditions on an unhampered market express the most strenuous efforts on the part of the shrewdest entrepreneurial minds to identify and correct existing discrepancies (between what *might* be done to best satisfy consumer preferences, and what *is* being done). Not only are these strenuous efforts being made at all times, these efforts have been made in the past, and current market prices have been modified (from those of the past) to the extent that the past shrewd judgments of entrepreneurs revealed those earlier plans to have been "false."

When Mises emphasized the virtues of those real world market prices and transactions which continually generate his "plain states of rest," he was not simply emphasizing the somewhat obvious, even trivial, insight that, in the best *ex ante* judgments of all market participants, their market exchanges on any given date make them better off. He was, instead, emphasizing the role being played by real world prices and transactions, in the exercise of consumer sovereignty—recall our earlier contrast between (a) seeing the market, in a production economy, as merely the extension of insights relevant to the pure exchange economy, and (b) seeing such a market as the arena in which Menger's vision is actualized. For Mises, the supremacy of the consumer is not simply a tendency manifested in the ongoing entrepreneurial-competitive market process; it is a reality fulfilled at every moment. Certainly such supremacy is not to be confused with any hypothetically "perfect" allocation of resources to correspond to the pattern of consumer preferences. Where neoclassical welfare economics focused exclusively on such possible correspondence, Mises's more, "dynamic," "process-oriented" mindset, focused on a quite different aspect of markets. In seeing the market as *continually striving*, as it were, better to satisfy consumer preferences, Mises's articulated an understanding and appreciation of free markets which, most unfortunately, relatively few of his readers have themselves understood and appreciated.

NOTES

1. For Mises's discussion of the "evenly rotating economy," see Mises (1966, pp. 246ff.).
2. The ideas briefly presented in this section have been developed more fully by the writer in his editorial Introduction to volume one of Kirzner (1994).
3. See Hutt (1936, ch. 16); Hutt (1940). Hutt used the term "consumer sovereignty" fairly frequently in his papers of the mid-1930s, see e.g. Hutt (1935) (reprinted as chapter 12 of Pejovich and Klingaman, 1975).
4. The late Murray N. Rothbard has sharply attacked Hutt's notion of consumer sovereignty (Rothbard, 1962, pp. 560–6). (Rothbard does not refer to Mises's very frequent references to the consumer sovereignty doctrine.) However Rothbard concedes that in a "formal" sense (in which the ultimate goals of producers are recognized as consumption goals) "consumer sovereignty, by definition, always, obtains" (Rothbard, 1962, p. 561). There is reason to believe that Rothbard's position is (regardless of its validity) not inconsistent with the interpretation of Mises being presented in this and subsequent sections of this chapter. However, there seems to be a link between Rothbard's critique of Hutt's notion of consumer sovereignty, and his critique of Mises's ideas on monopoly price. On the latter point see the writer's discussion in a later section of this chapter.

5. For further discussion of the Misesian theory of monopoly price (and a critique of some work of followers of Mises who have, in this writer's opinion, not adequately appreciated the Misesian theory), see Kirzner (1991).
6. Nor, it should be emphasized, is the case of monopoly price one that can be empirically identified and observed. Failure to use all the available supply of the monopolized resource may simply reflect the monopolist's entrepreneurial judgment that future consumer demand may be strong enough to justify postponing its use to the future. Even physical destruction of part of the supply *might* (admittedly far-fetchedly!) be the manner in which the monopolist is expressing his own consumer preferences . . .

REFERENCES

Hayek, Friedrich A. (1934) Introduction to *Collected Works of Carl Menger*, London: London School of Economics.

Hutt, William H. (1935) "The Nature of Aggressive Selling," *Economica*.

—— (1936) *Economists and the Public*, London: Jonathan Cape.

—— (1940) "The Concept of Consumers' Sovereignty," *Economic Journal* March.

Kirzner, Israel M. (1991) "The Driving Force of the Market: The Idea of 'Competition' in Contemporary Theory and in the Austrian Theory of the Market Process," in Richard M. Ebeling (ed.) *Austrian Economics, Perspectives on the Past and Prospects for the Future*, Hillsdale, MI: Hillsdale College Press, reprinted as chapter 12 in the present volume.

Mises, Ludwig von (1966) *Human Action, A Treatise on Economics* [1st edn, 1949], 3rd rev. edn, Chicago: Henry Regnery.

—— (1978) *Notes and Recollections*, South Holland, IL: Libertarian Press.

—— (1990) *Economic Freedom and Interventionism, An Anthology of Articles and Essays*, selected and edited by Bettina Bien Greaves, Irvington-on-Hudson, NY: Foundation for Economic Education.

Pejovich, Svetozar and Klingaman, David (1975) *Individual Freedom, Selected Works of William H. Hutt*, Westport, CT: Greenwood Press.

Rothbard, Murray N. (1962) *Man, Economy, and State, A Treatise on Economic Principles*, Princeton, NJ: Van Nostrand.

Salerno, Joseph T. (1993) "Mises and Hayek Dehomogenized," *Review of Austrian Economics* 6(2).

Streissler, Erich (1990) "The Influence of German Economics on the Work of Menger and Marshall," in Bruce Caldwell (ed.) *Carl Menger and his Legacy in Economics*, Durham, NC: Duke University Press, pp. 31–68.

Source: Mises and His Understanding of the Capitalist System, *Cato Journal*, forthcoming.

10

HEDGEHOG OR FOX?

Hayek and the idea of plan-coordination

George Shackle once wrote a paper entitled "The Hedgehog and the Fox, A Scheme of Economic Theory" (Shackle, 1966, ch. 12). He referred to a line from the poet Archilochus, made famous in contemporary discussion by Isaiah Berlin: "The fox knows many things, but the hedgehog knows one big thing" (ibid., p. 30 fn). Shackle explains that the

> hedgehog is the system-builder, the seeker after . . . a theory which explains everything by a unified conception of what the cosmos is . . . Such a theory might be itself compact, like the acorn, but able to unfold the whole glory of the heavens and the earth, like the oak which so massively arises . . . from the minute germ. The fox by contrast is the scientist who is content with . . . understanding one thing at a time by reference, in each case, to an ultimately arbitrary pattern.
>
> (ibid., p. 30)

Shackle himself suggests "that the economic theoretician must be content to know many things and not seek to know one big thing" (ibid., p. 31). (This is in contrast to a Paretian general equilibrium perspective which Shackle perceives as "perhaps an attempt to see the whole economic scene as the manifestation of the free operation of self-interest within a frame of law and order (ibid.). Shackle believes such an attempt must tacitly assume. that while "resources are scarce, knowledge is not scarce, but on the contrary every participant possesses, or can obtain, all knowledge relevant for his own choices" (ibid.).)

This chapter seeks an answer to the question whether Hayek is best understood as hedgehog or as fox. Certainly, in his extraordinarily long scholarly career, Hayek dealt with a remarkably extensive list of superficially disparate research areas, both inside and outside economics. Is it possible to see his work in all or most of these different areas—or at least his work in economics—as somehow flowing out of a single seminal insight ("one big thing")? Could one take, say, the idea of the dispersed character of knowledge and its implications for (both the need for and the possibility of) the coordination of individual plans and expectations in society, as the central unifying theme of Hayek's rich and multifarious scholarly output in the social sciences (or at least in his economics)? (Notice, however, that such a unifying theme, resting on the dispersed character of knowledge, would of course be the polar opposite of that "hedgehog" mentality which Shackle ascribed to the general equilibrium theorist.)

In his highly original and insightful survey of Hayek's contributions to economics, a survey written at a time when few in the economics profession were prepared to pay much attention to Hayek, Gerald P. O'Driscoll indeed took "the coordination of economic activities" as the unifying theme of Hayek's work: "Hayek's work is seen as variations of this theme" (O'Driscoll, 1977, p. xx). "Throughout all [Hayek's] work he maintained his conception of the 'economic problem' as a coordination problem . . ." (ibid., p. 28). O'Driscoll's book set out "to connect [Hayek's] many and diverse contributions to economics, and to show that they evidence an overall conception of economics as the study of decentralized planning and market coordination" (ibid., p. xxi). It is of considerable interest that in his 1975 Foreword to O'Driscoll's book, Hayek appears to endorse O'Driscoll's thesis (while confessing that he had himself *not* realized this unity in his own work). He notes the

> curious fact that a student of complex phenomena may long himself remain unaware of how his views of different problems hang together and perhaps never fully succeed in clearly stating the guiding ideas which led him in the treatment of particulars. I must confess that I was occasionally myself surprised when I found in Professor O'Driscoll's account side by side statements I made at the interval of many years and on quite different problems, which still implied the same general approach.
>
> (ibid., p. ix)

Notwithstanding the meticulous care and detail with which O'Driscoll's book examines Hayek's contributions to economics, however, it seems that the thesis which has inspired the book and its title (that the coordination theme unites all those contributions) has (despite the presence of a chapter entitled "The Coordination Problem") been left implicit in the book's expositions, rather that being explicitly *argued* anywhere in the book. It may therefore be of some value to assess this theme afresh in its own right, by direct reference to relevant statements to be found in Hayek's own writings over the central decades of his scholarly career.[1]

We shall find numerous references in Hayek's work to such concepts as "coordination," "economic order," "spontaneous order" and the like—but in a way which suggests a good deal less than a single "big" idea uniting these concepts, and creating a seamless unity among his many areas of research. What will emerge from this chapter is that Hayek was indeed largely driven, in most of his work, by a set of closely related ideas and concerns (relating to knowledge, its dispersed character, and to the phenomenon of the spontaneous coordination of the activities of numerous individuals with different, but equally incomplete, awareness of the circumstances surrounding their respective aims of making rational decisions). Rather than constituting a substantial unifying theme, however, it seems fairer to see these closely related ideas and concerns as constituting what Professor Butos (Butos, 1985, p. 110) has termed "a band of continuity" in "the expanse of Hayek's work." Continuity does not itself constitute unity. Neither hedgehog nor fox, Hayek turns out to be a social scientist whose work in numerous separate research areas has been repeatedly inspired and enriched by a series of related insights, questions and concerns involving dispersed knowledge, spontaneous order, the compatibility of plans and expectations, and the like. It may be suggested that our exploration into these matters can, by warning against a possible oversimplification in interpreting Hayek's economics, deepen our understanding of some of the complexities in Hayek's work.[2]

THE AUSTRIAN THEORY OF THE BUSINESS CYCLE AND THE IDEA OF COORDINATION

In an earlier essay (Kirzner, 1995) the writer drew attention to a certain penumbra of doubt which surrounds the question of whether Hayek's 1931 *Prices and Production* foreshadowed his later concern with the idea of coordination. On the one hand, the fact is that a reader of that work can find little or no explicit reference to the coordination notion. Yet a number of late twentieth-century references to the Austrian cycle theory which that work made famous, have interpreted it unambiguously as a theory of how "artificially" low rates of interest "discoordinate" the intertemporal market (in which investment decisions are made). Present decisions to undertake capital-intensive projects are misled (by the low rate of interest) overoptimistically to anticipate the future availability of capital resources. Present activity is thus generated, based on expectations concerning the future decisions of market participants which fail to dovetail with the future reality of those decisions. Thus Professor Garrison has more than once referred to "intertemporal coordination" (Garrison, 1985) and "intertemporal discoordination" (Garrison, 1989, p. 24) in regard to Austrian cycle theory. Stavros Ioannides has, in his critical exposition of Hayek's theory referred to the boom phase of that theory as distorting the structure of production "because the plans of producers and consumers are no longer compatible with each other" (Ioannides, 1992, p. 123). In similar vein Gerald O'Driscoll (whom we have already seen to emphasize the role of the coordination concept in Hayek's work) states that for Hayek "the crucial question for business cycle theory was the mutual correspondence of the plans of savers and investors and those of consumers and producers" (O'Driscoll, 1977, p. 73). Yet, as we have pointed out, Hayek's 1931 exposition of his cycle theory does *not* in fact emphasize this plan-coordination or plan-discoordination issue (or even the signalling function of prices, including rates of interest). Instead, that exposition is couched in terms of "misdirections of production" (Hayek [1931] 1935, pp. 105, 117). Now the idea of "misdirected production" is entirely consistent with the perspective of a central planner (whose central plan might replace all other possible individual plans, rendering the idea of plan coordination utterly irrelevant). Production might thus be considered "misdirected" (from the central planner's perspective), for example, if it involves currently-initiated long-term capital-intensive projects for which subsequently needed complementary resources turn out not to be available (in later stages of these projects, thus entailing their abandonment).

Yet it is the case that Hayek, in his 1981 lecture commemorating the fiftieth year since his original 1931 lectures at the London School of Economics (the lectures which were published as *Prices and Production*), recalled that the 1931 lectures "made use of what became the leading theme of most of my later work, an analysis of the signal function of prices in guiding production, a conception which I first expounded systematically . . . in . . . 'Economics and

Knowledge'" (Hayek, 1981, p. 2). Now certainly the latter paper (published in 1937 as the written version of a lecture given in 1936) did, as we shall discuss below, systematically expound the communication and coordinating role of prices. (And apparently by 1981 Hayek had become thoroughly persuaded, presumably by O'Driscoll's 1977 book, that the understanding of this coordinating role did indeed constitute the leading theme of most of his work subsequent to the 1931–7 period—despite his own earlier unawareness of any such unifying theme in his work!) And two European scholars have indeed fairly recently strongly and explicitly argued this very thesis, that Hayek's concern with the phenomenon of the business cycle early in his career, is to be seen as the opening phase of a lifelong research program on the theme of "coordination in economic process" (Schmidtchen and Utzig, 1989).

Certainly our broader question in this chapter concerning possible unity among Hayek's apparently disparate areas of research, must take note of these ambiguities concerning the role, if any, of the coordination concept in Hayek's 1931 book. It will, however, be at least equally helpful (in addressing the broader question) to examine carefully those parts of Hayek's work which deal most explicitly and directly with the notion of plan-coordination. To this we now turn.

THE TETRAD ON ECONOMIC COORDINATION[3]

There is no doubt that our interest in the place of the idea of plan-coordination in Hayek's economics has its source in four important papers (all republished in his *Individualism and Economic Order* (Hayek, 1949a, chs 2–5)). These papers were written within a 10-year span during perhaps the most important decade of Hayek's research career. These papers are: (i) "Economics and Knowledge" (Hayek, 1937); (ii) "The Facts of the Social Sciences" (Hayek, 1943); (iii) "The Use of Knowledge in Society" (Hayek, 1945); (iv) "The Meaning of Competition" (Hayek, 1949b). It was in these papers that Hayek articulated most clearly and originally his insights concerning the implications of incomplete and dispersed knowledge, concerning the signalling role of prices in such a world of dispersed information, and concerning the character of the competitive market process as one tending to coordinate the expectations, plans and activities of imperfectly informed market participants. Again and again Hayek would refer to the ideas developed in these papers (particularly the first of these four) as encapsulating what he considered his most important and potentially seminal ideas. For example, in a footnote to the 1939 republication of his 1933 Copenhagen lecture (Hayek, 1933), he referred to his 1937 paper as elaborating on and partly revising the discussion, in the 1933 lecture, of the relationship between equilibrium and foresight; in his 1941 *The Pure Theory of Capital* (Hayek, 1941a) he cited his 1937 paper as showing how the idea of general equilibrium refers to a relationship between the plans of different members of society; in his (1955) *The Counter-Revolution of Science: Studies on the Abuse of Reason* (Hayek, 1955) he referred to his 1937 paper in regard to the communication-of-knowledge function of market prices; and in a 1965 paper (Hayek, [1965] 1967) he referred to this (1937) paper as having been the starting point of his own development from being a "very pure and narrow economic theorist" into a scholar concerned with "all kinds of questions usually regarded as philosophical" (Hayek, [1965] 1967, p. 91).

Not only is it the case that, as we have noticed, Hayek believed that important parts of his subsequent work grew out of the ideas of this "coordination tetrad," it is also the case that Hayek believed these ideas to be relatively polished concepts which had themselves grown, in turn, out of earlier, less satisfactory formulations on his own part. We have noticed his linking his 1937 paper with ideas expressed initially in his 1933 Copenhagen lecture; in his above-cited 1941 *Pure Theory of Capital* reference to his 1937 paper, he also suggests that the ideas of that paper originated "in a rather unsatisfactory form" in his 1928 paper on intertemporal equilibrium (Hayek, [1928] 1994). So that these four "coordination" papers represent together for Hayek both a maturer development and articulation of earlier insights,[4] and a foundation, at the very least, for important aspects of Hayek's later scholarly contributions, both inside economics and beyond economics. It will therefore certainly be useful to analyze somewhat more carefully what Hayek understood by the ideas which illuminate the "coordination tetrad" (or which appear, perhaps less centrally, in several related Hayekian contributions).

COORDINATION AND OTHER RELATED IDEAS

The truth is that our references (following O'Driscoll) to the "coordination tetrad," needs to be qualified in a number of respects. These four seminal, classic Hayekian papers (as well as the other related contributions to which we will be referring) present an array of ideas which certainly *include* the notion of plan-coordination, but which also suggest a number of related insights which should *not* themselves be confused with the idea of plan-coordination. Let us take up some of the more obvious of these insights.

(a) *Order I*: The term "order" is used by Hayek not only to refer to a state of affairs in which the plans of different market participants are mutually supportive ("coordinated" in the sense to be distinguished below), but also to refer to any specified set of institutional arrangements. For example, in the third of the "coordination tetrad" papers, Hayek refers to "the problem of a rational economic order," to attempting "to construct a rational economic order" (Hayek, 1949a, p. 77); elsewhere he refers to "the task which faces the designer of a rational order of society" (Hayek, 1955, p. 98), to reproaches "of irrationality leveled against the existing economic order" (Hayek, 1949a, p. 81). He sometimes (e.g. Hayek, 1978, pp. 183ff.) refers to the "market order," sometimes to the "social order" (Hayek, 1949a, p. 1). In these references Hayek appears to be simply referring to the "economic system," the "market system," or to a "social system." He is not referring directly to the *orderliness* which may or may not be achieved within any of the identified (or unidentified) sets of institutional arrangements. Clearly this use of the word "order" has, then, nothing to do with our own focus of interest in this paper (that focus being the idea of plan-coordination). We mention this usage only to avoid possible confusion (and also to note a certain source of such possible confusion that may be generated, for example, by Hayek's title (to the important volume in which the "coordination tetrad" papers were published), *Individualism and Economic Order*).

(b) *Order II*: The use by Hayek of the word "order," that *is* relevant to the focus of this chapter, is that which implies the *orderliness* of some discussed set of activities or social arrangements. (And it is of course this use of the word "order" which is implicit in the correlative word "coordination," with which this chapter is directly concerned.) In a well-known paper written during the same years in which the "coordination tetrad" emerged, Hayek contrasts the view "which accounts for most of the order which we find in human affairs as the unforeseen result of individual actions," with "the view which traces all discoverable order to deliberate design" (Hayek, 1949a, p. 8). In this usage Hayek clearly understands "order" to refer to an orderliness which does *not* necessarily consist in the compatibility existing among independently-made individual plans. So that when we find Hayek identifying the "order" achieved by market competition as the "mutual adjustment of individual plans," involving "the circumstance that the expectations of transactions to be effected with other members of society, on which the plans of all the several economic subjects are based, can be mostly realized" (Hayek [1968] 1978, p. 184)—this is simply *one* kind of order. We can, in Hayek's terminology, envisage, at least, the possibility of designed order. Presumably such order would consist in the hypothesized successfully achieved consistency among the various distinct elements of a central design or plan; it would *not* relate to the dovetailing of individually made decisions and plans.

In his 1960 book *The Constitution of Liberty* (Hayek, 1960), Hayek cites an unidentified source for the following observation: "That there is some kind of order, consistency and constancy, in social life is obvious. If there were not, none of us would be able to go about his affairs or satisfy his most elementary wants." Hayek similarly points out that the "orderliness of social activity shows itself in the fact that the individual can carry out a consistent plan of action that, at almost every stage, rests on the expectation of certain contributions from his fellows" (ibid., pp. 159–60). In this, Hayek is illustrating the fallacy of the "enemies of liberty [who] have always based their arguments on the contention that order in human affairs requires that some should give orders and others obey" (ibid., p. 159).

From all this it appears that for Hayek, order in social phenomena consists in the mutual consistency displayed among individual elements that can be identified in those phenomena. We shall discover that this breadth in the conception of order in society has certain implications for Hayek's idea of coordination. We can also now understand what Hayek has in mind with his term "spontaneous order."

(c) *Spontaneous order*: Our discussion in the preceding subsection of Hayek's broad notion of "order," has already noticed Hayek's emphasis on the undesigned achievement, in a market economy, of order "as the unforeseen result of individual actions." This is Hayek's celebrated notion of "spontaneous order."[5] The order achieved spontaneously in the market has been demonstrated by economic theory. "One of the achievements of economic theory has been to explain how such a mutual adjustment of the spontaneous activities of individuals is brought about by the market" (Hayek, 1960, p. 159). "The study of spontaneous orders has long been the peculiar task of economic theory (Hayek, 1973, pp. 36–7). And just as the term "order" has its correlate in the term "coordination," so too does the term "spontaneous order" have its correlate, as we shall see, in one sense (out of other possible senses) of the term "coordination."

But just as we have seen that the notion of order in social phenomena is, for Hayek, not defined as the mutual adjustment of numerous independently made decisions, it is quite similarly the case that the term "spontaneous order" is not defined, for Hayek, as the spontaneous achievement of such mutual adjustment. By the notion of spontaneous order Hayek wished to refer more broadly, for example, to the circumstance that "the spontaneous collaboration of free men often creates things which are greater than their individual minds can ever fully comprehend. This is the great theme of Josiah Tucker and Adam Smith, of Adam Ferguson and Edmund Burke" (Hayek, 1949a, p. 7). Now the achievement of an outcome which no one has deliberately created, an outcome which is "greater" than anything the individuals (whose "spontaneous collaboration" spontaneously achieves this "greater" social outcome) could ever comprehend, does not require that that outcome be defined in terms of mutual compatibility of individual plans. Presumably when Hayek refers to the mutual compatibility of individually made plans that is achieved by the spontaneous interplay of market competition, he sees this as one example of something "greater" than what the individual market participants have been aiming at. Such compatibility is thus an example of spontaneous order rather than its defining characteristic.

It is worth emphasizing this aspect of the Hayekian spontaneous order concept. It might perhaps plausibly be argued that if one were to seek the "one big thing" that might qualify Hayek as "hedgehog," it might well be found in his concern with spontaneous order. Certainly some of Hayek's later work in the spontaneous evolution of benign social institutions focuses not so much upon the coordination of individual decisions, as upon the creation of something greater than anything which any of the innumerable individuals (out of whose actions these social institutions spontaneously emerge) could possibly have had in mind. Our purpose in drawing attention to this is not to support (or rebut) any such claim (concerning the centrality of the spontaneous order concept in Hayek's work). It is rather to point out that the "spontaneous" aspect of social outcomes must not be confined to outcomes that can be parsed as consisting of sets of mutually compatible individual decisions. Nor (given the breadth with which we have seen Hayek to have defined "order"), could we in good conscience even confine the concept of spontaneous order to the creation of benignly "greater" things (than the individuals could have had in mind). The same scientific fascination which surrounds the spontaneous emergence of benign social outcomes, should apply also to the spontaneous emergence of social outcomes which the individuals (out of whose activities these outcomes emerge) would abhor.[6] Any centrality in Hayekian thought of the spontaneous order concept must be distinguished from a possible focus upon plan-coordination.

(d) *Coordination I*: Closely related to the foregoing discussion is the notion of the coordination of the activities of many individuals in order to achieve some desired overall patterned outcome. Here the starting point is either (or both) of two realistic premises: (a) that individuals may be motivated by self-regarding goals that do not include the achievement of the desired social outcome; (b) that individuals may (as a result of the Hayekian phenomenon of dispersed knowledge) be only incompletely informed concerning the circumstances of time and place needed for the achievement of the desired social outcome. Given these premises, the achievement of the desired social outcome calls, as the most elementary economics recognizes, for a way of achieving coordination of individual activities. Certainly, as we have seen, Hayek's work drew attention again and again to the counterintuitive possibility of spontaneous market coordination to achieve a desirable social outcome. (The subtleties which Hayek certainly recognized surrounding the question of what constitutes the pattern of outcomes which is "desirable"—or whether indeed "desirability" involves any "pattern" at all—need not detain us for present purposes). It should be noticed, in regard to this coordination notion, that (just as we saw in regard to the notion of "order") such coordination is certainly not defined in terms of the mutual compatibility of independently made plans or independently held expectations—since such coordination includes (in principle) coordination sought to be achieved by central command, superseding individually made plans. The defining feature of this notion of coordination is the desired character of some social outcome.[7] Although most of the passages in which Hayek uses the word "coordination" are *not* referring to the central coordination of activities (by command) in order to achieve some desired social outcome (but refer instead to what we shall below term "Coordination II"), nonetheless it seems fair to say that at least sometimes it *is* the goal of achieving some desired overall outcome which underlies his use of the term "coordination." (An example of such a use is Hayek's 1941 reference to what individual entrepreneurs in a market economy "have to do in order to bring about that coordination of their efforts which a central planner could never achieve" (Hayek, [1941] 1997, p. 146).)

A second example seems to be present in a sentence in which Hayek states that "in a system in which the knowledge of the relevant facts is dispersed among many people, prices can act to co-ordinate the separate actions of different people *in the same way as subjective values help the individual to co-ordinate the parts of his plan*" (Hayek, [1945] 1949a, p. 85; emphasis added).

The same idea is surely implied in a number of passages in which Hayek draws attention to the circumstance that "the spontaneous actions of individuals will . . . bring about a distribution of resources which can be understood *as if it were made according to a single plan*" (Hayek [1937] 1949a, p. 54; emphasis added). It is, Hayek states, "the main merit of real competition that through it use is made of knowledge divided between many persons which, if it were to be used in a centrally directed economy, would all have to enter the single plan" (Hayek, 1949a, p. 202). Late in his career Hayek expressed unhappiness at the modern term "the economy," and made a plea that this term be reserved for describing "a complex of deliberately co-ordinated actions serving a single scale of ends" (Hayek, 1976, p. 108).

(e) *Coordination II*: Here we come to the place in Hayek of that central idea which has motivated the present chapter (and which, I believe, led Gerald O'Driscoll, as we have seen, to see all of Hayek's work as variations of the coordination theme)—namely, coordination as the state (or the process leading towards the state) in which the individual plans of independently-acting persons display mutual compatibility. Such compatibility may be couched, as in the preceding sentence, in terms of plans, or it may be couched in terms of decisions, or of expectations. The earmark of "coordination II" is that it refers to the dovetailing of individual purposeful efforts without any necessary concern with or interest in (either on the part of any of the individuals involved in these efforts, or on the part of the observing or theorizing scientist, or on the part of anyone else) the desirability or undesirability of the overall "social" outcome of these purposeful efforts. Certainly most of the references to coordination to be found in Hayek's work (while, as we have seen, they may sometimes if not always be defined in terms consistent with some overall social outcome that is somehow deemed desirable) in fact refer to the (spontaneous) coordination (through the market process) of the independently-made plans of market participants. In a 1939 paper[8] Hayek wrote of a market system achieving "effective coordination of individual effort," through "the free combination of the knowledge of all participants, with prices conveying to each the information which helps him to bring his actions in relation to those of others" (Hayek, [1939] 1997, p. 194). In a 1941 paper (in a passage with a thrust typical of numerous others, in which the word "coordination" may however not be explicitly used) Hayek stated that "in order to achieve the extensive division of labour on which our civilization is based, the direction of production must . . . be decentralized to a high degree, and some method must be found for coordinating these separate plans which does not depend on conscious central control" (Hayek, [1941] 1997, pp. 143ff.). The fundamental idea in this coordination concept is that we (the economic or social scientists) are interested in the extent to which the decisions made by an individual correctly anticipate (and take advantage of) the decisions in fact being made by others.

Perhaps the single most important and original insight which Hayek contributed to economic understanding is contained in his 1937 detailed interpretation of the state of equilibrium as being simply that state in which "the different plans which the individuals . . . have made for action in time are mutually compatible" (Hayek, [1937] 1949a, p. 41). This interpretation was first suggested in germinal form by Hayek, it appears, in his 1933 Copenhagen lecture, where the compatibility of plans was explicitly linked to the compatibility of expectations. The concept of equilibrium assumes, Hayek stated in that lecture, that everybody possesses correct foresight concerning "the behaviour of all the other people with whom he expects to perform economic transactions" (Hayek, [1933] 1939b, p. 140). From this interpretation of the equilibrium state it is possible to achieve an understanding of the market process which is hardly available to more conventional ways of seeing equilibrium (for example as the solution to a system of simultaneous equations of supply and demand functions, or as representing, as if in mechanics, a balance of the forces of supply and demand). It was this interpretation of equilibrium as expressing a pattern of mutually sustaining expectations, which enabled Hayek to highlight the role of dispersed information in market processes, and to perceive the signalling role of market prices in communicating information. And it was surely this interpretation which led Hayek to appreciate the possibility of a spontaneous order in which, without central direction, market prices generate an array of decisions on the part of independently-acting, independently-motivated, and independently-informed individuals which do, to a remarkable degree, reflect mutually sustaining expectations.

Having in this section briefly examined the various ideas and concepts surrounding the notion of "coordination II" to be found in Hayek's writings, (particularly those in, or influenced by his "tetrad on economic coordination"), we are in a position to summarize some of the separate (if overlapping) themes that we should identify in those writings. Although to do so is to do nothing new in regard to the substance of Hayek's contributions, it will enable us to raise doubts concerning possible claims that we can find any "one big thing" at the foundations of Hayek's work in so many different areas.

SOME SEPARATE (BUT OVERLAPPING) THEMES IN HAYEK

Several enduring themes pervade Hayek's work. These are well-known. Yet it may be helpful, for the purposes of this paper, to list some of them systematically here. The themes we select for this listing are those most salient in Hayek's "tetrad on coordination" (and thus most relevant to the possible identification of plan-coordination as the "one big thing" that might qualify Hayek for hedgehogdom).

(a) *Equilibrium*: In his famous 1933 Copenhagen lecture, Hayek pronounced "the fundamental problem of all economic theory," to be "the question of the significance of the concept of equilibrium and its relevance to the explanation of a process which takes place in time" (Hayek, [1933] 1939b, p. 138). There can be no doubt that this "fundamental problem" was never far from Hayek's concern as an economic theorist (and of course this is true for most economic theorists, of most schools of thought). Even when Hayek was to criticize "modern economists" for their "perhaps excessive preoccupation with the conditions of a hypothetical state of stationery equilibrium" (Hayek, [1935] 1949a, p. 167),[9] the relevance of the equilibrium concept and its centrality for economic understanding was not in question. Hayek is famous for having been a pioneer in the idea of intertemporal equilibrium (Hayek, [1928] 1994), and even after he expressed his impatience with the profession's preoccupation with the equilibrium concept, he considered intertemporal equilibrium to be a central building block for his own system of understanding.[10] In regard to the coordination problem, we note that Hayek did not object so much to the professional attention to what is called the state of "competitive equilibrium" (in which "the data for the different individuals are fully adjusted to each other"), as to its failure to explain "the nature of the process by which the data are thus adjusted" (Hayek, 1949a, p. 94). We have already noticed how important for Hayek's work on coordination, was his path-breaking reinterpretation of equilibrium in terms of the mutual compatibility of plans. Our purpose in identifying "equilibrium" as an important theme in Hayek's work is not to throw doubt on the importance for Hayek of the plan-coordination idea; it is simply to take note of the separateness of these ideas. To *interpret* equilibrium as expressing plan compatibility is not quite the same thing as to *replace* the role of equilibrium itself in economic understanding, by that of plan-compatibility.

(b) *Spontaneous order*: We have already taken note of the importance in Hayek's work of his celebrated notion of spontaneous order. For present purposes there is no need to elaborate further on what has already been said. Hayek's interest in spontaneous order clearly grows (as it does for most economists) out of his interest in the notion of equilibrium. It is Hayek's reinterpretation of equilibrium as expressing the mutual compatibility of independently-made plans which permitted him to see the price system as a signalling system, communicating information (concerning the actions of other market participants) to the entire market. Although we have seen that for Hayek the term "spontaneous order" is not defined in plan-compatibility terms, it remains a central feature of his spontaneous order that it refers, in a market system, to the spontaneous knowledge-communication process through which plan-compatibility can be approached.

(c) *The Knowledge Problem*: Distinct from, but of course closely related to the above, is the role of (what has come to be known as) Hayek's "Knowledge Problem." This refers to the "problem of the utilization of knowledge which is not given to anyone in its totality" (Hayek, [1945] 1949a, p. 78). The circumstance of dispersed knowledge came to be identified by Hayek as what renders plan-compatibility a challenge, and what renders central planning a virtual impossibility. So that this knowledge problem, a theme referred to again and again since the "coordination tetrad," is related to the possibility of spontaneous order, to the attainment (or at least to the tendency towards the attainment) of equilibrium. But it is, of course, distinct from each of them. (In fact, precisely in Hayek's emphasis on the difficulties which the knowledge problem poses for central planning, there is implicit the insight that this problem is *not* uniquely linked to the criterion of the compatibility of independently-made plans.)

(d) *The micro-basis for "macroeconomics" and cycle theory*: One theme which certainly runs through almost all Hayek's work is his recognition of what is now called the "microfoundations" of macroeconomics. This recognition was vigorously expressed already in Hayek's 1931 *Prices and Production*:

> it is on the assumption of a knowledge of the decisions of individuals that the main propositions of non-monetary economic theory are based. It is to this "individualistic" method that we owe whatever understanding of economic phenomena we possess . . . If, therefore, monetary theory still attempts to establish causal relations between aggregates or general averages, this means that monetary theory lags behind the development of economics in general. In fact, neither aggregates nor averages do act upon one another.
>
> (Hayek, [1931] 1935, p. 4)

Certainly this theme is of overriding importance for Hayek (and O'Driscoll rightly emphasizes this in his own emphasis on the centrality of plan-coordination in Hayek's work); but, of course, to insist on the micro-basis of the theory of the business cycle is, by itself, not the same as insisting on the centrality of plan-compatibility in such theory.

(e) *Plan-coordination*: This theme (which we identified above as "coordination II") is the focus of our interest in this chapter. Its importance in what we have seen O'Driscoll perceptively to have labelled Hayek's "tetrad on economic coordination," cannot be questioned. Into this concept of plan-coordination Hayek poured his deep and subtle understanding of individual decision-making, and in the social processes generated by the interactions among individual actions in markets. This concept embraces the implications of the dispersed character of knowledge in society, of the possibilities for the attainment of spontaneous order, and of the meaning of equilibrium and of equilibrating processes. Our understanding of the competitive process can, after appreciating the lessons of the coordination tetrad, never be the same. And certainly one can appreciate the insight of those recent expositions of Hayek's cycle theory which have, as we noticed very early in this chapter, read it directly in (intertemporal) plan-coordination terms. One does not have to accept the doctrinal-historiography of such expositions to understand sympathetically "where they are coming from." Yet our brief dissection of the various themes which we have identified as important for Hayekian economics must surely convince us that, whatever the degree of overlap with, and whatever the extent of other linkages between, the plan-coordination insight and the other themes, they must, at any rate, be recognized as distinct themes.

HAYEK AND THE WORLD OF SOCIAL SCIENCE BEYOND ECONOMICS

A fascinating theme which, I believe, has thus far been only partly explored, is the extent of and the source of the continuity between Hayek's work outside economics and his earlier purely economic work.[11] For the purposes of this chapter we take brief note of this as yet insufficiently examined issue only insofar as it may possibly throw light on our own search for the "one big thing" that could permit us to see Hayek as "hedgehog." A most revealing passage in a 1965 paper of Hayek's can perhaps be helpful. The year 1965 was several years after Hayek had published his *Constitution of Liberty*. The paper seems not only to reflect certain key ideas of that book, but also to anticipate a good deal of what Hayek would be expounding several years later in the three volumes of *Law, Legislation and Liberty*.

In this 1965 paper (Hayek, [1965] 1967) is making a plea against what he calls the "rational constructivism" of Bacon, Hobbes and Descartes, which contends "that all the useful human institutions were and ought to be the deliberate creation of conscious reason" (ibid., p. 85). This rationalism Hayek contrasts with the rationalism of the medieval thinkers who were "very much aware that many of the institutions of civilization were not the inventions of the reason but what, in explicit contrast to all that was invented, they called 'natural', i.e., spontaneously grown" (ibid., p. 84). Hayek, developing this latter (non-constructivist) rationalist perspective, suggests further "that in all our thinking we are guided (or even operated) by rules of which we are not aware, and that our conscious reason can therefore always take account only of some of the circumstances which determine our actions" (ibid., p. 87). This leads him to his now well-known conclusion that "the only manner in which we can in fact give our lives some order [in the face of ever new and unforeseeable circumstances] is to adopt certain abstract rules or principles for guidance, and then strictly adhere to the rules we have adopted in our dealing with the new situations as they arise" (ibid., p. 90). Hayek is then led to remark on what in his "personal development was the starting point of all these reflections," explaining how he "was led from technical economics into all kinds of questions usually regarded as philosophical" (ibid., p. 91). He sees it all to have begun with his 1937 "Economics and Knowledge" paper (the first of the "coordination tetrad"). That paper, he writes in 1965, showed how economics must explain "how an overall order of economic activity was achieved which utilized a large amount of knowledge which was not concentrated in any one mind."

Pursuing these insights further through "a re-examination of the age-old concept of freedom under the law, the basic conception of traditional liberalism, and of the problems of the philosophy of law which this raises," Hayek acquired, one gathers, "insight into the relations between the abstract rules which the individual follows in his actions, and the abstract overall order which is formed as a result of his responding, within the limits imposed upon him by those abstract rules, to the concrete particular circumstances which he encounters." These insights, it is made clear, have provided Hayek with "a tolerably clear picture of the nature of the spontaneous order of which liberal economists have so long been talking" (ibid., p. 92).

In other words, Hayek's insights into philosophy and political philosophy represent far-reaching extrapolation of ideas first outlined (within the narrow scope of purely technical economics) in the first of the coordination tetrad papers. We notice immediately that in this extrapolation the focus is no longer upon the simple coordination or dovetailing of individual decisions within a set of market institutions, but upon the achievement of an "abstract overall order," through rigorous adherence on the part of individuals to abstract rules, in broader social interaction, in the face of ever new and unforeseeable circumstances. The extension by Hayek of his economics insights of 1937 to his political philosophy insights of the 1960s is not so much a rigorous analytical development, as it is the pursuit of a fertile hunch based on an ingenious analogy. We notice also that Hayek saw this continuity in the development of his thinking outside narrow technical economics (as proceeding from his 1937 paper in the coordination tetrad), some 12 years before his 1977 statement (in his above-cited Foreword to O'Driscoll's book) in which he clearly appears to confess that, until he saw that book, he had been unaware of how the idea of plan-coordination had served as a guiding idea in most of his economic writings. It becomes thus very obvious that to recognize (as he did in 1965) that the coordination-of-dispersed-knowledge insights of his 1937 paper led him eventually to many of his later contributions to philosophy and political philosophy, is not at all inconsistent with unawareness at the very same time of the place of plan-coordination in his own post-1937 contributions to economics itself. All this confirms our scepticism concerning any "hedgehog"-understanding of Hayek's life-work in the social sciences, or even in economics proper. At the very time he was pursuing the fertile hunch (suggesting an analogy between the spheres of economics and of political philosophy—but in ways that did *not* involve individual plan-coordination) he was, in his work on the pure theory of capital, for example, (as in other economic contributions of the 1940s), engaging in technical economic analysis without consciously or deliberately invoking those coordination insights which loomed so prominently in his intellectual-autobiographical memory. We are now in a position to draw together what we have found.

CONTINUITY RATHER THAN UNITY

We have already cited Professor Butos's reference to "a band of continuity" running through Hayek's work. What we have seen in this chapter is confirmation that such continuity must be distinguished from unity. There is no "one big thing" that might permit us to see Hayek as "hedgehog," as developing an array of theories in various branches of social science, or of economics, that might all be recognized as flowing directly out of one, big seminal insight. Instead we find an array of overlapping themes and insights in Hayek's "tetrad," which appear to have inspired him to develop useful prescientific hunches, based on analogy, which his subsequent work—work of extraordinary scholarly devotion and breadth—permitted him to transform into systematically developed scientific contributions. Plan-coordination is one—very plausibly the most important one—of these enduring themes which inspired much of Hayek's work and which establishes that continuity of which Professor Butos wrote.

The truth seems to be that up until the mid-1930s Hayek's economics focused on two quite distinct areas, both of them involving the elaboration of pioneering contributions by Hayek's mentor, Ludwig von Mises. These two areas were (a) what came to be known as the Austrian theory of the business cycle,[12] and (b) the Austrian position concerning the difficulties surrounding the possibility of socialist economic calculation.[13] Now Mises himself never did focus explicitly on plan-coordination in all of his work; he never did focus on the dispersed character of knowledge, and on the consequent coordination problem. (This does not mean that Mises's seminal insights in each of the above two areas cannot be faithfully articulated in plan-coordination terms; it merely means that Mises himself never explicitly recognized this possible articulation.) Certainly for Mises these two areas of economics, while each of them reflected their common basis in the standard economic theory of prices, were quite separate areas of research. There is no reason whatever to suppose that, up until the mid-thirties (by which time Hayek's major contributions to both areas were virtually complete) Hayek saw these areas as anything but separate and distinct sets of theoretical argumentation.

It is true that (e.g. in his 1931 *Prices and Production*, and in his 1933 Copenhagen lecture) Hayek's work in both of these areas in the early 1930s was leading him to fresh insights which were to develop into his "tetrad on economic coordination." And it is this writer's conviction that these fresh insights constitute Hayek's enduring original contribution to economic understanding. (They also led him, as we have seen, to extend these insights, by analogy, to areas beyond economics proper. And this writer has elsewhere expressed reservations concerning some of Hayek's resulting conclusions; see Kirzner ([1990] 1992).) But what we have seen in this chapter must warn us against any sweeping thesis suggesting that, consciously or unconsciously, Hayek's entire work in economics, work extending from the 1920s to the 1970s and beyond, is to be seen as the consistent development of his plan-coordination insights.

Neither hedgehog nor fox, Hayek emerges as an extraordinarily fertile and broad scholar, one whose work in so many different areas can, naturally enough, be seen to reflect his consistent fascination with a series of related and overlapping themes and insights, to which he arrived in perhaps the central decade of his career as economist. Hayek's contributions to Austrian economics revolve around these overlapping themes; his lasting influence will, without question, depend on the extent to which these themes and insights will continue to inspire current and future Austrian scholars. In this centenary year commemorating Hayek's birth, we can pay no greater tribute to his work than to reaffirm the continuity which these themes and insights confer upon Hayek's lifelong scientific odyssey.

NOTES

1. It is perhaps worthwhile to remind ourselves that of course many economists (besides Hayek or other "Austrian" economists) have emphasized the idea of "coordination" (sometimes of "spontaneous coordination") as central to the understanding of economics. Thus, for example, Milton Friedman writes that the "basic problem of social organization is how to co-ordinate the economic activities of large numbers of people" (Friedman, 1962, p. 12). Axel Leijonhufvud titled a published collection of his essays in *macro*economic theory, *Information and Coordination* (Leijonhufvud, 1981), explaining (at p. v) that "macroeconomics," for Leijonhufvud, "is the study of the coordination of activities in large, complex, economic systems."
2. It should be emphasized that it is entirely possible, and perhaps even plausible, that O'Driscoll's book (as well as Hayek's above-cited Foreword to it) are not at all necessarily inconsistent with our conclusions in this chapter.
3. This phrase was perceptively coined by O'Driscoll (1977, p. 67).
4. And we have already noticed the possibility, at least, of tracing these coordination ideas to Hayek's earlier formulation of his business cycle theory. On this see further Kirzner (1995, pp. 38–40).
5. On the development of Hayek's insights into spontaneous order, see Leube (1994).
6. For a criticism of what this writer believes to be Hayek's insufficient appreciation of this possibility, see Kirzner ([1990] 1992).
7. In a recent subtle, provocative paper, Daniel B. Klein (Klein, 1997, pp. 325ff.) has read Hayek as speaking of coordination *exclusively* in terms of what we have called "Coordination I." He has labelled this coordination idea "metacoordination" (in order to distinguish it from another type of coordination, which he labels "coordination" *simpliciter*, or "Schelling coordination"). As will become evident in the subsequent subsection in the text ("Coordination II"), this writer believes that, at least part of the time, Hayek was using the term "coordination" not in the sense of Klein's "metacoordination," but in the sense of the achievement of mutual compatibility among independently-made individual plans (without regard to any overall desirability of this outcome). It is this latter sense of the term "coordination" (involving simply the objective criterion of mutual plan compatibility) which is the focus of our attention in this chapter. This sense of "coordination" is, in fact, closer to (but not identical with) Klein's "Schelling coordination." For a detailed exposition of what this writer believes to constitute "coordination" (i.e. what we call here "Coordination II"), including aspects of it which do not dovetail at all neatly with Klein's taxonomy, see Kirzner (1998).
8. In regard to this passage (and to other similar observations in other of his works) Hayek refers the reader to his 1937 paper (Hayek, [1937] 1949a).
9. For a similar criticism of the profession's preoccupation with equilibrium, see Hayek (1949a, ch. IX, p. 188).
10. See for example Hayek (1941, ch. II).

11. Our reference in this section is not to Hayek's early work in psychology (see Hayek, 1952), but to his work in political philosophy and other areas such as philosophy and the history of ideas.
12. For Hayek's reference to Mises's earlier work in this area see Hayek (1984).
13. See Hayek's acknowledgement of Mises's contribution in this area, in his introduction to the collection of essays on this problem which he edited in 1935 (Hayek, 1935).

REFERENCES

Butos, William N. (1985) "Hayek and General Equilibrium Analysis," *Southern Economic Journal* 52(October), pp. 332–43; page references are to the reprint in J.C. Wood and R.N. Woods (eds) (1991) *Friedrich A. Hayek, Critical Assessments*, Vol. IV, London and New York: Routledge.

Friedman, Milton (1962) *Capitalism and Freedom*, Chicago: University of Chicago Press.

Garrison, Roger W. (1985) "Intertemporal Coordination and the Invisible Hand: An Austrian Perspective on the Keynesian Vision," *History of Political Economy* 17(Summer), pp. 309–21.

—— (1989) "The Austrian Theory of the Business Cycle in the Light of Modern Macroeconomics," *Review of Austrian Economics* 9.

Hayek, Friedrich A. (1928) "Das intertemporale Gleichgewichtssystem der Preise und die Bewegungen des Geldwertes," *Weltwirtschaftliches Archiv* 28; English translation in Israel M. Kirzner (ed.) (1994) *Classics in Austrian Economics, A Sampling in the History of a Tradition*, Vol. III, London: William Pickering, pp. 161–98.

—— (1931) *Prices and Production*, 1st edn; page references are to the 1935 second edition, London: Routledge.

—— (1933) "Price Expectations, Monetary Disturbances and Malinvestments," reprinted as ch. IV in Hayek (1939b).

—— (1935a) *Collectivist Economic Planning*, London: Routledge and Kegan Paul.

—— (1935b) "Socialist Calculation, The State of the Debate," in Hayek (1935a); page references are to the reprint in Hayek (1949a).

—— (1937) "Economics and Knowledge," *Economica* 4(February); page references are to the reprint in Hayek (1949a).

—— (1939a) "Freedom and the Economic System," Public Policy Pamphlet No. 29, Chicago, University of Chicago Press; page references are to the reprint in Hayek (1997).

—— (1939b) *Profits, Interest and Investment*, London: George Routledge and Sons.

—— (1941a) *The Pure Theory of Capital*, Chicago: University of Chicago Press.

—— (1941b) "The Economics of Planning," *The Liberal Review* I, pp. 5–11; page references are to the reprint in Hayek (1997).

—— (1943) " The Facts of the Social Sciences," *Ethics* LIV(1); page references are to the reprint in Hayek (1949a).
—— (1945) "The Use of Knowledge in Society," *American Economic Review* XXXV(4), pp. 519–30; page references are to the reprint in Hayek (1949a).
—— (1949a) *Individualism and Economic Order*, London: Routledge and Kegan Paul.
—— (1949b) "The Meaning of Competition," in Hayek (1949a).
—— (1949c) "Individualism—True and False," in Hayek (1949a).
—— (1949d) "Socialist Calculation: The Competitive 'Solution,'" in Hayek (1949a).
—— (1952) *The Sensory Order*, London and Chicago: University of Chicago Press.
—— (1955) *The Counter-Revolution of Science: Studies on the Abuse of Reason*, Glencoe, IL: The Free Press.
—— (1960) *The Constitution of Liberty*, Chicago: University of Chicago Press.
—— (1965) "Kinds of Rationalism," *The Economic Studies Quarterly* XV(3); page references are to the reprint in Hayek (1967).
—— (1967) *Studies in Philosophy, Politics and Economics*, Chicago: University of Chicago Press.
—— (1968) "Competition as a Discovery Procedure"; page references to English version in Hayek (1978).
—— (1973) *Law, Legislation and Liberty*, Vol. 1, *Rules and Order*, Chicago: University of Chicago Press.
—— (1976) *Law, Legislation and Liberty*, Vol. 2, *The Mirage of Social Justice*, Chicago: University of Chicago Press.
—— (1978) *New Studies in Philosophy, Politics, Economics and the History of Ideas*, Chicago: University of Chicago Press.
—— (1979) *Law, Legislation and Liberty*, Vol. 3, *The Political Order of a Free People*, Chicago: University of Chicago Press.
—— (1981) Ms. of Introductory remarks to "The Flow of Goods and Services," lecture at the London School of Economics, January 27.
—— (1984) *Money, Capital and Fluctuations: Early Essays*, ed. Roy McCloughry, Chicago: University of Chicago Press.
—— (1997) *Socialism and War, Essays, Documents, Reviews*, Vol. 10 of *The Collected Works of F.A. Hayek* (ed. Bruce Caldwell), Chicago: University of Chicago Press.
Ioannides, Stavros (1992) *The Market, Competition and Democracy; A Critique of Neo-Austrian Economics*, Aldershot: Edward Elgar.
Kirzner, Israel M. (1990) "Knowledge Problems and Their Solutions: Some Relevant Distinctions," *Cultural Dynamics*; page references are to the reprint in Kirzner (1992).
—— (1992) *The Meaning of Market Process; Essays in the Development of Modern Austrian Economics*, London and New York: Routledge.
—— (ed.) (1994) *Classics in Austrian Economics, A Sampling in the History of a Tradition*, 3 vols, London: William Pickering.

—— (1995) "Hayeks Theorie der Koordination von Märkten," in *Vademecum zu Einem Klassiker Der Marktkoordination* (to accompany the facsimile republication of Hayek's *Preise und Produktion*), Dusseldorf: Verlag Wirtschaft und Finanzen GMBH.

—— (1998) "Coordination as a Criterion for Economic 'Goodness,'" *Constitutional Political Economy* 9, pp. 289–301, reprinted as chapter 7 in the present volume).

Klein, Daniel B. (1997) "Conventions, Social Order, and the Two Coordinations," *Constitutional Political Economy* 8, pp. 319–35.

Leijonhufvud, Axel (1981) *Information and Coordination, Essays in Macroeconomic Theory*, New York and Oxford: Oxford University Press.

Leube, Kurt R. (1994) "Law and Economics, Some Preliminary Remarks on Hayek's Early Student Years and his Development of the Theory of Spontaneous Order," in Christoph Frei and Robert Nef (eds) *Contending With Hayek: on Liberalism, Spontaneous Order and the Post-Communist Societies in Transition*, Bern: Peter Lang.

O'Driscoll, Gerald P. (1977) *Economics as a Coordination Problem, The Contributions of Friedrich A. Hayek*, Kansas City: Sheed, Andrews and McMeel.

Schmidtchen, Dieter and Utzig, S. (1989) "Die Konjunkturtheorie Hayeks: Episode in einem forscherleben oder Ausdruk eines lebenslangen Forschungsprogramms?" *Wirtschaftspolitische Blätter* 2 (in honor of Hayek's 90th birthday).

Shackle, George L.S. (1966) *The Nature of Economic Thought, Selected Papers, 1955–1964*, Cambridge: Cambridge University Press.

Source: Hedgehog or Fox? Hayek and the Idea of Plan-Coordination, *Journal des Economistes et des Etudes Humaines*, June/September 1999, IX(2/3), pp. 217–37.

Part IV

STUDIES IN THE THEORY OF COMPETITION AND ENTREPRENEURSHIP

11

COMPETITION AND THE MARKET PROCESS

Some doctrinal milestones

As the twentieth century nears its conclusion, economic policy-makers (if not the economic theory textbooks) have to a considerable extent come to recognize that the advantages of competition are to be found in the dynamics of the process of competition, rather than in the imagined state of affairs identified in the textbook model of competition. For most of the century, however, the general professional opinion was quite different. Any optimality properties a market system may possess, it was held, are those generated by its approximating the conditions of the perfectly competitive model. And the support for free markets which, it was generally understood, neoclassical economics (in its pre-1930 vintage) provided, rested (so ran the conventional wisdom during the central decades of this century) upon the dominant role played in neoclassical economics by the model of perfect competition. This chapter offers a brief survey of some significant milestones along the road which have led professional opinion away from these latter positions (emphasizing the role of perfect competition in achieving societal economic efficiency) towards the contemporary recognition of the greater relevance of the dynamic process of competition for an understanding of the achievements of free markets.

The story to be told is complicated by (and indeed includes) the following circumstance. We wish to provide insight into the gradual dislodgment of the perfectly competitive model from the center-stage of professional concern; but the story accounting for that earlier centrality of the perfectly competitive (henceforth "PC") model, is itself a complicated, confusing, and controversial one. In fact, we shall argue, an important early step along the road away from the dominance of the PC model, consisted in a drastic revision of what had become the orthodox account of the earlier rise of that model.

Indeed, as we shall see, the story of the late twentieth century (partial) decline of the PC model can be construed as being largely the story of continual critical reconsideration of the manner in which that model had, by the 1930s, captured the central attention of the profession. Our story of the decline of the PC model must then begin with an outline of the place of that model in the neoclassical world before 1930.

NEOCLASSICAL ECONOMICS AND THE PC MODEL

There is no doubt that the economics profession at mid-century believed that the PC model basically captured the way in which neoclassical economics had understood how markets work (before Edward Chamberlin and Joan Robinson). "The 'perfection' of the concept of competition, that is, the emergence of the idea of competition as itself a market structure, was a distinguishing contribution of neoclassical economics" (McNulty, 1968, p. 644). Indeed, in 1939 Hicks (deeply engaged in refining and polishing neoclassical economics) made an oft-quoted statement to the effect that "sacrificing the assumption of perfect competition" must threaten "wreckage of the greater part of general equilibrium theory" (Hicks, 1939, pp. 83–4).

It was, in this general view, the work of Chamberlin and Robinson—and nothing else—which challenged this dominance of the PC model (arguing that its lack of realism rendered it incapable of explaining real world market prices). (It was the Chicago School, in its mid-century incarnation, which held on methodological grounds that this lack of realism was unimportant and provided no grounds for questioning the practical usefulness of the PC model.)[1]

Yet this orthodox view (that the mainstream of neoclassical microeconomics before Chamberlin and Robinson focused primarily on the theory of PC price determination) has been riddled with challenges during the past several decades. Brian Loasby (1989, p. 62) cites Sraffa's famous 1926 paper as challenging the consistency of Marshall's theory of value because his insistence on increasing returns is incompatible with perfect competition. (Clearly Sraffa, like Hicks, understood neoclassical economics, and in particular Marshallian economics, to stand or fall with the PC model.) But, Loasby asserts, Sraffa was "quite wrong to assume that perfect competition was the basis of Marshall's theory of value" (ibid., p. 62). Indeed, Loasby has gone so far as to claim that "Marshallian competition is a Hayekian discovery process" (ibid., p. 55). In a recent work Frank Machovec has brilliantly reconstructed the place of competition in the history of economic thought (Machovec, 1995).

The main thrust of Machovec's *dogmengeschichtliche* revisionism concerns his denial of the view (propagated particularly by Stigler (1957)) that the classical economists were, in effect, thinking in terms of a (crude) PC model. But in developing his refutation of this widespread Stiglerian error, Machovec also challenged an equally widespread view concerning the neoclassical mainstream that dominated the profession from the 1880s. Machovec challenged the view that the major neoclassical economists (such as Marshall) grounded their theory in the PC model (or, more precisely, that the development of the neoclassical mainstream from the 1880s onward, consisted largely in a steady, gradual analytical refinement of the meaning and implications of perfect competition). In Machovec's view, nothing of the sort characterized the neoclassical mainstream before 1920. On the contrary, Machovec maintains, among the neoclassical economists around the turn of the century, Walras was virtually alone in resting his analytical system upon the PC conditions (a step to which he was inexorably pushed by the logic of his general equilibrium system) (Machovec, 1995, p. 241). It was only during the 1920s (in particular as an outcome of Knight's 1921 *Risk, Uncertainty and Profit*) that there occurred a "Kuhnian revolution—that is, a distinct change in concept and analytical apparatus . . . as the model of perfect competition became the keystone of analysis" (ibid., p. 159). Where conventional wisdom had seen the history of economics since Adam Smith as gradual refinement until the 1920s, of a single conception of competition, (that of competition as a completed state of affairs), Machovec maintained that the classical economists and also at least the earlier neoclassical writers saw competition as a dynamic process: "The process view of the classicists and the early neoclassical writers was purged during the 1920s as the profession adopted an exclusively equilibrium framework for its microeconomic theorizing" (ibid., p. 236).

The present writer would, at least in one respect, in fact push Machovec's revisionism even further. The dominance of the PC model in the economics profession of the 1930s, 1940s, and 1950s, was to a significant extent an outcome of the monopolistic competition revolution of the early 1930s. In contrasting their own (static) models of monopolistically competitive equilibrium with (what they certainly believed to be) the dominant earlier models, Chamberlin and Robinson were incidentally formalizing and emphasizing an analytical model of (perfect) competition which had, for most of the profession, hitherto remained less than precisely articulated. Paradoxically, therefore, it was the very effort to dislodge the PC model (in favor of the equally static, but less unrealistic model of monopolistic competition) which thrust that PC model into the analytical limelight. Certainly Chamberlin and Robinson shared the now-conventional view (disputed by Machovec) that the state of perfect competition was central to the earlier neoclassical theory of value. The efforts to challenge this centrality had the effect, we believe, of focusing more sophisticated analytic attention on the PC model. Their efforts to dislodge the PC model thus had the paradoxical effect of rendering truthful for the 1940s and 1950s, that dominance in economics (of the PC model) which they had not quite correctly attributed to pre-1920 economics.

FURTHER THOUGHTS ON THE EARLIER NEOCLASSICAL VIEW OF COMPETITION

As we have seen, Machovec has argued that the earlier neoclassicals had shared (with the classical economists) a process view of competition. It was, he maintained, only Walras's emphasis on the determinateness of general equilibrium which pushed the PC model to the center of his own system (until, under the influence of Knight, the Walrasian centrality for PC came, according to Machovec's reading, to be adopted by the profession in the twenties in rather revolutionary fashion). But this view (that the earlier neoclassical economists thought of competition primarily, if not exclusively, in its dynamic, process, sense) may be reading a little too much into their work. The circumstance that a writer describes competition in a manner at variance with the fully articulated Knightian version of the PC model, does not at all imply that that writer is necessarily thinking in process terms. This point is of some importance and requires some elaboration.

The most significant insight concerning the story of the PC model in the twentieth century is surely the following: until Hayek's 1946 paper, "The Meaning of Competition,"[2] no one in the profession, it appears, had seen (or at least made explicit) the crucial difference between competition as a state of affairs and competition as a driving, dynamic process.[3] There is little doubt that Machovec (following McNulty (1967) and others) is correct in reading the classical economists as seeing competition (not, as Stigler had believed, as a perfectly competitive state of affairs which they were not quite able to articulate correctly and precisely, but) as a rivalrous process. But, astounding as it must in retrospect appear, none of the host of writers before Hayek, during the first half of this century (and including those of the 1930s and later) who dwelt on the meaning and implications of the PC model, quite saw with clarity that this model was a strictly equilibrium model, from which all vestiges of process had been completely filtered out.[4]

To see this failure perhaps most clearly one can cite the 1952 work (published *after* Hayek's paper!) of Fritz Machlup, *The Economics of Seller's Competition* (Machlup, 1952). This mid-century volume is surely the most careful and complete analysis of the many possible meanings of the term "competition," of the entire century. There are few aspects of the competitive process and of competitive equilibrium, as they had been treated in a vast literature, which are not carefully and sensitively dissected and labeled (often with newly-coined labels), in this volume.[5] Yet it becomes clear that Machlup (who incidentally and surprisingly makes no reference whatever to Hayek's 1946 paper) was, quite amazingly, unaware that the PC model does indeed logically confine one to the equilibrium state. This is apparent in his lengthy discussion of the meanings attached to the term "perfect market" (Machlup, 1952, pp. 117–24). It also emerges almost dramatically in his following statement:

> The disparagers of perfect competition are badly mistaken if they regard perfect competition as inimical to progress. Of course, if they define it as instantaneous entry of newcomers, it is obvious that "perfect competition is not only impossible but inferior"—as we read in Joseph A. Schumpeter, *Capitalism, Socialism and Democracy* (New York: Harper, 1943), p. 106. But such a model of perfect competition serves no purpose except to confuse the issue. Instantaneous entry of newcomers, instantaneous appearance of imitators, is not only impossible but nonsensical.
>
> (Machlup, 1952, pp. 555–6, fn)

One is tempted to surmise that Machlup's "Austrian" training had such a profound influence on his thinking, that, despite the range of nuances which he was able to distinguish in the enormous literature on competition, it somehow became impossible for him to accept that a theorist could seriously think of perfect competition in the way which Schumpeter (surely correctly) ascribed to mainstream theorists!

Machovec is insightfully correct in attributing Walras's emphasis on perfect competition to his equilibrium perspective. And, as Machovec argues, the dominance within economics which the PC model attained, was attained concomitantly with the profession's adoption of the mathematical economist's primary concern with equilibrium conditions. But, at least until Hayek's paper, economists seemed (in retrospect, almost incredibly) entirely unaware of the sharp distinction between the two possible uses of the adjective "competitive," namely, either as describing a process or as describing the equilibrium outcome (of some undefined process) seen as an already attained and settled state of affairs. Although this failure seems, from today's perspective, to be difficult to comprehend, we will not, I suggest, adequately understand earlier neoclassical writing on competition without recognizing the *fact* of this failure.

In particular we should, therefore, avoid the possible error of interpreting references in earlier neoclassical writing, to acts of competitive entry, as firm evidence of a process view of competition. As a result of the failure (to recognize the distinction we have emphasized), such references to acts of competitive entry may have been understood as aspects of a competitive *structure* (rather than as implying any understanding that such competitive acts of entry are strictly and inherently inconsistent with any equilibrium state).

This writer would therefore tend to see the development of neoclassical ideas on competition between the 1880s and 1930s as a more gradual analytical change than Machovec is prepared to accept. In brief, it would appear that, under the influence of increasing analytic formalization (manifested partly but not exclusively in increased use of geometrical—and eventually more general mathematical—tools) neoclassical economics came to focus more and more on the *outcomes* of economic processes and less and less on these processes themselves. As part of this change, references to competition came gradually to refer less and less to competitive processes and more and more to the results of such processes. Because the distinction between a competitive process and a "competitive" state of affairs was as yet entirely unclear, the neoclassical economists (such as Knight) engaged in explicit articulation of a precise characterization of competition (and who were, perhaps unselfconsciously, thinking in equilibrium terms) were able to nudge their fellow economists towards thinking within a structural, rather than a process framework. It is, then, not so much that an earlier dominant purely "process" view of competition succumbed to a revolution in favor of the "state-of-affairs" view of competition—as that an earlier somewhat nondescript view of competition (in which elements of process and of outcomes were rather confusedly jumbled together) came gradually to be purged of its process elements. While, from a late twentieth century perspective this change may appear negative in its extrusion of elements of process understanding, we can at least recognize that the achieved internal consistency (attained through exclusively structural understanding of perfect competition) may have had much to do with the new dominance of the PC model, and the length of its period of such dominance.

HAYEK AND THE MEANING OF COMPETITION

Hayek's 1946 paper was undoubtedly a by-product of his concern in the late 1930s and early 1940s with the role of markets in disseminating mutual knowledge among markets participants. The remarkable series of papers which emerged from this concern were published in Hayek's 1949 *Individualism and Economic Order*. His paper "The Meaning of Competition" is described in that book as reproducing the substance of a lecture delivered at Princeton in May 1946. Hayek begins his paper recognizing that "some valiant attempts" had been made to bring discussion of the meaning of the term competition "back to earth."[6] But he quickly points out that the general view is still that "the so-called theory of 'perfect competition' provides the appropriate model for judging the effectiveness of competition in real life, and that, to the extent that real competition differs from that model, it is undesirable and even harmful" (Hayek, 1949, p. 92).

Hayek vigorously disputed this view. He pointed out in particular that this general view "throughout assumes that state of affairs already to exist which, according to the truer view of the older theory, the process of competition tends to bring about . . . and that, if the state of affairs assumed by theory of perfect competition ever existed, it would not only deprive of their scope all the activities which the verb 'to compete' describes but would make them virtually impossible" (ibid.). Hayek proceeded to articulate with utmost clarity that the "modern theory of competition deals almost exclusively with a state of what is called 'competitive equilibrium' in which it is assumed that the data for the different individuals are fully adjusted to each other, while the problem which requires explanation is the nature of the process by which the data are thus adjusted" (ibid., p. 94).

Hayek's paper reads like a breath of fresh air. Cutting through a veritable forest of confusion in the literature, he was putting his finger on the root difficulty with the profession's preoccupation with the PC model: its being an equilibrium model inherently incapable of offering help in understanding how equilibrium might possible be approached. (It should be noted that his approving references to J.M. Clark and to Fritz Machlup[7] do not at all suggest that Hayek's fundamental insight had been anticipated by these writers. Rather they were being cited as lone writers who at least recognized that real world competition may have merit that does not depend on its being a close approximation to the PC model.)

THE SCENE AFTER HAYEK'S 1946 PAPER

Hayek's paper appears to have been virtually ignored in the subsequent literature (perhaps, in part, because it was not published in a journal). Mises (in his 1949 *Human Action* (p. 278, fn)) approvingly cited Hayek's paper as refuting the doctrines of monopolistic or imperfect competition. (Although Hayek did not in fact directly criticize these theories themselves in his paper, Mises obviously recognized the profound implications of Hayek's insights for the way in which Chamberlin's and Robinson's work had been interpreted by the profession.) Mises, whose own understanding of competition was, emphatically, steeped in the process mode,[8] instantly appreciated Hayek's contribution. But this writer has not found other references to Hayek's paper in the literature immediately after 1946.[9]

It was not that the profession failed to see the (obvious) difference between the term "competition" as used by businessmen and that term as used by economists.[10] But very few writers recognized that this difference reflected completely different perspectives on the market, *each* of which might be able to make a (separate) crucial contribution to economic understanding. Rather, the businessman's perception of active, rivalrous competition was dismissed as a crude expression of the way in which imperfect reality falls short of the sophisticated analytical ideal which the PC model expresses. In other words, the businessman's usage was seen as an uncouth use of language which fails to recognize that the market which he describes as competitive is, in fact, riddled with monopolistic elements—or, more pointedly, that precisely those elements which he sees as competitive, are, in fact, more properly to be labeled as monopolistic.

It is true that when this writer wrote his *Competition and Entrepreneurship*,[11] he was able in 1973 to trace a handful of references in the literature of the 1950s and 1960s to the need to supplement the theory of competitive equilibrium by a process theory, and to recognition that the PC model provides only the former.[12] Yet what were perceived as the most authoritative mainstream voices in those decades continued to articulate the conventional PC doctrine with renewed emphasis. George Stigler's well-known 1957 paper was, indeed, so emphatic in this regard that it may have, precisely as a result of that emphasis, provoked something of a reaction to the orthodoxy which he offered.[13]

Stigler offered a history of the PC model from the time of the classical economists until his own time. He treated Adam Smith's references to rivalrous competition as the early and somewhat crude articulation of a notion of competition which was to receive its refinement and precise formulation only in later generations, specifically in the pioneering mathematical work of Cournot (1838) and, finally, in the careful pronouncements of J.B. Clark and (in particular) of Frank Knight. It was this understanding of the classical economists' notion of competition which was to be challenged in the important (and above-cited) work of McNulty and, most recently, of Frank Machovec.

One important (and fairly prominent) contribution, published, as it happens, in the same year as Stigler's paper, challenged key aspects of the mainstream perception of the place of the PC model in early twentieth century neoclassical economics. This was the paper by Shorey Peterson, "Antitrust and the Classic Model".[14] In his paper Peterson maintained that it was not the case (as seemed to be argued by the later theories of monopolistic and imperfect competition) that the mainstream economic theory of the 1920s and earlier was one dominated by the PC model. The idea of such a "classic" model's having dominated "pre-Chamberlinian thought" seems "mildly shocking" to Peterson (who described himself as one of the "economists trained in the 1920s and before" (Peterson, 1957, pp. 60–3).

Instead, Peterson insisted, the economics which was learned from the treatises of J.B. Clark and Alfred Marshall understood that the rough and ready competition of the real world, particularly when buttressed by the threat of potential competition, sufficed to protect the consumers from the most serious of the distortions with which monopoly elements in the market might menace them. We should notice that in dwelling on this theme, Peterson does not seem to be disagreeing with the terminology in which all departures from the PC conditions are termed "monopolistic." Rather he appears to claim (on behalf of the mainstream economics of the 1920s and earlier) that the vigorous "imperfect" competition of the real world, riddled though it may be with such "monopolistic" elements, may suffice to impose efficiency and "order" upon market phenomena. It is this which supports Peterson's contention that John Maurice Clark's work on "workable competition" was not trying to "close a gap caused by failure of the older theory" (Peterson, 1957, p. 78), but was rather seeking to stem policy misunderstandings likely to be generated by "recent refinements of the competitive model" (ibid.). And it is was this which led Peterson to express surprise that Schumpeter[15] should have read neo-classical doctrine as inconsistent with his own emphasis on the competition of new and better products and on the force of potential competition. Schumpeter's emphasis in these respects was rather to be seen as "essentially an unfolding of earlier thought" (ibid., p. 74).

An intriguing paper of the 1950s by John Maurice Clark (which served as the basis for his subsequent book (Clark, 1961)), was entitled "Competition: Static Models and Dynamic Aspects" (Clark, 1955), and was presented at the 1954 American Economic Association meetings. Despite the surprisingly ill-tempered remarks with which Machlup commented on this paper (Machlup, 1955), Clark was clearly groping towards a sound critique of the place which the PC model was playing in mainstream economics at mid-century. It is perhaps relevant to note that, while Clark was certainly thoroughly aware of (indeed insistent upon) the distinction between competition as a "static" state of affairs and competition as a "dynamic process," his distinction is not quite the same as that which distinguishes between the PC state and the competitive process which might hypothetically produce that PC state. For Clark, dynamic competition was not primarily important as a possibly equilibrating force, but rather as a more general force relevant, in particular, for economic progress and growth (as well as for the protection of the consumers against monopolistic exploitation). (It should perhaps be emphasized that our observation here is not intended to be in any way critical of Clark.) This crusade by Clark (which, as Machovec points out (Machovec, 1995, p. 293), was in reality a "struggle [that] was hopeless" in the face of the cold reception it received in the profession) sought to dislodge the dominance of the static PC model. It made no attempt to point out that that model, and the very idea of determinacy in market outcomes—

surely the heart of neoclassical theory—acquires relevance only by being supplemented by a theory of competitive process.[16]

REFLECTIONS ON MAINSTREAM ECONOMICS IN THE 1940s AND 1950s

Our brief sampling of the literature of the central decades of this century has revealed a certain confusion in regard to the perceived role of the PC model. As has become increasingly apparent since the 1950s, the central body of (contemporary) neoclassical theory saw (and still sees) the PC model as its primary tool, and as the main pillar upon which to build a normative case for a free market economy. For a George Stigler, or a Milton Friedman,[17] for example, questions of realism were relatively unimportant. They believed the pragmatic usefulness of the PC model justified its dominant role in economic theory. On the other hand, we have seen that there existed (quite apart from Hayek's completely developed, but virtually ignored, contribution) a definite if rather disorganized set of dissident views, associated with such names as Schumpeter, J.M. Clark, and Shorey Peterson. These writers were challenging (not so much the meaningfulness of an economic theory virtually confined, for its central understanding of the workings of a market economy, upon the PC models, as) the attitude which saw all observed departures from the PC conditions as representing harmfully monopolistic features of reality. Their critiques certainly set their work decisively apart from the extensive literature in the area of industrial organization which explored industries described as oligopolistic, seeing them as variants of monopoly situations (see, for example, Peterson, 1957, p. 76). We do not perhaps adequately appreciate how much the very perception of an analytical box labeled "oligopoly," sprang from the dominance of that orthodoxy in which the word "competitive" means nothing but one particular market structure, the PC model. Once one refuses to grant use of the adjective "competitive" to describe any act of entrepreneurial entry aimed at winning pure profit (on the grounds that such acts are, as a matter of definition, "monopolistic"), one has firmly closed one's eyes to the obvious (and surely genuinely competitive) feature which is common to all situations characterized by freedom of entry. What remains is only the task of classifying different combinations and/or degrees of quasi-monopoly—a task to which so much of oligopoly theory has in fact been devoted.

What distinguishes these dissident views (from those that would emerge in the subsequent decades) is perhaps their linkages to earlier pre-Chamberlinian conceptions of competition (which had not yet been pressed into what would turn out to be the PC mold). They were not Young Turks rebelling at an existing orthodoxy which they found in place; rather they were expressing dismay at the fashion in which this orthodoxy had displaced a less formal, but more meaningful and useful, earlier orthodoxy. Their work no doubt played a role in keeping alive the notion of active competition in the profession. But a retrospective survey of late twentieth-century economics shows that these voices were drowned out by a textbook literature in which the PC model continued to occupy a more and more central position in economic explanations of market economies.

THE LATE TWENTIETH-CENTURY TURN

During the latter several decades of the century, however, new voices have emerged to question the dominance the PC model. These new voices have not in any sense constituted a unified "school"; often these voices clashed with each other. Yet the overall outcome achieved by the work expressed in these voices has been to dislodge the PC model (if not from its dominance of the textbooks, yet) from its long-established position of almost unchallenged dominance in professional understanding of how the market economy in fact works. In the space available here we certainly cannot adequately describe the way in which these new challenges to the PC model emerged and broadly reinforced each other. What we can attempt to do is to list briefly and identify some of these new voices, so that we can gain appreciation for the way in which, discordant though they may have been, they have nonetheless drilled a certain scepticism into professional consciousness in regard to the relevance of the PC model—a skepticism along an entirely different dimension from that introduced a half-century earlier by Chamberlin and Robinson.

Voices emphasizing the process character of market effectiveness include work from the early 1960s onwards by such writers as G.B. Richardson (1960), who was a pioneer in understanding the role of the interactive flow of information in the competitive market process; Murray N. Rothbard (1962), who (although barely mentioning Hayek's work) pursued Austrian ideas on competition with admirable consistency to some of their radical implications; and Paul J. McNulty (1967, 1968), who in the late 1960s articulated the Hayekian insights with great skill and effectiveness and deployed them to offer (as we have already seen) a powerful history-of-thought critique of George Stigler's views on the history of the PC model.[18]

Voices emphasizing the powerful effectiveness of freedom of potential entry include Sylos-Labini who, early in the 1960s had published a much discussed work on oligopoly (Sylos-Labini, 1962),[19] in which the role on entry was extensively explored. Although much of the subsequently-inspired work on the role of entry was conducted within the conventional "structural" framework, this work did focus attention on an aspect of real world competition which the PC model tended to suppress or at least ignore.[20] A powerful 1969 paper by Yale Brozen (Brozen, 1969) sharply criticized the way in which the term "barriers to entry" had been used, in the conventional literature, to include such dynamically competitive activities (or arenas) as advertising, economies of scale, and product differentiation.

Closely related to the foregoing were voices questioning that orthodoxy which defined degrees of monopoly and competition in terms of numbers. Harold Demsetz, in a pioneering paper on the regulation of public utilities (Demsetz, 1968) (one which had far-reaching implications for monopoly theory in general), sharply challenged the standard doctrine on "natural monopoly." There is, Demsetz pointed out, "no clear or necessary reason for *production* scale economies to decrease the number of *bidders*. Let prospective buyers call for bids to service their demands. Scale economies in servicing their demands in no way imply that there will be one bidder only. There can be many bidders and the bid that wins will be the lowest" (ibid., p. 57). It was this insight, so strange to conventional wisdom at the time it was introduced, that would subsequently generate the theory of "contestable" markets (see Baumol, Panzar and Willig, 1982). While that theory was largely developed within the mainstream framework on market structures, it did much to widen economists' horizons on the nature and role of competition.

Much in the spirit of the foregoing was the new work of the early 1970s which challenged the then existing so-called "structural approach" to the evaluation of oligopoly situations. Some of that work was summarized in a prominent paper by J. Fred Weston (Weston, 1972). Weston, who himself contributed to this research, was particularly concerned to demonstrate empirically the competitive processes which take place in concentrated markets. Clearly this line of work, conducted primarily in the "applied" area of industrial organization (and eventually to be dubbed "the new learning"[21]), had important implications for the theory of competition. This line of work has indeed had continual influential impact on industrial organization theory and on antitrust economics, during the latter decades of the century.

A RETROSPECTIVE REFLECTION

Although it may seem that the contrast emphasized in this chapter (between competition as a process or competition as a state of affairs) is purely semantic, this is not at all the case. It would be a mistake to understand the shift in recent professional thinking about competition, as one primarily concerned with the meaning of the word—or even about the economic policy implications of the use of that word. Rather, the shift we have briefly surveyed constitutes a gradual deepening of professional understanding of how a market economy works. As long as the PC model dominated microeconomic theory, appreciation for the economic success of the market economy saw that economy as more-or-less closely approximating the state of perfect competitive equilibrium, with its prices and quantities emerging spontaneously as if from a magic computer. As professional understanding of the dynamic character of the competitive process has deepened, the contributions of the market have come to be glimpsed more profoundly and more accurately. It is the rivalrous competition described by Adam Smith, the entrepreneurial process described by Ludwig von Mises, and the knowledge-discovery procedure described by Friedrich Hayek, which has been "rediscovered" by a significant proportion of the economics profession, as this century reaches its conclusion. This encouraging development should serve as a firm foundation for future research into the competitive process, during the decades ahead.

NOTES

1. On this issue see Knight (1946), Stigler (1949), and Chamberlin (1957).
2. This paper was read as a lecture in 1946 and published in Hayek (1949). It is of interest that Hayek had incautiously described as competition the situation in which "the individual producer has to adapt to price changes and cannot control them" (1944, p. 49). Galbraith read this as requiring that demand curves facing individual sellers "be completely elastic at the ruling price" (1948, p. 111, fn 29). Certainly this would not be in the spirit of Hayek's 1946 paper. For a looser reading of Hayek than Galbraith's, see Shorey Peterson (1957, p. 75).

3. The following statement of George Stigler (written 11 years after Hayek's paper—which he does not cite) is of interest in this regard. Stigler is referring to Adam Smith's use of the term "competition" in the rivalrous sense. Stigler comments: "Competition is a process of responding to a new force and a method of reaching a new equilibrium" (1957, p. 235). The fact that, as noted in the text, Stigler saw Adam Smith as something of a crude forerunner of Knight's (equilibrium) PC model, suggests that Stigler was himself perhaps not fully alive to the significance that might be read into his sentence.
4. A careful reading of Schumpeter (1942, pp. 77–80, 103–6) may arguably, but not conclusively, suggest an exception to the statement in the text.
5. On the use of new labels to distinguish between subtly different aspects of competition, see Machlup (1952, p. 105, fn 17).
6. In this regard Hayek cites Clark (1940) and Machlup (1942).
7. See above, note 6.
8. See especially Mises (1949, pp. 273–9).
9. Among the earliest references to Hayek's 1946 paper are perhaps the papers by McNulty (1967, 1968).
10. For some references on this point see Kirzner (1973, p. 89, fn).
11. Kirzner (1973). This work cited Hayek's paper as "penetrating and pioneering" (p. 91) in regard to the distinction with which the present chapter is concerned.
12. See Kirzner (1973, esp. p. 93, fn 13, and p. 89, fn 1).
13. The reference is to Stigler (1957); it was this paper to which McNulty (1967) was primarily responding.
14. The reference is Peterson (1957). This paper was included in the influential AEA-sponsored volume of readings in industrial organization (Heflebower and Stocking, 1958).
15. Peterson was referring to Schumpeter (1942, chs VII and VIII).
16. It would be a mistake to conclude this section without any reference to a valuable (but almost entirely neglected) work of the 1950s, which was thoroughly out of step with the static ("state-of-affairs") notion of competition. This was Lawrence Abbott's *Quality and Competition* (New York: Columbia University Press, 1955). Abbott's emphasis on the dynamics of quality competition differs in spirit (although not perhaps in policy implications) from the work on "quality-as-a-variable" of E.H. Chamberlin (see Chamberlin, 1957, ch. 6). For an appreciative awareness of Abbott's work, see Rothbard, 1962, vol. II, p. 906, n. 28).
17. See Friedman (1953).
18. One of this writer's own books (Kirzner, 1973) was deeply influenced by Hayek and McNulty in this regard.
19. The standard work on barriers to entry had been Bain (1956).
20. For an example of such work see Needham (1969, ch. 7), reprinted in Breit and Hochman (1971).
21. Important samples of this and related literature were creatively assembled and edited by Yale Brozen (Brozen, 1975).

REFERENCES

Bain, J.S. (1956) *Barriers to New Competition*, Cambridge, MA: Harvard University Press.

Baumol, W.J., Panzar, J.C., and Willig, R. D. (1982) *Contestable Markets and the Theory of Industry Structure*, New York: Harcourt, Brace and Jovanovich.

Breit, William and Hochman, Harold M. (1971) *Readings in Microeconomics*, 2nd edn, New York: Holt, Rinehart and Winston.

Brozen, Yale (1969) "Competition, Efficiency, and Antitrust," *Journal of World Trade Law*; reprinted in Brozen (1975).

—— (ed.) (1975) *The Competitive Economy, Selected Readings*, Morristown, NJ: General Learning Press.

Chamberlin, Edward H. (1957) "The Chicago School," and "The Product as an Economic Variable," in E.H. Chamberlin, *Towards a More General Theory of Value*, New York: Oxford.

Clark, John Maurice (1940) "Toward a Concept of Workable Competition," *American Economic Review* XXX(June).

—— (1955) "Competition: Static Models and Dynamic Aspects," *American Economic Review* XLV(May).

—— (1961) *Competition as a Dynamic Process*, New York: Brookings.

Demsetz, Harold (1968) "Why Regulate Utilities?" *Journal of Law and Economics* 11(April).

Ellis, Howard S. (ed.) (1948) *A Survey of Contemporary Economics* (published for the American Economic Association), Homewood, IL: Irwin.

Friedman, Milton (1953) "The Methodology of Positive Economics," in *Essays in Positive Economics*, Chicago: University of Chicago Press.

Galbraith, John Kenneth (1948) "Monopoly and the Concentration of Economic Power," in Ellis (1948).

Hayek, Friedrich A. (1944) *The Road to Serfdom*, Chicago: University of Chicago Press.

—— (1949) *Individualism and Economic Order*, London: Routledge and Kegan Paul.

Heflebower, Richard B. and Stocking, George W. (eds) (1958) *Readings in Industrial Organization and Public Policy* (published for the American Economic Association), Homewood, IL: Irwin.

Hicks, J.R. (1946) *Value and Capital* (1st edn, 1939), 2nd edn, Oxford: Clarendon Press.

Kirzner, Israel M. (1973) *Competition and Entrepreneurship*, Chicago: University of Chicago Press.

Knight, Frank H. (1946) "Immutable Law in Economics: Its Reality and Limitations," *American Economic Review* May.

Loasby, Brian J. (1989) *The Mind and Method of the Economist*, Aldershot: Edward Elgar.

Machlup, Fritz (1942) "Competition, Pliopoly, and Profit," *Economica* IX(new ser.: February and May).

—— (1952) *The Economics of Sellers' Competition, Model Analysis of Sellers' Conduct*, Baltimore, MD: The Johns Hopkins University Press.

—— (1955) "Discussion," *American Economic Review* XLV(May), pp. 480–3.

Machovec, Frank M. (1995) *Perfect Competition and the Transformation of Economics*, London and New York: Routledge.

McNulty, Paul J. (1967) "A Note on the History of Perfect Competition," *Journal of Political Economy* 75(August).

—— (1968) "Economic Theory and the Meaning of Competition," *Quarterly Journal of Economics* 82(November).

Mises, Ludwig von (1949) *Human Action*, New Haven, CT: Yale University Press.

Needham, Douglas (1969) *Economic Analysis and Industrial Structure*, New York: Holt, Rinehart and Winston, ch. 7; reprinted in Breit and Hochman (1971).

Peterson, Shorey (1957) "Antitrust and the Classic Model," *American Economic Review* XLVII(March).

Richardson, G.B. (1960) *Information and Investment*, Oxford: Oxford University Press.

Rothbard, Murray N. (1962) *Man, Economy, and State: A Treatise on Economic Principles*, Princeton, NJ: Van Nostrand.

Schumpeter, Joseph A. (1950) *Capitalism, Socialism and Democracy* (1st edn, 1942), 3rd edn, New York: Harper.

Stigler, George J. (1949) *Five Lectures on Economic Problems*, London: Macmillan.

—— (1957) "Perfect Competition, Historically Contemplated," *Journal of Political Economy* 65(February); page references to Stigler (1965).

—— (1965) *Essays in the History of Economics*, Chicago and London: University of Chicago Press.

Sylos-Labini, P. (1962) *Oligopoly and Technical Progress*, Cambridge, MA: Harvard University Press.

Weston, J. Fred (1922) "Implications of Recent Research for the Structural Approach to Oligopoly," *Antitrust Law Journal* 41.

Source: Competition and the Market Process: Some Doctrinal Milestones, in J. Krafft (ed.) (1999) *Le processus de concurrence*, Editions ECONOMICA.

12

THE DRIVING FORCE OF THE MARKET

The idea of "competition" in contemporary economic theory and in the Austrian theory of the market process

The crucial role played by the notion of dynamic competition in Austrian economics is by now well known. It is widely appreciated that perhaps the critical respect in which the modern Austrian paradigm differs from the mainstream approach consists in the Austrian rejection of the centrality in the latter of the perfectly competitive model, and its replacement by the idea of the entrepreneurial-competitive market process. In this process the essential element is the steadily expanding field of mutual awareness on the part of potential market participants. Whereas the perfectly competitive model expresses the equilibrium pattern of decisions expressing already attained, complete mutual knowledge, the competitive market process expresses the course of mutual discovery through which an equilibrium may possibly be approached.[1]

Although this fundamental difference has been articulated by the Austrians now for several decades,[2] there has been disappointingly little impact upon mainstream contemporary theory. Precisely during a period in which mainstream theorists have come to recognize the limitations of their models in explaining the equilibrating process,[3] and have come to appreciate the importance of changing knowledge in determining market outcomes,[4] the textbook paramountcy of the perfectly competitive model appears to be as solidly ensconced as ever. Despite the "uprising" of contestable market theory,[5] the perfectly competitive model appears not to have been dislodged. More to the point, perhaps, there is little in this uprising itself which reflects the insights of the theory of the dynamic competitive process.

I shall not attempt yet another Austrian assault on mainstream perfect competition orthodoxy. Instead I shall briefly review the principal insights embodied in the Austrian approach to understanding competition, in order to place emphasis upon certain insufficiently noticed features of this approach. Beyond these points of emphasis (and an attempt to illustrate the significance of this emphasis by reference to certain recent disagreements among Austrians), there will be very little new here.

The point upon which I wish to place emphasis can be stated simply: economists contrast monopolistic markets with competitive markets. But while this contrast is appropriate within the equilibrium understanding of the meaning of competition, this is not the case for a theory concentrating on the competitive market process. In the context of the theory of market process, competition should be recognized as universal—even for the market process which operates to bring about monopoly prices. To speak of the competitive market process is in fact to engage in periphrasis. There *is* no market process other than the competitive one. Competitive activity is the activity which constitutes the market process. So it is misleading to inquire, for example, into the conditions required to render the market process competitive. To understand the dynamic motion of competition is at the same time to grasp the nature of the market process—with or without monopoly. Although this insight is certainly not new,[6] it appears not to have been sufficiently emphasized. I will suggest in this chapter that this insight offers a useful vantage point from which to appraise certain issues debated in modern Austrian literature.

THE MODEL OF PERFECT COMPETITION

The equilibrium character of the perfectly competitive market model is now widely understood. The model presumes satisfaction of a series of conditions which together assure a pattern of decisions by market participants insulated from the possibility of disappointment or regret. No decision to buy or to sell can fail to be accepted in this model. Nor can hindsight ever reveal to any buyer or seller that a more attractive market opportunity has been missed. Each potential buyer (seller) correctly anticipates the lowest (highest) price available in the market, and, moreover, correctly expects to be able to buy (sell) as much as he wishes to buy (sell) at this price. The price which all market participants correctly anticipate is that price which, when indeed anticipated by all, inspires the decisions to buy and sell which dovetail completely. It is not merely that the buying and selling decisions so made do indeed mesh perfectly; it is, in addition to such "pre-reconciliation of plans,"[7] that the sets of expectations underlying and inspiring each of these plans have somehow come to correctly and mutually anticipate what each of the other plans will in fact bring about. In fact, the perfection of knowledge underlying the model is, ultimately, more than simply the correct anticipation by each participant of the actions of others; it involves, in the final analysis, the correct and self-fulfilling anticipation by each of the (correct and self-fulfilling) anticipations by each of the others, of the (correct and self-fulfilling) anticipations, *et cetera*, *et cetera*, *ad infinitum*.

To put the matter concisely, the perfectly competitive model portrays (as does each and every equilibrium model of a market) a pattern of mutual anticipations and executed decisions which, if somehow attained, would lead no participant to wish that he had acted differently. It was this equilibrium character of the model to which Hayek was referring when, over forty years ago, he criticized it as blandly assuming that "situation to exist which a true explanation ought to account for as the effect of the competitive process."[8] *If* such a perfectly competitive situation in fact exists, Hayek was exclaiming, the scientific challenge is surely to account for the chain of events which has led to the quite remarkable fulfillment of the extraordinarily demanding set of relevant conditions. Of course no such account can be expected from the model itself.

Unless one adopts a methodology in which the truthfulness of the assumptions of models is of no concern, all this must render the model of perfect competition far less useful than the standard microeconomics textbooks appear to believe. The model cannot be used to "explain" market prices; the model presumes that everyone has, somehow, correctly and self-fulfillingly guessed what the market price is going to be. The circumstance that (quite apart from the assumed correctness of the anticipated price) the model treats each market participant as a price-taker further underscores the uselessness of the model as an explanation for the manner in which prices are adjusted. No one in the model ever does change his price bids or offers.

These limitations of the model have not altogether escaped mainstream acknowledgment. One recent writer on the perfectly competitive model pointed out that "the competitive model is inherently unable to contemplate economic activity out of equilibrium."[9] An entire issue of the *Journal of Economic Theory* was devoted, several years ago, to exploring the rationale for the perfectly competitive model.[10] Yet the centrality of the model in mainstream microeconomics seems to continue virtually unchallenged. Even more disturbing, perhaps, is the circumstance that, where attention is paid to the need for a theory of the equilibrating process, and even where it is recognized that such a theory must involve systematic processes of knowledge and expectations modification, it is somehow not perceived that the notion of dynamic competition is precisely the analytical device needed for the required theoretical task.

COMPETITION AS AN ENTREPRENEURIAL/ DISCOVERY PROCEDURE

The emphasis by Austrians in recent decades upon dynamic competition has been part of their comprehensive attack on the dominance, in modern economics, of equilibrium analysis. Following Ludwig von Mises in his conception of the market as a dynamic entrepreneurial *process*, rather than as an array of mutually sustaining optimal exchange decisions, Austrians have drawn the attention of economists back to an earlier classical notion of competition as a rivalrous process.[11] This notion, so congenial to the experience of the businessman, underscores competition not in the sense of individual powerlessness in the face of the presence of competitors, but in the sense of a procedure inspired by the incentive of outstripping one's competitors in order to achieve market success. As Austrians came to appreciate, the essence of this rivalrous process lies in the pressure it applies, and the incentives it offers, to competing market participants to recognize the opportunities created by earlier decisions (which failed to offer the best possible conditions to other market participants), and the disappointments to be avoided in repeating earlier decisions (which erroneously insisted on unattainable exchange terms). To put it concisely, Austrians came to understand competition as process of discovery. Both over-optimism and undue pessimism, as expressed in earlier rejected bids and offers and in earlier regrets (at attained, but less than optimal, exchange transactions) may come to be replaced in this process by more realistic assessments of market opportunities.

In other words, the changing patterns of bids and offers made in the course of the market process reflect, in the perspective of this Austrian approach, the lessons learned, rightly or wrongly, during that process. If the course of this competitive market process turns out to be equilibrating, this is seen, from this dynamic perspective, as the result of the systematic improvement in mutual knowledge (among market participants) generated by the competitive pressures. The possibility of systematic equilibrating tendencies is underscored by recognition of the entrepreneurial character of the competitive process.

Initial errors by market participants generate a disequilibrium pattern of market bids and offers. Some bids and offers are rejected as hopelessly unattractive. Prospective buyers may have been prepared to offer better terms, but had erroneously overestimated the eagerness of the potential sellers. And so on. Market experience may teach more realistic estimates in this regard. Again, bids and offers may be accepted, but may generate regret as market experience demonstrates that even more advantageous market opportunities might have been grasped. The changes in bids and offers stimulated by these market experiences represent entrepreneurial discovery of the true dimensions of market opportunities. Without deliberate search (by prospective buyers and sellers) for the best terms consistent with the attitudes of other market participants, decision makers come to learn how to avoid disappointment and elude regret. Their alertness to earlier disappointments and to regrettably overlooked opportunities teaches them, during an equilibrating process, to adopt more accurate attitudes in anticipating the reactions of others.

The net result is that, to the extent that entrepreneurial alertness indeed induces steadily more realistic estimates of the attitudes of others, the course of market transactions becomes steadily closer to a pattern avoiding both disappointments and regrets. The competitive-entrepreneurial process then becomes an equilibrating process leading, possibly, close to that very state of affairs assumed from the very beginning by the modelists of perfect competition. To the extent that economic history ever does display market conditions roughly consistent with the perfectly competitive model, this can then be accounted for by reference to the achievements of the dynamic process of competition. To the extent that economic history (as it invariably does) displays features which are thoroughly inconsistent with the perfectly competitive model, this may be accounted for by understanding how the dynamic process of competition has, as yet, not fully run its equilibrating course. Features of real world markets will typically reflect the errors which it is the function of the competitive process to identify and correct.

What drives this competitive process is the alertness of market participants to the profit possibilities created by past errors, and, to the unfortunate frustrations that would be the result of repeating past errors. This entrepreneurial process is competitive in the sense that it relies upon the freedom of alert entrepreneurs to enter markets and exploit these possibilities. It is the possibility of such entry which not only provides an incentive for alert potential entrants, but also, through acting as a threat, inspires parallel alertness on the part of incumbent market participants, spurring them to anticipate potential entrants through their own entrepreneurial decisions. Constantly looking over their shoulders, market participants are inspired alertly to notice and implement opportunities for offering superior options to the market. The competitive process is driven by the entrepreneurial element in each human being, by the propensity to notice the implications of earlier errors (which propensity is the essence of entrepreneurship). The competitive process itself consists of the systematic series of revised decisions on the part of market participants, generated by their entrepreneurial discoveries. I am now in a position to spell out more fully the point in this approach to competition which I wish to emphasize in this chapter.

COMPETITION AND MONOPOLY

It is ordinarily assumed that competition and monopoly are at opposite poles of a single continuum. Along this spectrum, being "more monopolistic" means being correspondingly "less competitive." At the one extreme one has the perfectly competitive market, at the other a market characterized by pure monopoly. (Theories of imperfect or monopolistic competition were designed to avoid confining economic theory strictly to these polar cases.) Each type of market is, in this perspective, characterized by a series of defining criteria. The criteria defining the polar cases are mutually exclusive; those governing intermediate cases partly overlap with those defining one or both of the polar models.

My claim here is that this way of looking at competition and monopoly might be appropriate for the classification of alternative static equilibrium models. To the extent, for example, that the demand curve confronting a firm is less than perfectly elastic, this may be interpreted as reflecting a degree of "market power" possessed by the firm. With perfect competition defined in terms of total absence of such power, a degree of power expressed in a downward-sloping demand curve may plausibly come to be labelled a degree of monopoly. This was indeed the approach expressed in Abba Lerner's classic attempt to conceive of a measure of monopoly power.[12]

But, I wish to point out, for an approach which puts the emphasis on competition as a dynamic process, the idea of competition and monopoly being at opposite poles of a single spectrum is confused and almost incoherent. For this approach, competition is the essential defining characteristic of the market process itself. No matter what the institutional contours of the market may be, no matter what the economic power possessed by market participants may be, the market process (if such a process does exist and occur) is itself necessarily competitive. It is a process during which entrepreneurial, competitive-minded market participants, whether incumbent participants or merely potential participants, discover the true shape of market possibilities and constraints. The only situation in which competition can be said to be absent is one in which markets do not operate. Such a situation presumes, as in the centrally planned economy, the existence of institutional prohibitions on market exchanges. In any *market* situation, however, no matter what the degree of monopoly may be (and regardless of how monopoly is to be defined), the market process itself must be a competitive one. There simply is no market process other than that consisting of competitively inspired discoveries of opportunities for gain through exchange.

If, for example, a firm is the monopolist in an industry (whether as the result of unique control over some essential input or as the result of governmental grant of exclusive privilege), the manner in which the monopolist's price and quantity of sales is determined in the market is one that emerges from the competitive interplay of the decisions of potential buyers (of the monopolized commodity) as well as of those of participants in related markets. There is no other procedure governing the sequence of prices and quantities as determined in a world of open-ended uncertainty. Textbooks present, of course, the monopolized market as one in which the monopolist is confronted by a given and known demand curve, from which he at once selects his profit-maximizing price–quantity combination. But in fact no monopolist knows his demand curve in advance. It is the market process that reveals what the contours of the market possibilities really are, so that for the monopolized market it is the competitive process that tends to ensure that the monopoly equilibrium is in fact approached.

It is reasonable to try to formulate the conditions defining a monopolized market, but it is almost incoherent to ask for the conditions that must be satisfied in order for a market process to be described as being competitive. A market process is competitive by the very nature of being a market process. Sometimes I try to characterize the competitive nature of the market process by drawing attention to "freedom of entry" (or its correlate, "absence of privilege"), but it would be confusing to state that a market process is competitive according to the extent to which it permits free entry. A market process consists of the decisions of those who enter or who might enter. At most one can say that the extent to which a social process can be described as a market process depends on the extent to which freedom of entry to buy and sell are permitted. Freedom of entry is indeed a defining characteristic of competition, but only because the market process is, by definition, a competitive one.

Admittedly all this does create a certain difficulty for economic terminology. A market may be monopolized or it may not be monopolized. How am I to describe a market in which exclusive monopolistic privilege is absent? Surely the adjective "competitive" has a reasonable claim, in economic history and in the history of economic theory, to be the label describing the absence of exclusive privilege? The terminological difficulty is a real one, and is, probably, responsible in part for the extraordinary confusion which has surrounded the concepts of monopoly and competition during the twentieth century. It is, therefore, useful to examine one recent example of the problem, an example taken from an internal disagreement within Austrian economics.

THE MISESIAN THEORY OF MONOPOLY

Standard theory defines competition in terms of the degree of elasticity of demand facing the firm. In the case of perfect competition this elasticity is infinite; there are so many firms in the industry, and knowledge is so perfect, that no one of them can sell anything above the going market price. The polar opposite case is then that of a single firm selling in a well-defined market. With outside entry somehow absent, this monopolist then confronts the market demand curve, and chooses his profit-maximizing position accordingly. Clearly, if this monopoly position does indeed yield pure profit, the question arises as to why outside entry is indeed absent. Why don't others enter in an attempt to grasp some of this profit? It was this insight which inspired Mises to recognize that, within the market system itself, the only possible source for monopoly was sole ownership of some scarce essential input. (Of course Mises made it clear that government intervention in a market system can—and has historically very frequently indeed—generated monopolized markets.) If government forbids others to compete with a licensed producer, this certainly places him in a monopoly position, able to earn a supernormal return (which competition will be unable to "compete away").

Without government blocking of competitive entry, the number of firms in an industry, no matter how small, does not insulate them from the cold winds of potential competition; they are subject to the threat of the process of competitive entry. With the possibility, however, of a single owner of a scarce essential resource, Mises argued, we must recognize the possibility that this owner may be able to obtain greater revenue out of his resource by withholding part of it from the market. Whether he uses the resource in production himself or whether he sells it to other producers, his revenues may turn out to be greater as a result of his refusing to sell all that he, in his capacity as resource owner, might be prepared to sell were he to be only one of a number of such resource owners. Mises did not consider this possibility to be of much practical importance. Certainly he was convinced that most situations usually described as monopolistic are either not monopolistic at all or are likely to be the result of government obstacles against entry, rather than being the result of unique resource ownership. Yet, from the theoretical perspective, the possibility of a true monopoly occurring within a market is an interesting one and Mises pursued it for the sake of theoretical completeness.

With exclusive resource ownership, the extra monopoly revenue (that results from withholding some of the available supply from the market) is clearly not in the nature of any pure entrepreneurial profit. Rather it is an extra rent obtainable from the scarce resource as a result of the economic power created out of the peculiar pattern of ownership coupled with the absence of close substitute resources:

> Entrepreneurial profit has nothing to do with monopoly. If an entrepreneur is in a position to sell at monopoly prices, he owes this advantage to his monopoly with regard to a monopolized factor *m*. He earns the specific monopoly gain from his ownership of *m*, not from his specific entrepreneurial activities.[13]

There is, therefore, no problem of explaining why entrepreneurial entry does not compete away this surplus revenue; this surplus revenue is not an entrepreneurial profit, it can be obtained only by virtue of ownership of the resource.

Just as in the case of other markets, price in the monopolized market emerges through the rough and tumble of competing entrants. Of course, with exclusive resource ownership the entrants are (apart from the competing potential buyers) the owners of (possibly distant) substitute resources, or producers of competing products. It is the process of such competition that guides the monopoly resource owner to his best obtainable position. Mises points out that the "monopolist does not know the shape of the curve of demand" for his resource.[14] Clearly Mises is relying on the competitive market process to guide the monopolist to the profit-maximizing position obtainable by withholding some of the resource.

MISES: A NEOCLASSICAL?

I shall not deal comprehensively with the various criticisms from within Austrian economics which the Misesian theory has drawn.[15] I shall concern myself here only with one line of criticism which I believe can be traced to the terminological ambiguities cited earlier.

Several years ago, Gerald O'Driscoll argued that the theory of monopoly presented by Mises is "a variant of the neoclassical theory."[16] By the neoclassical theory of monopoly, O'Driscoll means the approach which (a) ignores the case of monopolies created by the state, and (b) ignores, in effect, the problem of why monopoly profits do not attract competitive entry (or, at any rate, provide untenable solutions to this problem). "[Neoclassical] theory lacks any defensible, coherent answer to the entry question. Monopoly is postulated without being explained."[17] O'Driscoll contrasts the neoclassical theory of monopoly with the "property-rights" approach. In the property-rights approach, entry will indeed occur:

> A profitable open-market monopoly is not a stable situation and hence is not one to concern either the economist or the policymaker. The property-rights tradition is to concentrate on the many varied ways in which governments create, foster, and maintain monopoly.[18]

Although O'Driscoll exonerates Mises from the charge of ignoring the cases of state-created monopoly,[19] he charges him with having a neoclassical monopoly theory in two senses. First, resource monopoly is one source of neoclassical monopoly. Second, Mises's theory "is no more successful at answering the entry question than is neoclassical theory."[20] In what follows I shall not deal directly with the unimportant issue of the neoclassical label which O'Driscoll has polemically pinned on to the Misesian theory. Instead I will attempt to address the substance of O'Driscoll's quite astonishing charge that Mises has ignored the problem of competitive entry.[21]

O'Driscoll's charge is astonishing primarily because in any reading of Mises's vehement disagreements with the standard theories of perfect competition, pure monopoly, and monopolistic competition, the absolutely central role must surely be assigned to his insistence on the driving force of competitive entry (actual and potential) into profitable markets. It was precisely this Misesian insistence on the power of dynamic competitive entry that has inspired the revival of interest, within contemporary Austrian economics, in the market as a process, rather than as an equilibrium configuration. It was undoubtedly precisely because of this concern with competitive entry that Mises offered his drastic idea (as it must be judged by the standards of neoclassical equilibrium theory) of restricting the notion of monopoly (and its "welfare" consequences) to the level of resource ownership.

And this brings us to a second sense in which O'Driscoll's charge against Mises (that he ignored the problem of competitive entry) appears astonishing. Mises avoided the entry problem entirely by deliberately restricting the notion of monopoly, in its primary sense, to the resource owner. The entrepreneur-producer is never a monopolist *qua* entrepreneur. If he is a monopolist it is only due to the circumstance that earlier (possibly entrepreneurial) transactions may have made him, at a given point in time, the sole owner of a scarce essential resource. (In this case he is a monopolist *qua* resource owner, *not qua* entrepreneur.) To ask why competitive entry does not compete away a monopoly resource owner's monopoly gain, is, one suspects, to misunderstand that gain as a sub-species of pure entrepreneurial profit.

O'Driscoll states the central theoretical issue to be solved by a monopoly theory as being that of explaining why, if "monopoly yields a net revenue or surplus . . . does entry of new firms not occur? The profitability of monopoly should ensure its own demise."[22] The answer which Mises's theory of resource monopoly offers to the question of why competition does not wipe out the monopolist's special gain (attributable to his monopoly position) is that this special gain is, "admittedly" (if that is the appropriate adverb) by hypothesis, a result of his exclusive ownership of this (apparently essential) resource.[23] One presumes that O'Driscoll would argue that, if we accepted this interpretation of Mises, this will mean that (as O'Driscoll remarks on Ricardo) Mises has then "trivialized the central question" which O'Driscoll believes must be dealt with by any monopoly theory. Our point here is that for Mises (perhaps even more than for the writers whom O'Driscoll labels the "property-rights theorists"), the entry problem in fact erases the monopoly case completely from the agenda of the theorist insofar as concerns the entrepreneur. "A profitable open-market monopoly," at the entrepreneurial level, "is not a stable situation and hence is not one to concern either the economist or the policy-maker."[24] Even more to the point, for our purposes, a "profitable open-market monopoly" at the entrepreneurial level is simply, for Mises, an unfortunate misnomer. When a single entrepreneur in an open market engages in a profitable venture he has, in Misesian terminology, engaged in it competitively, not monopolistically. Others could have entered into this line of activity. Their not having done so, so far from rendering the profit-making entrepreneur a monopolist, simply means that they have been out-competed by him. His activity is part of the entrepreneurial competitive process.

The only sense in which the idea of a monopoly retains any meaning for Mises is in the context of resource ownership. As explained in the preceding section, the monopoly gain that may, under appropriate conditions, be made by the monopoly resource owner, has nothing to do with entrepreneurial gain. It is a gain, obtainable by virtue of ownership of his resource, which would not have been forthcoming were the resource supply to be owned by more than one independent owner. There simply is no ignored "entry problem" that needs to be addressed by the Misesian theory of monopoly.

THE SOURCE OF THE MISUNDERSTANDING

That so perceptive and so Austrian an economist as O'Driscoll came to misunderstand Mises in this regard seems to illustrate the terminological difficulties and confusions referred to earlier. It seems evident that O'Driscoll, recognizing the Austrian emphasis on the competitive process, has thought of monopoly as a case to be contrasted with that process. It is in this context that O'Driscoll raises the entry problem. "No one would seek a monopoly position . . . unless he expected to earn returns in excess of revenues forgone. Why then do others not follow suit or imitate the first rent seeker, thus breaking down the monopoly and competing away that monopoly rent?"[25] Clearly O'Driscoll is thinking of an entrepreneur who has successfully sought a monopoly position. But this was not Mises's approach at all. He thought of a monopoly position somehow already existing (as a result of historical patterns of resource ownership, or whatever).[26]

In regard to the competitive-entrepreneurial process itself, it is utterly vain to search for any monopoly case. There can be none, such as we have seen, not merely because any monopoly gains, so won in an open market must tend to be competed away, but also because in an open market *every* action is taken competitively (i.e., with full awareness of the need to anticipate the actions of others, actual or potential competitors). And here we have a source of misunderstanding. Mises contrasted the special case of "monopoly price" with the more general case of "competitive price."[27] This use of terminology is readily understandable but may, I fear, easily lead to a degree of confusion. It might be understood that, by using the contrasting terms, "competitive price" and "monopoly price," Mises was implying that monopoly is the opposite of competition in the sense of the competitive entrepreneurial process. Perhaps, as we have seen, O'Driscoll was led so to assume. But we have seen how this would be incorrect. The Austrian process of entrepreneurial competition has no contrast within the market. So long as there is a market at all, or to any degree to which a market is able to proceed, it proceeds through the sequence of transactions generated by dynamic competition.

Monopoly, for Mises, has been reduced to a particular, not-very-important case, of a resource-owner who, by virtue of history and market conditions, happens to be the sole owner of a scarce essential ingredient in the production of a good. Market outcomes in this context are, as always, determined through the course of the competitive market process. Monopoly resource ownership does not compromise the competitive character of the market process; it merely diverts it from the particular pattern which that process might have taken in the absence of monopoly resource ownership. Had this resource not been exclusively owned, the driving forces of competition among entrepreneurs seeking to buy the resource from competing sellers of the resource, would have tended to make it desirable for resource owners to sell all of their resource supplies (beyond what they might retain for their own consumer purposes or for speculation). With all supplies of the scarce essential resource concentrated in the hands of one owner, the forces of market competition may not tend to induce him to sell all of his supply; they may teach him how to enhance his sales revenue from the resource by throwing some of it into the sea.

Such a possibility, Mises argued, would, if ever realized, pit the interests of the consuming public against those of the exclusive resource owner. It was this theoretical possibility that Mises recognized (without considering it to be of much practical significance).

COMPETITION AS THE FUNDAMENTAL PRINCIPLE IN MARKET THEORY

In his doctoral dissertation, Frank Machovec documented the thesis that the dynamic notion of competition pervaded the bulk of economics in the neoclassical period up until the 1920s.[28] It was only during the twenties and thirties that equilibrium thinking, and thus the static model of perfect competition, assumed its current dominance in mainstream economic thought. It was presumably this prevalence of the dynamic notion of competition which led Mises into believing, as late as 1932, that the various schools of twentieth-century economic thought shared a common basic understanding of the workings of the market economy.[29]

Whatever the degree of shared understanding may have been, and whatever the diverse directions toward which these schools were respectively pointing,[30] the prevalence of the dynamic notion of competition at this time may lend support to a thesis I recently suggested. Our emphasis here has been upon the universality in market processes in all contexts, of the dynamically competitive element. Recently I suggested that it is the character of the discoveries which make up this dynamically competitive process to which the central economist's assumption of universal self-interest in fact pertains.[31] The self-interest assumption in economics, this suggestion argues, does not so much identify a particular pattern of choices among given available options, as it illuminates the discovery process through which market participants identify the options available to them. The self-interest assumption sees market participants as purposeful human beings alert to changing conditions and to the new opportunities these may create. The alertness which inspires the discoveries made by market participants in the course of the market process, is an alertness fueled, not necessarily by selfish or materialistic goals, but by concern to further one's goals, whatever these may be. What is being suggested, then, is that the critical place filled by the self-interest assumption is not in the theory of the consumer decision, or the theory of the producer's decision, but in the entrepreneurial decision. Because all market participants are, to some degree, entrepreneurial, the self-interest assumption has universal relevance. From this perspective it turns out that the competitive character of market processes, and the self-interested character of market behavior, are simply two sides of the same coin.

Something of this seems to have been present in the thinking on competition of major economists at the turn of the century. "Broadly defined," Herbert J. Davenport observed, "economic competition is a struggle for maximum economic rewards (minimum sacrifice)."[32] The rivalrous character of dynamic competition and the self-interested purposefulness of individual market behavior "fold into" each other. The ubiquity in markets of self-interest, and the universality in markets of dynamic competition turn out to be one and the same.

NOTES

1. Reekie (1984, pp. 37ff.); O'Driscoll and Rizzo (1985, ch. 6); Littlechild (1981); Shand (1984, pp. 65–71).
2. See especially Mises (1966, chs XV, XVI); Hayek (1948, 1978); Kirzner (1973).
3. See, for example, Fisher (1983).
4. See, for example, Frydmann (1982).
5. See Baumol (1982).
6. See, for example, Kirzner (1973, pp. 19ff.).
7. See Shackle (1972, pp. 54, 124, 137ff.).
8. Hayek (1948, p. 94).
9. Silvestre (1986, p. 197). Earlier references include Arrow (1959); Richardson (1960); Clark (1961).
10. 22(2) (April 1980).
11. On this see McNulty (1967).
12. Lerner (1934).
13. Mises (1966, p. 360).
14. Ibid., p. 378.
15. See, for example, Armentano (1978).
16. O'Driscoll (1982, p. 190). O'Driscoll's sentence reads: "Some [modern Austrians], such as Ludwig von Mises and Israel Kirzner, present a variant of the neoclassical theory." Certain of O'Driscoll's criticisms (pp. 205–6) do relate especially to this writer's presentation of the Misesian theory (in *Competition and Entrepreneurship*). However, the remarks in the text relate strictly to the sense in which O'Driscoll finds Mises's own theory to be neoclassical. Accordingly no further references will be made to O'Driscoll's specific criticisms of this writer's presentation.
17. Ibid., p. 199.
18. Ibid.
19. Ibid., p. 205.
20. Ibid.
21. O'Driscoll's charge is all the more surprising in that he uses, as the epigraph introducing his paper, a quotation from Mises explicitly empha-

sizing that in dealing with cases of monopoly price "one must first of all raise the question of what obstacles restrain people from challenging the monopolist" (ibid., p. 189).

22. Ibid.
23. It must certainly be recognized that, in the Misesian theory of resource monopoly, this monopoly is, to use O'Driscoll's language, "postulated without being explained" (ibid., p. 199). The theory deals with the implications of a particular possible situation. That is all.
24. Ibid.
25. Ibid.
26. For a discussion of the forces that might lead entrepreneurs to attempt to win the position of a Misesian resource monopolist, see Kirzner (1973, pp. 199ff.).
27. See, for example, Mises (1966, p. 357).
28. Machovec (1986).
29. Mises (1960, p. 214).
30. See Kirzner (1989, pp. 2ff.).
31. Kirzner (1990).
32. Davenport (1905, p. 201).

REFERENCES

Armentano, Dominick T. (1978) "A Critique of Neoclassical and Austrian Monopoly Theory," in Louis M. Spadaro (ed.) *New Directions in Austrian Economics*, Kansas City: Sheed, Andrews and McMeel.

Arrow, Kenneth (1959) "Toward a Theory of Price Adjustment," in Abramowitz *et al.* (eds) *The Allocation of Economic Resources*, Stanford, CA: Stanford University Press.

Baumol, William J. (1982) "Contestable Markets: An Uprising in the Theory of Industry Structure," *American Economic Review* March.

Clark, J.M. (1961) *Competition as a Dynamic Process*, Washington, D.C.: Brookings Institution.

Davenport, Herbert J. (1905) *Outlines of Economic Theory*, New York: Macmillan.

Fisher, Franklin M. (1983) *Disequilibrium Foundations of Equilibrium Economics*, Cambridge: Cambridge University Press.

Frydman, Roman (1982) "Towards an Understanding of Market Processes: Individual Expectations, Learning and Convergence to Rational Expectations Equilibrium," *American Economic Review* 72.

Hayek, Friedrich von (1948) "The Meaning of Competition," in *Individualism and Economic Order*, Chicago: University of Chicago Press.

—— (1978) "Competition as a Discovery Procedure," in *New Studies in Philosophy, Politics, Economics and the History of Ideas*, Chicago: University of Chicago Press.

Kirzner, Israel M. (1973) *Competition and Entrepreneurship*, Chicago: University of Chicago Press.

—— (1989) "The Economic Calculation Debate: Lessons for Austrians," *The Review of Austrian Economics* 2.

—— (1990) "Self-Interest and the New Bashing of Economics: A Fresh Opportunity in the Perennial Debate?" *Critical Review* 4(1–2).

Lerner, Abba P. (1934) "The Concept of Monopoly and the Measurement of Monopoly Power," *Review of Economic Studies*, June.

Littlechild, Stephen C. (1981) "Misleading Calculation of the Social Costs of Monopoly Power," *Economic Journal*.

Machovec, Frank (1986) "The Destruction of Competition Theory: The Perfectly Competitive Model and Beyond," unpublished doctoral dissertation, New York University.

McNulty, P.J. (1967) "A Note on the History of Perfect Competition," *Journal of Political Economy* 75.

Mises, Ludwig von (1960) *Epistemological Problems of Economics* (first published 1933, Princeton, NJ: Van Nostrand.

—— (1966) *Human Action*, 3rd rev. edn, Chicago: Henry Regnery.

O'Driscoll, Gerald P., Jr. (1982) "Monopoly in Theory and Practice," in Israel M. Kirzner (ed.) *Method, Process, and Austrian Economics, Essays in Honor of Ludwig von Mises*, Lexington, MA: D.C. Heath.

O'Driscoll, Gerald P., Jr. and Rizzo, Mario J. (1985) *The Economics of Time and Ignorance*, Oxford: Basil Blackwell.

Reekie, W. Duncan (1984) *Markets, Entrepreneurs and Liberty: An Austrian View of Capitalism*, New York: St. Martin's Press.

Richardson, G.B. (1960) *Information and Investment*, London: Oxford University Press.

Shackle, George L.S. (1972) *Epistemics and Economics: A Critique of Economic Doctrines*, Cambridge: Cambridge University Press.

Shand, Alexander H. (1984) *The Capitalist Alternative: An Introduction to Neo-Austrian Economics*, New York: New York University Press.

Silvestre, Joachim (1986) "The Elements of Fixprice Microeconomics," in Larry Samuelson (ed.) *Microeconomic Theory*, Boston: Kluwer-Nijhoff.

Source: The Driving Force of the Market: The Idea of "Competition" in Contemporary Economic Theory and in the Austrian Theory of the Market Process, in R. Ebeling (ed.) (1997) *Austrian Economics; Perspectives on the Past and Prospects for the Future*, Hillsdale College Press.

13

CREATIVITY AND/OR ALERTNESS

A reconsideration of the Schumpeterian entrepreneur

The purpose of this chapter is to reconsider the difference between Schumpeter's portrayal of the entrepreneurial role, and my own, earlier (1969, 1973) portrayal of that same role.[1] In 1969 and in 1973, in the course of developing, my own understanding of the entrepreneurial character of the competitive, equilibrative market process, I emphasized these differences as I then saw them. Schumpeter's entrepreneur, I pointed out, was essentially disruptive, destroying the preexisting state of equilibrium. My entrepreneur, on the other hand, was responsible for the tendency through which initial conditions of disequilibrium come systematically to be displaced by equilibrative market competition. The outcome of the present reconsideration will be, not a thoroughgoing "reconciliation" of these two conceptions of the entrepreneurial role—I still believe that these views are, at least in part, contrasting ones—but a clearer understanding of how each of these apparently conflicting views can be seen as plausible and realistic; and how each can usefully advance economic understanding (of respectively different aspects of the capitalist economy).

The central theme of this reconsideration can be expressed in the following four propositions:

1. For understanding the psychological profile typical of the real-world entrepreneur as we know him, Schumpeter's portrayal is valid and accurate.
2. For understanding the "creative destruction" which Schumpeter sees as the central and distinguishing feature of the capitalist system, Schumpeter's portrayal is valid and essential; to the extent that policy objectives include the stimulation of such creative destruction, careful attention will indeed have to be

paid to that Schumpeterian psychological profile to which we have referred.

3. For understanding the equilibrative tendency of markets in general, my own view of the entrepreneur as alert to opportunities (created by, or able to be created by, independently-initiated changes), is valid and significant.
4. To see the entrepreneurial role of a real-world entrepreneur as essentially that of being "merely" alert to opportunities created (or able to be created) by independently-initiated changes, is not *necessarily* inconsistent with a Schumpeterian perspective on the activity of that same entrepreneur (which sees him as aggressively and actively initiating change).

THE ENTREPRENEUR AS I SAW HIM IN 1973

My 1973 book, *Competition and Entrepreneurship* sought to offer an Austrian (i.e., a Misesian) perspective on markets which would highlight the dynamically competitive character of the market process. In that process markets tend continually (in the face of equally continual exogenous changes in the relevant independent variables) towards equilibrium, as the consequence of continually-stimulated entrepreneurial discoveries. These discoveries are discoveries of earlier errors made in the course of market exchanges. As a result of those earlier errors, market participants have been led (i) over-optimistically to insist on receiving prices that are "too high" (to enable them to sell all that they would like to sell at those prices) [or on paying prices that are "too low" (to enable them to buy all that they would like to buy at those prices)]; or (ii) over-pessimistically to enter into transactions that turn out to be less than optimal in the light of the true market conditions as they in fact reveal themselves (e.g., a buyer discovers that he has paid a price higher than that being charged elsewhere in the market; a seller discovers that he has accepted a price lower than that which has been paid elsewhere in the market). The first of these latter two consequences of error (i.e., of errors of over-optimism) leads inevitably to frustrated plans: would-be buyers return home without having bought goods, would-be sellers return home with their unsold goods (in spite of the fulfillment of the conditions needed for mutually gainful exchange to be feasible among potential buyers and sellers). The second of the afore-mentioned two consequences (arising out of over-pessimism) expresses itself as the phenomenon of unexploited pure profit opportunities (the same good is being sold at different prices in different parts of the same market). The entrepreneurial role is that of alertly noticing ("discovering") where these errors have occurred, and of moving to take advantage of such discoveries, and thus of nudging the market systematically in the direction of greater mutual awareness among market participants. (Since equilibrium is the state in which all market participants are, in effect, fully and correctly aware of what all others are doing, the entrepreneurial discovery process is one whose tendency is systematically equilibrative.)

This perspective on the entrepreneurial role and of its equilibrative character was articulated, in my 1973 book, primarily in the simplest of contexts, i.e., in markets for single commodities, within a single time period. For the purposes of that work I believed it important deliberately to abstract, for the most part, from the complications introduced by consideration of production, and of the passage of time. Readers of that work may be excused for concluding that phenomena associated with innovative production and with the uncertainty that accompanies time-consuming processes of production (and certainly time-consuming innovative processes of production) are basically irrelevant for the entrepreneurial role as portrayed in that work.

The entrepreneur who played the equilibrative role for me in 1973, fulfilled his essential function not by introducing new products, or technologically more efficient methods of production (in fact he was not a producer at all)—but simply by noticing earlier errors (manifested, most importantly, by the availability of pure profit opportunities existing in the multiple-price-for-the-same-good situation generated by those earlier errors). The emphasis was thus on the entrepreneur as the person who alertly (but "passively") simply *noticed* the opportunities generated by the earlier errors, which errors were seen as arising from unanticipated independently-caused, changes in underlying market circumstances.

Indeed, in that 1973 work (based on insights first developed in a 1969 paper) I was careful to distinguish sharply between the entrepreneurial role as I saw it, and that role as portrayed by Schumpeter. Let us turn to see how I presented that distinction.

THE SCHUMPETERIAN ENTREPRENEUR—AS I SAW HIM IN 1973

It was important for me in 1973 to emphasize the differences between Schumpeter's entrepreneur and my own, because a superficial reader of my exposition of the dynamically competitive market process might easily and understandably be misled by the very significant parallels between my exposition of that process and Schumpeter's understanding of the competitive process. Schumpeter had vigorously rejected the orthodox emphasis on the perfectly competitive market.[2] He emphasized the entrepreneurial character of real-world dynamically competitive processes.[3] In these respects my own expositions of the competitive process (expositions based on my understanding of Ludwig von Mises's monumental 1949 work, *Human Action*) overlapped considerably with those of Schumpeter.[4] Yet, as we shall see, my ("Misesian") understanding of the market economy differed significantly from Schumpeter's understanding of capitalism as a "perennial gale" of "creative destruction." In seeking to clarify this difference I found it convenient to draw attention to the different roles played, within these different expositions of the competitive process, respectively, by the entrepreneur.

For Schumpeter "the essence of entrepreneurship is the ability to break away from routine, to destroy existing structures, to move the system away from the even, circular flow of equilibrium. . . . For Schumpeter the entrepreneur is the disruptive, disequilibrating force that dislodges the market from the somnolence of equilibrium."[5] The primary consequence of Schumpeter's entrepreneurship was the long-run economic development of the capitalist system.

> The opening up of new markets, foreign or domestic, and the organizational development from the craft shop and factory to such concerns as U.S. Steel illustrate the same process of industrial mutation . . . that incessantly revolutionizes the economic structure *from within,* incessantly destroying the old one, incessantly creating a new one. This process of Creative Destruction is the essential fact about capitalism.[6]

The Schumpeterian entrepreneur is a *leader* (contrasted with the many "imitators" who follow the innovative lead of the entrepreneurs). All this contrasted, I pointed out, with the way I saw the entrepreneurial role. For me the essential element in that role was its potential of impinging on an initial state of disequilibrium, and, through alertly noticing ("discovering") those errors of which this state consists, moving equilibratively to correct them. I pointed out[7] that Schumpeter's exposition was "likely to generate the utterly mistaken view that the state of equilibrium can establish itself without any social device to deploy and marshall the scattered pieces of information which are the only sources of such a state." (I also drew attention to Hayek's work[8] in regard to the role of mutual ignorance in disequilibrium, and to his critique of Schumpeter in the latter's seeming to fall prey to precisely that "mistaken view" mentioned in the preceding sentence.)

The contrast between the two views was concisely reflected in my following complaint concerning Schumpeter's view of entrepreneurial activity:[9] "Instead of entrepreneurs grasping the opportunities available, responding to and healing maladjustments due to existing ignorance, the entrepreneur is pictured as generating disturbances in a fully adjusted circularly flowing world in which all opportunities were already fully and familiarly exploited." The contrast between Schumpeter's view and my own, which I saw in 1969 and in 1973, came to be variously commented on by several writers during subsequent years. A number of valuable insights emerged from these comments.

CONFLICTING APPRAISALS OF THE "CONTRAST"

One reaction was to treat the contrast which I had perceived between Schumpeter's view and my own, as exaggerated. "Superficially," Hébert and Link[10] declared in 1982, "the Kirznerian entrepreneur appears to be the antithesis of the Schumpeterian entrepreneur, but fundamentally their differences are more apparent than real . . . one vision seems to complement the other."[11] This complementarity consists in the circumstance that while Schumpeter's innovating entrepreneur is responsible for creating disequilibrium "in the first place," it is the "Kirznerian" entrepreneur who "springs into action upon recognizing a disequilibrium situation." One gathers from Hébert and Link that, while the differences between the two views are real, they arise not from two fundamentally inconsistent views of the economic process, but from the necessarily different emphases relevant to the two parts of the same market process, to which these views respectively pertain. (What is not made clear, however, is how a single economic function, the entrepreneurial function, can be simultaneously identified with two contrastingly different sets of characteristics.)

Two other papers have similarly perceptively criticized the sharpness of the contrast drawn between Schumpeter's view and my own. Donald J. Boudreaux[12] argues that *both* Schumpeterian and

Kirznerian entrepreneurs should be seen as equilibrating (since both tend to push the market towards fulfillment of as yet unfulfilled potential). The different views should be seen as complementary: Schumpeter usefully draws attention to dimensions of improvement in product quality (dimensions which Boudreaux believes to be necessarily outside any picture based on my own entrepreneurial discovery process); Kirzner, on the other hand, usefully draws attention to the equilibrative sense in which all social opportunity-grasping, including (by extension) Schumpeterian innovation, can be perceived.

Young Back Choi, after a discussion (rather similar to Boudreaux's) in which the similarities between Schumpeter's entrepreneur and my own are emphasized, reaches the following conclusion: "the concern over whether the entrepreneur is equilibrating or disequilibrating [seems] similar to the debate whether a glass is half-full or half-empty."[13] What Choi means is that the two views are not so much complementary (referring to different segments of the same market process) as in fact *identical* (differing only as a result of "a difference in perspective" reflecting merely "what Schumpeter and Kirzner take as the basis"[14]).

Brian Loasby, like several of these above-cited writers, considers the possibility of complementarity between the two views of the entrepreneurial role, but is led to dismiss it. "Kirzner's entrepreneur profits by assisting cohesion, Schumpeter's by disruption. Each might be regarded as providing opportunities for the other; yet they do not fit together all that well. They are linked to quite different conceptions of profit, and to substantially different conceptions of the working of the economy."[15] Elsewhere he has emphasized the differences as follows: "Whereas Kirzner's entrepreneurs respond to changing data, Schumpeter's cause the data to change."[16]

Stephan Boehm, too, tends to agree with existence of irreconcilable differences between the two views. "Schumpeter's and Kirzner's entrepreneur share a number of characteristics, but they are outweighed by some important dissimilarities."[17]

Affirmation of the contrast which I emphasized in 1973 (between Schumpeter's view of the entrepreneur and my own) does not, however, imply acceptance of my own characterization of the entrepreneurial role. In fact a number of writers generally sympathetic to a Misesian view of the competitive market process, have felt uncomfortable with my emphasis on the entrepreneur as "passively" noticing (and profiting by) independently created changes that have occurred in the data. The Schumpeterian view of the aggressive, active, innovative entrepreneur appears, to these critics, to be too faithful a portrayal of real-world business entrepreneurs to be given up simply in order to achieve the somewhat obscure analytical purposes claimed on behalf of my own entrepreneurial portrait. A number of these critics seem to have been particularly disturbed by what they saw as my deliberate abstraction from uncertainty. Because Mises himself emphasized the place of uncertainty in the context of entrepreneurship, and because the boldness needed to grapple confidently with uncertainty seems more similar to the aggressiveness of Schumpeter's entrepreneur (the success of whose innovations must be inextricably bound up in the uncertainty of an open-ended world) than to the passivity of the Kirznerian entrepreneur—these Misesian critics tended to be critical of my own characterization of the entrepreneur.[18]

ENTREPRENEURSHIP AND UNCERTAINTY

In a 1981 paper[19] I sought to address these criticisms by exploring the role of uncertainty in Misesian entrepreneurship. The relevance of such an exploration to the differences between Schumpeter's entrepreneur and my own can be recognized by noticing that I introduced my exploration with the observation[20] that the character of the market process is, for Mises, "decisively shaped by the leadership, the initiative, and the driving activity displayed and exercised by the entrepreneur." Clearly, I wished to emphasize that the uncertainty which envelops entrepreneurial activity evokes these "Schumpeterian" qualities of "leadership, initiative and driving activity." Although no explicit mention was made, in that 1981 paper, of the contrast which I had earlier emphasized as existing between Schumpeter's entrepreneur and my own, the issues discussed in that paper, concerning the place of uncertainty in entrepreneurship, are profoundly significant for the "reconsideration" in which the present paper is engaged. Because my 1981 paper was concerned with the role of uncertainty, it deliberately extended my earlier discussions of entrepreneurship from the single period (in which uncertainty can be, in one sense, ignored)[21] to the multi-period case (in which scope for uncertainty must be granted). It was this extension which implied, in addition, recognition for imagination and innovativeness:

> [T]he futurity that entrepreneurship must confront introduces the possibility that the entrepreneur may, by his own creative actions, in fact *construct* the future as *he*

> wishes it to be. In the single-period case alertness can at best discover hitherto overlooked current facts. In the multi-period case entrepreneurial alertness must include the entrepreneur's perception of the way in which creative and imaginative action may vitally shape the kind of transactions that will be entered into in future market periods. . . . To be a successful entrepreneur one must now possess those qualities of vision, boldness, determination and creativity.[22]

Some comments upon this paper seem to wish to assert that it may have misleadingly understated the extent to which it acknowledges, in effect, the inadequacies which earlier critics found in my 1973 exposition.[23] They read that (1981) paper as constituting a rather significant modification of my earlier position—a more significant modification than I was apparently prepared to admit. Some further clarification may be helpful. The truth is that (while the extension presented in my 1981 paper did permit explicit attention to the psychological characteristics of Schumpeter's entrepreneur that were absent from my own 1973 entrepreneur) it was not (and is not) my understanding of the extension from single-period to multi-period entrepreneurship that it entails any modification of my conception of the entrepreneurial role. The key to that conception is, following Mises, to recognize the arbitrage element in all entrepreneurial activity, whether single-period or multi-period.

In discussing pure entrepreneurial profit Mises pointed out that what is responsible for such profit "is the fact that the entrepreneur who judges the future prices of the products more correctly than other people do buys some or all of the factors of production at prices which, seen from the point of view of the future state of the market, are too low."[24] The crucial element in intertemporal entrepreneurship is thus captured in the entrepreneur's perception of a price gap between present inputs and (appropriately discounted) future output. My 1973 work found it expedient to focus upon this, the essential feature of entrepreneurship, through the device of abstracting from all other aspects of the real-world exercise of entrepreneurship. This device consists in imagining how entrepreneurship might be exercised in a world in which all those other aspects are imagined to be absent—i.e., in a single-period world without production and without the uncertainty that arises from awareness of futurity. It was certainly not the intention, in deploying this analytical device, to deny that in the real world of production and (consequently) of multi-period decision-making and radical uncertainty, entrepreneurship is exercised only by calling upon the entrepreneur's qualities of boldness, innovativeness and creativity. Conversely, in extending the single-period entrepreneur to my 1981 multi-period context, it was not the intention to modify what I understood to be the Misesian conception of pure entrepreneurial activity, viz the perception (and thus the inevitable grasping) of a divergence between two prices at which the "same" item can be bought and sold. In recognizing how, (in order to act entrepreneurially in the uncertain context of time-consuming production possibilities) the entrepreneur will need to display qualities of boldness and creativity, there was no intention (and no need) to see these qualities as essential to the pure entrepreneurial role, as that role enters into our analysis and understanding of the market process. In acknowledging that, for Mises, the uncertainty within which the entrepreneur operates is an essential defining condition for the situations in which scope for entrepreneurship exists, there was no intention (and no need) to see boldness and creativity as anything more than the psychological qualities needed in order for the entrepreneur effectively to recognize, in peering into the future, those pure price differentials in which prospective entrepreneurial profits are to be won. (Consider the factor service "labor." For many real-world employment situations (perhaps all), the psychological profile of a successful laborer will include the quality of "obedience." Yet this does not require us to *define* the laborer's decision to sell labor, in terms of obedience. We simply define the essence of the laborer's decision as that of selling his human services.) Perhaps this can be more clearly expressed in the following assertions: (a) Were we to be able to imagine a world without uncertainty in regard to the future, we would (as Mises taught us) be unable to find scope in that world for pure entrepreneurship. With the future knowable with certainty, we could hardly imagine those errors being made that create the scope for entrepreneurship in our own, open-ended, world. (b) Entrepreneurship, in the context of production possibilities, consists in one's conviction that one has perceived earlier errors in the market to have created a differential between the price at which one can buy inputs and the price at which it will be possible to sell outputs. (c) While psychological and personal qualities of boldness, creativity, and self-confidence will doubtless be helpful or even necessary in order for a person to "see" such price-differentials in the open-ended, uncertain world in which we live (with "seeing" defined as necessarily implying the grasping of the opportunity one has seen), the analytical essence of the pure entrepreneurial role is itself independent of these specific qualities.

So that while the explicit introduction of uncertainty into my portrayal of the entrepreneurial context[25] certainly fleshes out and improves that portrayal ((a) by bringing it closer to the real-world context, and (b) by relating that context to Mises's own explicit insistence on the presence of uncertainty as the defining feature of that context), it does *not* embody any change[26] in the pure, analytical conception of the entrepreneur who, in my 1973 work, was responsible for the tendency towards market equilibration. The equilibrative properties of entrepreneurial activity still consist purely in perceiving price differences. Aggressive, creative or other "Schumpeterian" characteristics often or typically displayed by successful real-world entrepreneurs, play no analytical role in the dynamically competitive market process driven by entrepreneurial activity.

THE SCHUMPETERIAN ENTREPRENEUR RECONSIDERED

Despite this insistence (my critics may consider it obstinacy) on my part in asserting that my 1981 paper did not (contrary to a number of commentaries upon it) represent any essential modification of my earlier understanding of the entrepreneurial role, it must certainly be recognized that that paper encourages a far more sympathetic appreciation, on my part, for the Schumpeterian entrepreneur. Once we permit the multi-period character of real-world entrepreneurial behavior to be explicitly considered, the relevance of the active, aggressive characteristics of Schumpeter's entrepreneurs becomes understandable and important. Entrepreneurial alertness, in this essentially uncertain, open-ended, multi-period world must unavoidably express itself in the qualities of boldness, self-confidence, creativity and innovative ability. In order to make a discovery, in this world, it is simply not sufficient to be somehow more prescient than others; it requires that that "abstract" prescience be supported by psychological qualities that encourage one to ignore conventional wisdom, to dismiss the jeers of those deriding what they see as the self-deluded visionary, to disrupt what others have come to see as the comfortable familiarity of the old-fashioned ways of doing things, to ruin rudely and even cruelly the confident expectations of those whose somnolence has led them to expect to continue to make their living as they have for years past. Recognition of all this is no doubt responsible for the difficulties which my critics had with my earlier discussion of the pure, alert entrepreneur without these Schumpeterian characteristics. Perhaps it was this which led them to read my 1981 paper as a belated concession to the inadequacy of my earlier simple notion of the entrepreneur as merely the ("passive" but alert) noticer of hitherto overlooked changes—a concession compelled, they believed, immediately one takes the step of extending analysis of entrepreneurial behavior beyond the highly artificial context of the single period.

Our discussion in the preceding section of this paper will, I trust, have made it clear how I can both eat my cake and have it (i.e., recognize how the multi-period world requires its entrepreneurs to display the Schumpeterian qualities, while still maintaining that it does not require me to surrender one iota of my earlier view of the entrepreneurial role as one of pure, alert, discovery of hitherto overlooked, exogenously created, changes.) To be sure, the entrepreneurial exercise of alert prescience calls for aggressive, bold, creative, leadership qualities. But this simply means that the seer who can imagine how the world might be improved by a radical innovation, but who lacks the needed boldness and initiative (to shoulder the risks which he would have to assume in order actually to introduce this innovation to reality in a world fraught with uncertainties)—has in fact not yet really discovered an available, attractive opportunity for innovation. If he has not seen that opportunity in so shining a light that it drives him to its implementation in spite of the jeering scepticism of others, and in spite of the possibility of its ultimate failure—then he has not really "seen" that opportunity. To imagine how, under hypothesized conditions, (not confidently believed to be in fact feasible), a true opportunity might exist, is not yet to have seen that opportunity as a tempting available option. For the possibility of genuine "alertness" in the multi-period, uncertain world, that alertness must indeed express itself in the boldness, self-confidence, and daring of the Schumpeterian leader. My "obstinacy" consists in my continuing to insist that what is important for analytical purposes is not these leadership qualities in themselves, but the pure "alertness" which these qualities express and sustain.

ENTREPRENEURIAL INNOVATION—COORDINATIVE OR DISRUPTIVE?

It may be helpful, in this regard, to consider an objection which many have raised in the past in regard to my emphasis on the coordinative tendencies set in motion by (successful) entrepreneurship. This objection has deeply worried a number of otherwise sympathetic scholars, in regard to my notion of the entrepreneurial role. Surely, they argue, every successful entrepreneurial venture constitutes a shock to the market, more or less severely disrupting the existing plans of those who, failing to anticipate these changes, have invested all or parts of their careers in the methods of production which the new venture is about to displace. We may grant, the objection concedes, that this shock may be seen as beneficial to the consumers; but surely, they claim, these benefits to the consumer are obtained only through drastically *dis*coordinating and frustrating the plans of those in the displaced industry. To pronounce these disruptive shocks as essentially coordinative and equilibrative, as I have, is to twist language outrageously. My use of language in this way, my critics tend to believe, is not unrelated to my obstinate refusal to recognize (as Schumpeter did) that successful entrepreneurship is indeed disruptive, to concede that while the destruction it sets in motion may indeed be "creative," it is destructive nonetheless.

To see why and how I believe it possible and accurate to insist on my use of the term "coordinative" to describe the entrepreneur's behavior, it will be useful to focus on an example of bold, creative, innovative Schumpeterian entrepreneurship responsible for a dramatic technological breakthrough, revolutionizing an entire industry. Consider the invention and innovation of the automobile in the U.S. This innovation, we may be sure, devastated the livelihoods of many who had built their entire careers around the horse-drawn carriage industry. Virtually overnight, we may be convinced, enormous loss of value occurred in capital investments that had been made in that industry; large numbers of skilled professional workers in that industry find that the market value of their skills has fallen catastrophically. Yet, while understanding how Schumpeter can focus on the creative destruction which this successful and dramatic entrepreneurial innovation has wrought, I maintain that we must, at the same time, recognize the coordinative quality of this innovation, *even in regard to the horse-drawn carriage industry*.

The truth surely is, we now see with 20–20 hindsight, that the horse-drawn carriage industry, for all its placid, normal-profitability over many decades, was an industry in grave disequilibrium *before* the automobile actually appeared. This was so, we now realize, in that the means (and even, in a sense, the technology) to replace expensive, inconvenient, time-consuming horse-drawn transportation by lower-cost, convenient and rapid motorized transportation was available at an acceptable cost, at the very moment when the horse-drawn carriage industry (as far as the superficial vision of the person in the street could discern) seemed normally prosperous and secure. The truth is, we now know, that the investments made in physical and human capital were *mal*investments. The value of the output of the horse-drawn carriage industry was, as we now know, far lower than the value which the market *at that very moment* would have been prepared to place upon the outputs of comparable inputs directed into an automobile-producing industry.

The consumers paying substantial prices for (what we now know to have been) inefficient and inconvenient horse-drawn transportation were in fact "wasting" their money; opportunities, as yet unnoticed, existed for far superior motorized transportation to be provided at prices that would have been highly attractive to many consumers. Production was, in this sense, being conducted inefficiently; capital and labor were being misallocated—invested and specialized in directions and skills that were (in the light of the true conditions which hindsight reveals to have existed) utterly mistaken.

The brash, bold entrepreneurs who introduced the automobile to the U.S. market indeed set in motion market movements which, in one sense, disrupted the plans of many investors and workers in the industries they displaced. But their doing so, we now see, constituted not an act of destruction in itself, but one which *revealed* the wastefulness and the misallocated character of the enormous volume of investor and labor decisions that mistakenly committed resources to the horse-drawn carriage industry. The superficial placidity of the situation in that industry on the eve of the emergence of the automobile was indeed just that, merely superficial. The truth, as we now know, is that it was an industry sitting on a powder keg waiting to explode. The essential entrepreneurial contribution of the automobile pioneers was unmistakably to make clear what that disequilibrium situation really was. Those entrepreneurs alertly saw better ways of using resources; their putting into effect the productive possibilities they saw was coordinative in the sense that it brought the pattern of resource allocation into a higher degree of coordination both with the true pattern of technological possibilities and the pattern of consumer preferences, than had the leaders of the horse-drawn carriage industry. While we can readily understand how, at a superficial level, it seems obvious that it is the actions of the automobile entrepreneurs that have directly destroyed the capital and labor-skill values built up in the horse-drawn carriage industry, we must recognize that, at a deeper level, these losses, while as yet unnoticed, had already occurred at the times the investments (in the horse-drawn carriage industry) were made. From this perspective, the automobile entrepreneurs can no more accurately be described as the agents of "destruction," than can the physician whose diagnosis sends an apparently healthy person (undergoing a routine medical examination) to hospital with a newly-identified severe heart condition, be described as having ruined that patient's health.

SEMANTICS AND SUBSTANCE

We may readily grant to my critics[27] that a certain semantic ambiguity is partly responsible for the possibly overemphasized differences (between Schumpeter's views and my own) which I had asserted in 1969 and 1973. As I had recognized as early as 1963,[28] so long as one can imagine that "there are *always* unknown technological possibilities that future generations will discover," we can describe a market system as necessarily always being "in a state of disequilibrium, with respect to the infinity of knowledge that is beyond (contemporary) human reach." While this use of the term disequilibrium would permit us to see each and every "Schumpeterian" technological innovation as "equilibrating" (as I appeared to wish to argue in 1969 and 1973), such a semantic usage is neither required nor necessarily advisable. Ordinarily we do describe as an equilibrium that Walrasian state of affairs which fully and adequately incorporates all currently available technological knowledge. Surely, then, Schumpeter was not out of order in seeing entrepreneurial technological innovation as disruptive and disequilibrating. It must seem that my insistence on seeing even Schumpeterian entrepreneurial activity as coordinative and equilibrative, does involve a confusing and unfortunate use of language.

The following may permit me to plead non-guilty to this latter offense. There *is* an important sense in which we must indeed see the entrepreneur who achieves Schumpeterian technological revolutions, who engages in what Schumpeter valuably identifies as "creative destruction," as (Schumpeter's use of language to the contrary notwithstanding) equilibrative. This sense is that in which we wish to understand the *economic* forces at work in generating such technological revolutions. Schumpeter correctly identified the economic forces so responsible as being driven by entrepreneurial activity. What Schumpeter's use of language (i.e., his identification of this activity as disruptive and disequilibrative) obscured, I maintained (and still maintain), is that this entrepreneurial activity is, after all (and most significantly) stimulated and motivated by the possibility of winning pure profit. What Schumpeter's use of language (and indeed his "vision" of how capitalism works) obscured, is that the entrepreneurial activity with which he is dealing is, at a deep level, responding to the conditions of the market. To fail to see that the entrepreneurs in the automobile industry were responding to the economic inefficiencies and resource misallocations (and the resulting profit opportunities) already present in the horse-drawn carriage industry, is surely to fail to see a most important aspect of the market process. My 1973 book was built on the idea that it is this aspect of the market (present but overlooked in Schumpeter's account of long-run technological change) which is responsible for that tendency for market equilibration which is at the very core of economic understanding—even in the imagined world in which technological change is absent.

I believe the foregoing permits me to sum up the "reconsideration" undertaken in this chapter, by simply reiterating the four propositions announced at its very outset:

1. For understanding the psychological profile typical of the real-world entrepreneur as we know him, Schumpeter's portrayal is valid and accurate.
2. For understanding the "creative destruction" which Schumpeter sees as the central and distinguishing feature of the capitalist system, Schumpeter's portrayal is valid and essential; to the extent that policy objectives include the stimulation of such creative destruction, careful attention will indeed have to be paid to that Schumpeterian psychological profile to which we have referred.
3. For understanding the equilibrative tendency of markets in general, my own view of the entrepreneur as alert to opportunities (created by, or able to be created by, independently initiated changes), is valid and significant.
4. To see the entrepreneurial role of a real-world entrepreneur as essentially that of being "merely" alert to opportunities created (or able to be created) by independently initiated changes, is not *necessarily* inconsistent with a Schumpeterian perspective on the activity of that same entrepreneur (which sees him as aggressively and actively initiating change).

To put the matter somewhat differently: The reconsideration here undertaken indeed permits us to see how both the Schumpeterian view of the entrepreneurial role and my own view can both be simultaneously accepted. Schumpeter is concerned to enable us to see, from the outside, as it were, what constitutes the essence of capitalism (viz. its being characterized by continual technological change driven by innovative, creative entrepreneurs). My own focus on the entrepreneur was inspired by the objective of enabling us to see the inside workings of the capitalist system (its ability to offer pure profit incentives that can evoke entrepreneurial perception of available opportunities—some (but not all!) of which opportunities may consist in the potential for technological revolution (implementation of which calls for the "Schumpeterian" qualities of boldness, initiative, and creativity)). To the extent, however, that Schumpeter's language and his picture of capitalism lead us to see the placid, old-fashioned-technology world as one in which actions have long come to be fully and efficiently mutually and smoothly coordinated, with no "gaps" crying out for alert entrepreneurial notice—until the placidity is rudely disrupted by exogenous "entrepreneurial" creative innovation, I must continue to assert that my own view of entrepreneurial activity permits and requires us to see a quite different picture even in that very same sequence of Schumpeterian events.

NOTES

1. Although the objective of this chapter is to throw light on the nature of the entrepreneurial role (rather than to clarify what this writer "really meant" in earlier, almost forgotten writings), it does focus distressingly abundantly, upon some of that earlier work. I can only apologize for this.
2. Schumpeter (1942, 1950, pp. 103ff.).
3. Schumpeter (1942, 1950, p. 84).
4. On this see also Kirzner (1990, pp. 245–9).
5. See Kirzner (1973, p. 127).
6. Schumpeter (1942, 1950, p. 83).
7. Kirzner (1973, pp. 73ff.).
8. Hayek (1945. 1949).
9. Kirzner(1969, 1979, p. 118).
10. Hébert and Link (1982, p. 99).
11. In a recent paper (Holcombe, 1997) Professor Randall G. Holcombe states that "at least a part of the difference between Schumpeter's and Kirzner's views might be semantic, based on different understandings of the meaning of the word equilibrium."
12. Boudreaux (1994).
13. Choi (1995, p. 62).
14. Ibid.
15. Loasby (1982, p. 224).
16. Loasby (1989, p. 178).

17. Boehm (1990, p. 229). See also McNulty (1987, pp. 536ff.) ("Schumpeter's entrepreneur is a disequilibrating force . . . Kirzner's entrepreneur plays an equilibrating role."). See also Ricketts (1994, pp. 63ff.).
18. See e.g., Greaves (1974); Hazlitt (1974); White (1976); High (1980); see also High (1990, p. 41).
19. Kirzner (1982, 1985, ch. 3).
20. Kirzner (1982, 1985, p. 40).
21. Although the single-period context (upon which my 1973 discussion of entrepreneurship focused) permits us to "ignore uncertainty," this is *not* inconsistent with Mises's insistence that (as my critics pointed out) the entrepreneurial role can be defined only in the context of uncertainty. What Mises meant by that insistence, it is my understanding, was that scope for entrepreneurial discovery (of errors being made by others) cannot be imagined to exist except in a world in which "sheer ignorance" (i.e., undeliberate, costlessly-removable ignorance which "inefficiently" remains after all *known* worthwhile, cost-benefit-calculated efforts have been made to remove known ignorance) is essentially present. In the world in which we live the element within it which creates scope for such sheer ignorance is the uncertainty of the future. Were the future to be "determined" (and thus essentially knowable), the only ignorance of it which would remain would be "efficient" ignorance (i.e., ignorance the costly removal of which would be seen as not worthwhile). My device, in 1973, of focusing on the single-period context for entrepreneurship, required the deus-ex-machina-*assumption* of the possibility of sheer ignorance in that context (*without* the multi-period uncertainty which renders sheer ignorance plausible or inevitable in the real world). The analytical core of the 1973 treatment is, I believed (and still believe), identical with that which Mises develops in his own treatment of entrepreneurship in the multi-period real world.
22. Kirzner (1982, 1985, pp. 63ff.).
23. Hébert and Link (1982, pp. 97ff.), High (1982).
24. Mises (1962, p. 109).
25. That portrayal did point out very explicitly that uncertainty was being deliberately abstracted from (see Kirzner, 1973, pp. 86ff.).
26. Although Professor Vaughn disagrees with much of my position, she has recognized the essentially unchanged core of that position over the years. See Vaughn (1994, pp. 148ff.). For a disagreement with Vaughn on this, see Rizzo (1996, pp. xviiiff. and fn 7).
27. For references see above, notes 11, 12, 13.
28. Kirzner (1963, p. 258 fn).

REFERENCES

Boehm, Stephan (1990) "The Austrian Tradition: Schumpeter and Mises," in Klaus Hennings and Warren J. Samuels (eds) *Neoclassical Economic Theory, 1870–1930*, Boston/Dordrecht/London: Kluwer.

Boudreaux, Donald (1994) "Schumpeter and Kirzner on Competition and Equilibrium," in Peter J. Boettke and David L. Prychitko (eds) *The*

Market Process: Essays in Contemporary Austrian Economics, Aldershot: Edward Elgar.

Choi, Young Back (1995) "The Entrepreneur: Schumpeter vs. Kirzner," in Peter J. Boettke and Mario J. Rizzo (eds), *Advances in Austrian Economics*, Vol. 2, Part A, Greenwich, CT and London: JAI Press.

Greaves, Percy L., Jr. (1974) Review of Kirzner (1973), *Wertfrei.*

Hayek, Friedrich A. (1945) "The Use of Knowledge in Society," *American Economic Review* XXXV(4), reprinted in Hayek (1949) *Individualism and Economic Order*, London: Routledge and Kegan Paul.

Hazlitt, Henry (1974) Review of Kirzner (1973), *Freeman* 24.

Hébert, Robert F. and Albert N. Link (1982) *The Entrepreneur, Mainstream Views and Radical Critiques*, New York: Praeger.

High, Jack (1980) Review of Kirzner (1979), *Austrian Economics Newsletter.*

—— (1982) "Alertness and Judgment: Comment on Kirzner," in Israel M. Kirzner (ed.), *Method, Process and Austrian Economics, Essays in Honor of Ludwig von Mises*, Lexington, MA: D.C. Heath.

—— (1990) *Maximizing, Action, and Market Adjustment, An Inquiry into the Theory of Economic Disequilibrium*, Munich: Philosophia Verlag.

Holcombe, Randall G. (1997) "The Origins of Entrepreneurial Opportunities," unpublished manuscript, Florida State University.

Kirzner, Israel M. (1963) *Market Theory and the Price System*, Princeton, NJ: Van Nostrand.

—— (1969) "Entrepreneurship and the Market Approach to Development," reprinted in Kirzner (1979).

—— (1973) *Competition and Entrepreneurship*, Chicago: University of Chicago Press.

—— (1979) *Perception, Opportunity and Profit*, Chicago: University of Chicago Press.

—— (1982) "Uncertainty, Discovery, and Human Action," in Israel M. Kirzner, *Discovery and the Capitalist Process*, Chicago: University of Chicago Press.

—— (1990) "Commentary" on Stephan Boehm.

Loasby, Brian J. (1982) "The Entrepreneur in Economic Theory," *Scottish Journal of Political Economy* 29.

—— (1989) *The Mind and Method of the Economist, A Critical Appraisal of Major Economists in the Twentieth Century*, Aldershot: Edward Elgar.

McNulty, Paul J. (1987) "Competition: Austrian Conceptions," in John Eatwell, Murray Milgate, and Peter Newman (eds) *The New Palgrave: A Dictionary of Economics*, Vol. 1, London: Macmillan.

Ricketts, Martin (1994) *The Economics of Business Enterprise—An Introduction to Economic Organization and the Theory of the Firm*, 2nd edn, New York and London: Harvester Wheatsheaf.

Rizzo, Mario J. (1996) "Introduction: Time and Ignorance After Ten Years," in Gerald P. O'Driscoll and Mario J. Rizzo (eds) *The Economics of Time and Ignorance*, 2nd edn, London and New York: Routledge.

Schumpeter, Joseph A. (1942) *Capitalism, Socialism and Democracy*, New York: Harper and Row (reprint, 1950).

Vaughn, Karen I. (1994) *Austrian Economics in America—The Migration of a Tradition*, Cambridge: Cambridge University Press.

Mises, Ludwig von (1949) *Human Action, A Treatise on Economics*, New Haven, CT: Yale University Press.

—— (1962) "Profit and Loss," in Ludwig von Mises (ed.) *Planning for Freedom and Other Essays and Addresses*, 2nd edn, South Holland, IL: Libertarian Press.

White, Lawrence H. (1976) "Entrepreneurship, Imagination and the Question of Equilibration," unpublished manuscript.

Source: Creativity and/or Alertness: A Reconsideration of the Schumpeterian Entrepreneur, *Review of Austrian Economics*, 1999, 11, pp. 5–17.

14

RATIONALITY, ENTREPRENEURSHIP, AND ECONOMIC "IMPERIALISM"

In 1976 Gary Becker's *The Economic Approach to Human Behavior* introduced into social science a radical emphasis on the relevance of individual rationality in human behavior of all kinds, and argued that this rendered the conclusions of economic theory directly and overridingly applicable to areas of social interaction which had traditionally been treated as the "turf" of other social sciences. Brian Loasby was one economist who expressed serious reservations concerning what others have seen as "economic imperialism." Loasby was disturbed by a perspective which sees all areas of social science as being rendered subfields in a "universal" applied economics. "Becker . . . has claimed that this principle of coherent rationality not only provides a unified framework for the analysis of all human behaviour—itself a claim of astonishing ambition, if not arrogance—but that it is the only such basis—the only firm spot on which to stand" (Loasby, 1989, p. 191). Becker's position, which has been described as "hardboiled economism" (Green, 1996, p. 28), raises important issues relating to the very foundations of economic science.

In one sense, Becker's position reflects an old lesson which economists learned from Lionel Robbins in 1932,[1] viz. that economics does not deal with one specific *area* of human behavior, but rather with one specific *aspect* of *all* areas of human behavior. The self-same economizing, allocative aspect of human behavior which is salient in, say, the commercial areas of life conventionally dealt with in economic theory, is present, Robbins taught us, also in the religious or cultural fields of human endeavor. Wherever human purposefulness encounters the imperative to choose, imposed by scarcity of the necessary means needed to achieve all of one's goals, human beings will economize, allocate, and engage in constrained maximization. Similarly, Becker's position reminds us of the assertion by Ludwig von Mises that economics is merely "a part, although the hitherto best elaborated part, of a more universal science, praxeology."[2] Praxeology is the general science of human action (with human action seen as deliberative choice under conditions of radical uncertainty). And human action manifests itself in all areas of endeavor:

> Choosing determines all human decisions. In making, his choice man chooses not only between various material things and services. All human values are offered for option. All ends and all means, both material and ideal issues, the sublime and the base, the noble and the ignoble, are ranged in a single row and subjected to a decision which picks out one thing and sets aside another. Nothing that men aim at or want to avoid remains outside of this arrangement into a unique scale of gradation and preference."[3]

Both for Robbins and for Mises, economics is seen as the science of rational choice, and rational choice is seen as governing human action in all its departments. It might seem, then, that Becker's extension of economic analysis to govern explanation in all departments of social science is simply the consistent application of the "Austrian" (Robbins–Mises) position. The purpose of this chapter is to dispel such an impression. The Austrian tradition in economics which both Robbins and Mises were articulating, does not by itself lead to the economic imperialism of which Becker has, not without cause, been accused. There is an important difference between (a) the sense in which Becker understands the relevance of rational choice to areas outside the conventional scope of economics, and (b) the significance of Austrian insights concerning the universality of rational choice.

In fact there is something of an exquisite paradox here. On the one hand it is the universality of rational choice for Becker, which leads him almost ineluctably to see all possible explanations in social science as being reducible to applications of the standard theorems of economics. On the other hand, it will be shown that it is precisely the universality of rational choice for Mises, which entails our conclusion that the Austrian tradition which Mises represents, is unable to accept the direct applicability of the standard theorems of economics to the intellectual areas marked out by economic imperialists for annexation. All this requires careful explanation. Our explanation begins by way of an illustrative digression.[4]

A WORLD OF PERENNIAL OPTIMALITY: A DIGRESSION

What is generally known as the Coase Theorem draws attention to the possibilities which exist in free markets for spontaneous internalization of externalities through direct trading (between decision makers generating externalities, and the beneficiaries/victims of those externalities). Simple economics shows that all suboptimalities attributable to externalities correspond to unreaped potential gains from such trade. In the absence of transactions costs, it is therefore argued, it follows that all such potential gains from trade will be grasped; *all* externalities will have been spontaneously internalized. Furthermore, it came to be maintained, even in the presence of positive transactions costs, Coaseian logic argues for spontaneous market optimality despite the continued presence of externalities. After all, if transactions costs are positive, this simply means that gains from trade will be forgone due to the costs of the resources required to consummate such trade. But this merely means that such unconsummated possibilities for spontaneous internalization of externalities are, indeed best left unconsummated: the social benefits are simply not worth the costs.

This kind of logic has been pushed to the bitter end to seriously argue that all conceivable kinds of apparent suboptimalities (e.g. those attributable to the exercise of monopoly power) must ultimately be declared (at least absent transactions costs) to be entirely consistent with social optimality, after all. As Calabresi put it:

> A misallocation exists when there is available a possible reallocation in which all those who would lose from the reallocation could be fully compensated by those who would gain, and, at the end of this compensation process, there would still be some who would be better off than before. [But this] . . . and other similar definitions of resource misallocation merely mean that there is a misallocation when a situation can be improved by bargains. If people are rational, bargains are costless, and there are no legal impediments to bargains, transactions will *ex hypothesis* occur to the point where bargains can no longer improve the situation; to the point, in short, of optimal resource allocation.[5]

And what Calabresi suggests as true for a zero-transaction-cost world, would, it is clear, *mutatis mutandis*, also be true for a world in which transactions are costly: *all* misallocations would be spontaneously traded away—since those not so traded because of transactions costs turn out not to have been net misallocations after all.

But all this leads us still further. Suppose government regulation blocks some negotiations or some trades. It might at first glance seem that if markets are not permitted to function, this surely permits misallocation to persist. But the economic logic we have cited has been applied even to this situation. Even here, the Coase–Calabresi logic *seems* to indicate, the world must be the best of all possible worlds since, after all, the regulations which block the reaping of potential gains from trade must be beneficial to some agents in society (or else it would pay those thwarted by those regulations from reaping gains-from-trade, to incur the financial and/or political costs needed to eliminate such regulation). Clearly the benefits enjoyed by those whose protected positions are secured by regulation, are so considerable that we cannot pronounce the elimination of such regulation (even though it would ensure the reaping of potential gains from trade) to be a net social gain. The late George Stigler, pursuing this logic to its bitter end (an end many are likely to consider a *reductio ad absurdum*), argued that an economist pointing out an unwise (i.e. a misallocative) public policy, is really merely disagreeing with the valuations placed upon potential transactions by agents in the economy (or with the ethical validity of the manner in which decision-making rights are distributed among those agents). To declare a public policy to be economically "wrong" is therefore not to assert a scientific conclusion; it is merely to engage in "preaching." The world, according to its own lights, is *always* in an optimal state.[6]

But all this seems, surely, abundantly perverse. We know by casual observation that many situations in the world *are* suboptimal—not merely in "our" subjective evaluation of the alternatives, but, quite clearly and obviously, also in the evaluations of all the affected parties themselves. It is simply not the case, it is abundantly apparent, that at each and every moment the world has exhausted all relevant net-beneficial opportunities for mutually gainful negotiations. Economic logic seems to have somehow led seriously astray—even in the context of potential market activities which seem to fall squarely within the scope of conventional, non-imperialistic, economics.

THE ILLUSION OF PERENNIAL OPTIMALITY EXPLODED: DIGRESSION CONCLUDED

The most simple and obvious explanation for where and how our economic logic has led us astray lies, it seems to us, in the assumption concealed in that economic reasoning, to the effect that each and every opportunity for mutually net-beneficial exchange between each and every pair of individuals *must* be taken advantage of at the very instant when such an opportunity emerges into existence. This assumption simply rules out, even for the briefest span of time, the possibility of an available, as-yet unexploited opportunity for mutually net-beneficial exchange. (This assumption thus formalizes the old, weak, joke in which an economist asserts that there are *never* any lost dollar bills to be found in Times Square, because any such lost bills that *would* be in Times Square, will already have been picked up.)

This obviously false assumption underlies and vitiates almost every conclusion reached, on the basis of economic logic, in the preceding section of this chapter. It is not true that, with zero transactions costs, all externalities must necessarily be spontaneously internalized; it is not true that all net misallocations of resources must instantaneously have been corrected (through the instantaneous exploitation of the entailed available potential gains from trade); it is not true that an economist pointing out an obviously economically-flawed public policy measure is necessarily merely preaching. All these assertions are false simply because it is entirely possible for an individual to pass up an available opportunity for pure gain, without taking advantage of it. He may fail to take advantage of it not because the costs of doing so (e.g. the costs of gaining the necessary information to do so) render this opportunity no longer one offering net gain. He may fail to take advantage of such opportunity *simply because he is not aware of its availability*. To be unaware of the availability of an opportunity for pure gain (and thus to fail to exploit it), is not deliberately to reject it because of the infinite cost of knowing about its existence; it is not to be irrational; it is unwittingly to pass up an attractive opportunity staring one in the face.

The assumption frequently encountered in economic theory that denies any such possibility of unwittingly passing up an attractive opportunity, is based, in effect, on the assumption that the existence of available opportunities (including particularly opportunities to acquire needed information at a worthwhile cost) is always known to all relevant parties. Austrian economics rejects this assumption, and thus insists on having us grapple with the very real possibility of unexploited opportunities for pure gain. In particular this requires us to recognize the possibility that pairs of individuals between whom exists the potential for mutually gainful trade may simply overlook such opportunities. And once we admit this very real possibility into our theoretical discussions, the idea of necessary perennial optimality immediately evaporates into thin air. There is nothing in economic reasoning which entails any such perennial optimality; the possibility of misallocated resources, of overlooked opportunities for mutually gainful exchanges, with or without transactions costs, and the possibility of genuinely economically wrong public policy, is alive and well—and fully consistent with economic analysis, properly understood.

ECONOMIC REASONING RECONSTRUCTED

Yet the theorems of economics which assume that all such opportunities have already been grasped and corrected, are certainly not without usefulness. Austrian (and, for that matter, non-Austrian) economists may not wish to see the economy as if it were, at each and every moment, in that state of affairs in which no available opportunities for gainful exchange remain. But, at the same time, they may recognize the existence of powerful tendencies which, in the absence of exogenous change, might eventually *be imagined* to culminate in such a state of affairs. There may indeed be important lessons to be learned by contrasting the world in which we live (characterized by unexploited opportunities for mutually gainful exchange) with a hypothesized world in economic equilibrium (in which no such unexploited opportunities remain). This does not reinstate equilibrium analysis as the central tool of economic understanding, but it does permit us to use equilibrium constructs as tools in helping us understand the phenomena of markets in disequilibrium. Austrian economics has indeed proceeded in this way, drawing attention (by careful analysis of such contrasting views of conceivable worlds) to the forces which are set in motion by the lure of pure entrepreneurial profit (opportunities for which exist whenever unexploited gains from trade are available for the taking).

In this perspective, understanding of market dynamics flows from the circumstance that opportunities for pure gain are created precisely when the conditions for equilibrium have not been fulfilled—so that disequilibrium conditions, by "switching on" entrepreneurial alertness to opportunities for pure profit, tend to initiate entrepreneurial actions which move towards the elimination of those disequilibrium conditions. (After all, every action taken to grasp pure entrepreneurial profit, tends to eliminate the price discrepancy of which that opportunity consists.) So that sound economic reasoning *does* show how equilibrating forces (that is, tendencies towards the disappearance of unexploited opportunities for mutually gainful exchange) are continually—despite the equally continual interference of exogenously created new opportunities—being set in motion.

DISCOVERY AND THE RELEVANCE OF INSTITUTIONAL SETTING

It should be noticed that this entrepreneurial process of becoming alert to as-yet ungrasped opportunities for pure profit, depends crucially on the circumstance, unique to the institutional setting of the market, that earlier errors do translate into identifiable lumps of pure prospective net gain. A number of perceptive readers of (earlier drafts of) this chapter have pointed out that even in an institutional setting which does not translate errors into such identifiable lumps of pure gain, we might expect a systematic tendency for error correction. After all, if unexploited opportunities exist for mutual gain through exchange between two parties, A and B, in an institutional world in which no entrepreneurial arbitrage activity is permitted, we may nonetheless postulate eventual mutual discovery of each other, by A and B, simply as a result of the "entrepreneurial" propensity of alert human individuals to become aware of opportunities available to them—even if the gain available as a result of exchange cannot be isolated as a pure lump of gain available to any imagined "pure" entrepreneur. Our response to this thoughtful observation is that the phenomenal rapidity with which we observe markets to absorb and respond continually to new information does clearly appear to depend upon the remarkable circumstance which characterizes markets—namely that unexploited opportunities for interpersonal mutually gainful exchange, become translated into pure profit opportunities, available to pure arbitraging entrepreneurs. While there is indeed an entrepreneurial element in all human action, it is the scope offered by markets, for pure arbitraging entrepreneurship to be exercised, which is responsible for the swift adjustments of markets to exogenous changes.

It is markets, under institutional arrangements which include especially the possibility of buying at a low price in order to resell at a higher price, which are responsible for the initiation of those systematic processes of error-correction which we understand as making up the process of equilibration. While interaction between alert human beings can be expected to result in some relevant gradual mutual discovery under any institutional circumstances, the speed of such discovery processes within markets is clearly of an entirely different order of magnitude than is conceivable outside markets.

What is responsible for the initial existence of potential lumps of pure gain, under market institutions, is not any cost of transacting, of gaining knowledge, or the like, but merely sheer ignorance, utter unawareness of these opportunities (including, as we have seen, the opportunities available for deliberately acquiring relevant knowledge). The spontaneous learning required in order for misallocations (represented by unexploited exchange opportunities) to be corrected, is inspired by the circumstance that this sheer ignorance translates itself (within the institutional setting of individual rights to property and thus to market arrangements) into pure profit opportunities. Were this translation not to occur, we would be unable to rely upon any economic forces for the generation of those discoveries which had hitherto not been made. Ignorance attributable to the costs of deliberate learning may be expected to be eliminated by deliberate learning as (and if) these costs become lower. But the sheer ignorance which we have seen to occur even in the absence of costs of deliberate learning, cannot be expected systematically to disappear with any rapidity without definite cause. The lure offered by pure profit opportunities represents such a possible cause. It is only within the market setting that this cause can operate. Outside the market context we have nothing, within the realm of economic theory, upon which we can rely to generate any systematically rapid processes of mutual discovery that might tend to eliminate episodes of social suboptimality (caused by sheer ignorance).

RATIONALITY, EQUILIBRIUM, AND THE SOURCE OF ECONOMIC IMPERIALISM

Examination of the foundations of ventures to extend the scope of economic reasoning to govern territories conventionally treated in other social sciences, reveals that the key "economic" assumptions claimed to characterize also those territories, include especially not only universal rationality, but also universally attained equilibrium. As Becker put it: "The combined assumptions of maximizing behavior, market equilibrium, and stable preferences, used relentlessly and unflinchingly, form the heart of the economic approach."[7] In Jack Hirshleifer's words:

> What gives economics its imperialist power is that our analytical categories—scarcity, cost, preferences, opportunities, etc.—are truly universal in applicability. Even more important is our structural organization of these concepts into the distinct yet intertwined processes of optimization on the individual decision level *and equilibrium on the social level of analysis*. Thus economics really does constitute the universal grammar of social science.
>
> (Hirshleifer, 1985, p. 53; emphasis added)

An examination of Becker's work in applying the economic approach to areas usually reserved to other social sciences, indeed reveals that the assumption of universally attained equilibrium is taken very seriously and quite self-consciously. Thus in his well-known analysis of marriage Becker is explicit, not only in assuming that "each person tries to find a mate who maximizes his or her well-being, with well-being measured by the consumption of household-produced commodities," but also in hypothesizing that "the 'marriage market' is assumed to be in equilibrium, in the sense that no person could change mates and become better off."[8]

Now, as we have seen, (and despite our unhappiness at the overemphasis of economists upon equilibrium analysis) there is considerable usefulness, within economics, in the ideas of equilibrium and of equilibration. The central thesis of this chapter is, however, that such usefulness cannot simply be assumed to apply also to these ideas within the territories conventionally treated by other social sciences (especially in the absence of market institutions). Equilibrium is a useful notion within the economic analysis of markets, because we understand how, within the institutional setting of the market, disequilibrium conditions tend to inspire that spontaneous process of mutual discovery of which equilibration consists. But, as pointed out in the preceding section, we have no basis whatever, in economic theory, for concluding that any similar processes of equilibration can tend systematically to exist in areas of social interaction outside the market setting.

An approach to explanation in the areas conventionally dealt with in other social sciences (that is, in areas outside the setting created by market institutions) which relies heavily on the assumption of universally attained equilibrium must therefore, in our view, be fundamentally flawed. It is one thing to postulate universal rationality in human decision-making; it is quite another thing (and, in our view quite unjustified) simply to assume as an empirical matter that all human decisions are at all times universally arranged in equilibrium patterns. (To *assume* that no married person could change mates and become better off thus appears as a totally unjustified and unrealistic assumption, thoroughly undermining the usefulness of the "economic approach" in the marriage "market.")

In the succeeding sections of this chapter we explore how and why this latter distinction is implicitly denied in the literature of "economic imperialism." This discussion will permit us to savor the paradox referred to early in this chapter. That paradox consisted, we said, in that the universality of rational choice for Becker *does* rigorously entail subordination of other social sciences to economics, while for the Austrian tradition, it is precisely the universality of rational choice (in the Mises sense) which rigorously entails our *in*ability to extend the applicability of the theorems of economics, uncritically, to other areas of social interaction.

RATIONALITY AND EQUILIBRIUM—THE MAINSTREAM VIEW

The truth is that the mainstream assumptions which, we saw in an earlier section, lead to a picture of the world as being in a perennial state of optimality, are merely the logically derived consequences entailed by the mainstream understanding of the rationality assumption itself. The very assumption of rational choice which undergirds economic theory must, if this assumption is understood as it is understood by the mainstream, necessarily mean that we are also, at the same time, assuming the equilibrium state.

For the mainstream, to assume rational choice is, as we have seen, to assume universal awareness, at each and every instant, of all the circumstances relevant to choice. (Although, ever since George Stigler's pioneering article of 1961,[9] economists have incorporated the need to search for information (in order to reduce ignorance) into microeconomic analysis, this does not in any way compromise the omniscience implied in the mainstream interpretation of the rationality assumption. The theory of search still stoutly assumes that each individual is aware, at each and every instant, of all the circumstances relevant to choice—and thus of all opportunities for worthwhile search. The only ignorance recognized as conceivable in this Stiglerian world is "optimal" ignorance, that is, ignorance which it is too costly to remove. To undertake the search necessary to remove such ignorance would be a mistake; efficiency *requires* this ignorance.) But this assumption (of universal awareness of all circumstances relevant to choice) conceals within it also the assumption that the decisions being made (besides—or rather as a result of—their all being rational) have all somehow already been modified and coordinatively arranged in a mutually sustaining (i.e. an equilibrium) pattern. No two decisions made (by two rational individuals) can be imagined as being made without these decisions having been somehow prearranged so as to be mutually sustaining—i.e. each must be such as not to frustrate the possible implementation of the other, and, further, each must not be such as to render the other decision as less than the best which its maker could possibly have made. To imagine that these two decisions are *not* mutually sustaining, is to imagine either that one decision-maker is presuming circumstances (on which he is relying) to exist which do not in fact exist, or to imagine that that decision-maker is failing to take advantage of opportunities actually available to him. In other words, to imagine that decisions are not mutually sustaining is to give up the assumption of universal rationality in decision-making—at least in the context of the mainstream interpretation of this assumption.

But it is immediately clear that if the rationality assumption implies that each pair of decisions made in the market are necessarily mutually sustaining, then the rationality assumption is also revealed to require that all decisions being made throughout the market system make up a complete system of general equilibrium. So that, for mainstream understanding of rationality, there really is no way of understanding individual behavior (for which understanding we must rely on the rationality assumption) without assuming complete market equilibrium somehow already to exist at all times. It follows, similarly, that any claim of universally rational behavior (in areas of social activity not conventionally covered in economics) must also imply the prior attainment of universal equilibrium in all areas of social interaction. If (in the preceding section) we found this universal equilibrium assumption unacceptable, and hence found the attempts to subordinate explanation in other areas of social science to the hegemony of economic theory, to be flawed, what is to blame in this regard is the assumption of universal rationality (in its mainstream interpretation). And it is here that we encounter the paradox mentioned earlier. For the "Austrian" sense in which rationality is a universal aspect of all human action, it turns out that it is precisely this universality of rationality which led us to challenge definitively the direct relevance of the equilibrium pattern in areas of social interaction outside the conventional scope of economics.

UNIVERSAL RATIONALITY IN THE MISESIAN FRAMEWORK

As was recognized already in the 1930s[10] the notion of rationality central to economics was understood by Mises to mean, essentially, purposefulness. For Mises the rationality of human action does not mean that decisions are made with full awareness of the circumstances relevant to choice. For Mises there is necessarily an element (which this writer has identified as the entrepreneurial element) in human action (a notion applicable only in a world of open-ended uncertainty) which grapples with the inherent uncertainty in which the agent is enveloped.[11] The assumption of rationality therefore means not any relevant omniscience, but simply the intent purposefulness of the human agent which inspires his alertness to opportunities (or to dangers) which he might otherwise overlook (or has in the past overlooked). It is this sense of rationality which, for Mises, characterizes human action in all its manifestations, in all areas of human interaction.

But this focus upon (what we have identified as) the entrepreneurial element in Misesian human action entails the insights developed in earlier sections of this chapter. Those insights led us to argue for a sharp difference between human action as it occurs within the institutional setting of the market, and human action as it occurs outside that setting. Within the setting of the market the entrepreneurial element in human action can be expected to set in motion a process of mutual discovery. The reasonableness of such processes of mutual discovery in markets renders the notions of equilibrium and equilibration relevant, at least, for our understanding of market phenomena. But outside the market setting, we argued, there is nothing in the character of interpersonal interaction which suggests any systematic discovery process (analogous to the discovery processes inspired, in markets, by the lure of pure entrepreneurial profit). Precisely because the notion of universal rationality, in the Misesian framework, includes the powerful possibility, at very least, of entrepreneurial error, our recognition of such universality ignites a red light warning against the uncritical transfer, to areas outside the conventional scope of economics, of the notion of equilibrium. To the degree that any extension of the applicability of economic theory requires us to invoke equilibrium notions, such extension must, for the Austrian-Misesian tradition, remain thoroughly suspect.

UNIVERSAL PRAXEOLOGY AND GAINS FROM INTERDISCIPLINARY TRADE

It is quite true that Mises envisaged a general science of human action based on the universality of the rationality aspect of action. Certainly this common feature of human action in all its manifestations suggested for Mises that this feature can serve as the starting point for the development of theorems that cover both conventional economic interaction and other areas. We do not know (and Mises did not claim to know in any way specifically) how such theorems can in fact be developed. The universal notion of human action, Mises was convinced, could serve as an intellectual key to open up new areas of understanding. This conviction seems to have been in the nature of a prescientific hunch, which has as yet not been validated. Of one thing, however, we can be quite sure: Mises did not envisage any general science of praxeology that might be anchored in the assumption of universal, omniscience-based, equilibrium.

At the same time, while recoiling from that economic imperialism which, for Becker and Hirshleifer, derives from the assumption of universal equilibrium, we certainly need not and should not fail to recognize possible usefulness in interdisciplinary trade. No doubt many of the insights of economics (even in its mainstream version!) can be usefully incorporated into areas outside the conventional scope of economics. Much of Becker's work can no doubt be hailed in these terms. As Demsetz (1996, p. 3) put it, interaction between economics and other social sciences has, thus far, resulted in a "strong export surplus" being maintained by economics "in its trade in areas and methods with the other social sciences." Nothing in this chapter need contradict Demsetz's statement, or the spirit of interdisciplinary trade in ideas which it represents. Economics, through its insights concerning the universality of human reason and purposefulness, can, one can confidently hope, be of enormous benefit to other social sciences, *without* transforming them into colonial subdisciplines of applied economic theory.

NOTES

1. Robbins (1932, ch. 1).
2. Mises (1996, p. 3).
3. Ibid.
4. This digression is based on ideas developed earlier, out of the work of Mises and Hayek. See especially Kirzner (1973, ch. 6). The mode of exposition in the following section has benefitted from listening to a lecture by Professor Mancur Olson.
5. Calabresi (1968, p. 68).
6. See the title essay in Stigler (1982).
7. Becker (1976, p. 4).
8. Ibid., p. 232.
9. Stigler (1961).
10. See for example, Robbins (1932; 2nd edn, 1935, p. 93 and fn). See also Kirzner (1960, pp. 165–72).
11. See Kirzner (1973, pp. 32–7).

REFERENCES

Becker, G. (1976) *The Economic Approach to Human Behavior*, Chicago: University of Chicago Press.

Calabresi, G. (1968) "Transaction Costs, Resource Allocation, and Liability Rules: A Comment," *Journal of Law and Economics* 11(April).

Demsetz, H. (1996) *The Economics, An Explanation of the Comparative Success of Economics in the Social Sciences*, Jena: Max Planck Institut.

Green, David G. (1996) *Community Without Politics. A Market Approach to Welfare Reform*, London: IEA Health and Welfare Unit.

Hirshleifer, Jack (1985) "The Expanding Domain of Economics," *American Economic Review* 75(6).

Kirzner, Israel M. (1960) *The Economic Point of View*, Princeton, NJ: Van Nostrand.

—— (1973) *Competition and Entrepreneurship*, Chicago: University of Chicago Press.

Loasby, Brian J. (1989) *The Mind and Method of the Economist. A Critical Appraisal of Major Economists in the Twentieth Century*, Aldershot and Brookfield, CT: Edward Elgar.

Mises, Ludwig von (1966) *Human Action. A Treatise on Economics*, Chicago: Contemporary Books.

Robbins, Lionel (1932) *The Nature and Significance of Economic Science*, London: Macmillan.

Stigler, George J. (1961) "The Economics of Information," *Journal of Political Economy* 69(June).

—— (1982) *The Economist as Preacher and Other Essays*, Chicago: University of Chicago Press.

Source: Rationality, Entrepreneurship, and Economic "Imperialism," in Sheila C. Dow and Peter E. Earl (eds) (1999) *Economic Organisation and Economic Knowledge: Essays in Honor of Brian J. Loasby*, Edward Elgar.

Appendices

THREE OBITUARIES

1

LUDWIG VON MISES

1881–1973

ON THE MARKET

In paying tribute to the memory of an inspiring teacher and towering scholar and thinker, it seems eminently appropriate to draw attention to the major intellectual "vision" which sparked and sustained the master's contributions to his science. To those who knew him, Ludwig Mises was, in the face of shocking neglect by so many of his contemporaries, a living exemplar of incorruptible intellectual integrity, a model of passionate, relentless scholarship and dedication. It will not be easy to forget these stern lessons which he so courageously personified. But what will surely live on even longer in future histories of economic thought will be those distinctive elements of Mises' extraordinary contribution which set it so clearly apart from the dominant economics of his age. It was into the enunciation of these elements that Mises poured a lifetime of what can almost be called intellectual martyrdom. It is for the brief exposition of one of these brilliantly seminal ideas—the perception of the market exclusively in process terms—that these lines are set down.

In the sweep of the development of economic ideas over the past two centuries, the concept held by the various thinkers concerning the market has been crucial. The pioneers of modern economics after 1870, reinvigorating the contributions of the earlier classical economists by the infusion of powerful new insights into the nature of demand, offered a view of the operation of the market society which was of enormous significance. Henceforth economic literacy could not fail to embrace the understanding of the way in which the free interaction of the decisions of owners of resources, of producers, and of consumers in the market systematically generates determinate patterns of prices, output quantities and qualities, methods of production, and resource allocation.

However, in the ferment of intellectual developments in economics during the twentieth century, this understanding came, in the work of the dominant schools, to be perceived within a mechanistic framework which did violence to the subtle insights a more profound awareness of the market is able to confer. The market came to be seen as a kind of computer, grinding out the equilibrium solution compatible with the basic data of the system—a task which presumes that the economic actors already possess perfect knowledge. The theory of the market came to mean the solving by the theorist of the computation problem. Moreover this theory came to be seen as equally well suited to the needs of societies choosing to allocate their resources by central direction; the socialist planner could, it came to be thought, simulate the success with which the market allocates resources by merely addressing himself to the very same computation problem which it was thought to be the function of market theory to solve.

It was this view of the market which Mises denied with every ounce of energy. It is no exaggeration to say that this denial was central to the major portion of Mises' disagreements with the various economic doctrines of his age. Future economists, when they come to accept, as in time they surely must, the validity of the Misesian critique of the faulty perception of the market, will find it necessary to re-examine many of the doctrines of contemporary economics with which Mises took issue. For Mises the market is not a computer grinding out equilibrium solutions to sets of simultaneous equations. Rather the market is a delicate *process* whereby, against the background of continually changing conditions, and with information available only in limited and piecemeal fashion, the decisions of market participants are, through their interplay in the market, brought into steadily more dovetailing adjustment. In this process the key roles are played by restless, active, ever alert entrepreneurship, and by its counterpart, the merciless, ceaseless, impartial court of active competition. Both these latter roles—completely absent in the dominant equilibrium versions of market theory—are crucial in the emergence of the kaleidoscopically changing patterns of market prices.

* * *

It was the "process" perception of markets and of market prices that led Mises unerringly to dismiss all attempts to recognize "non-market prices" as devices through which socialist planners might simulate the achievements of the market economy. The notion of non-market prices can have relevance only in a world of equilibrium situations; it bears no analytical or functional resemblance to the prices which emerge, during disequilibrium, in markets revealing the impact of entrepreneurial competition against a background of widespread ignorance.

It was the "process" perception of markets and of market prices that led Mises to deplore with such sharpness the dominance over economics achieved by mathematical techniques during his own lifetime. Such techniques, useful though they may be to the derivation of the conditions for equilibria of various kinds, must inevitably mask the more subtle processes of entrepreneurial change which (because they depend on essentially extra-economic flashes of awareness) do not permit analysis within the procrustean bed of maximization techniques.

And it was the "process" perception of markets and of market prices that led Mises to reject the various attempts by economists since the 1930s to build theories of the market based on notions of monopolistic or imperfect competition. Such models fail, Mises believed, because they reveal precisely the central weaknesses of the theories they seek to replace, viz., an exclusive concern with equilibrium, and a failure to understand the active entrepreneurial-competitive process.

No economist perceived more thoroughly and sadly than Mises how the rejection of his ideas was leading Western societies relentlessly down a path along which the free interplay of independent, individual decisions in the market was being steadily replaced by the centralization of more and more political and economic power in the hands of governments and their functionaries. If Western society ever achieves a reversal of this trend, if it ever learns to respect the decisions of free men interacting within a framework of rigorously maintained individual rights, it can only be as a result of Mises' vision and insight into the true character of the market society. Here indeed we have a monument to Mises the construction of which is well worth our diligence and our dedication.

Source: Tribute to von Mises: On the Market, *National Review*, November 9, 1973, pp. 1246, 1260.

2

FRIEDRICH A. VON HAYEK

1899–1992

A concise obituary evaluation of a scholar of the magisterial caliber of the late Friedrich A. Hayek must necessarily aim to be far less than comprehensive. Hayek's work has been so extensive, both in sheer volume and in the variety of areas explored, that a short essay can hope, at best, only to highlight some selected feature held to be central to that work. Certainly any detailed review of Hayek's personal biography can and must be dispensed with: this scholar's scientific achievements attained an eminence which render the details of his life story, except where they directly contribute to a deeper appreciation and understanding of his work, of distinctly secondary interest.

The present essay has evolved as a result of two observations made concerning the many obituary notices which appeared soon after Hayek's death. First, these notices presented Hayek invariably in terms of his ideological profile. Hayek's eulogists tended to see his scholarly contributions as being primarily important for the support they provided to the political program of classical liberalism. And indeed, while remaining fully aware of the obvious scientific integrity and objectivity of Hayek's work, we must at the same time recognize that very little of his writing is wholly unrelated to his commitment, spanning more than six decades, to a societal ideal based on individual rights and limited government. Certainly Hayek's fame in the wider world of lay intellectual opinion rests on this latter circumstance. Therefore, one cannot complain too loudly about the tendency of Hayek's obituaries to highlight his political commitments.

What is less understandable is that the obituary notices have almost invariably ignored or underestimated Hayek's role as a key figure in the twentieth-century history of the Austrian school of economics. This hiatus suggests widespread misunderstanding of

Hayek's thought. The truth is that very little of his work, both in economics and outside it, can be properly appreciated, especially insofar as it relates to his classical liberalism, without recognizing the "Austrian" character of Hayek's economics. The following pages express one economist's appreciation of Hayek's contributions, *qua* economist, to the understanding of how a capitalist society works (and how and why a socialist society does not). We shall find that this contribution is indeed rooted in the economics of the Austrian tradition, and did itself importantly enrich the insights which characterize that tradition. It is precisely this Hayekian version of Austrian economics which constituted the foundation upon which Hayek's celebrated case for classical liberalism has been consistently built. A more extensive and ambitious evaluation might well go on to explore possible problems to be found in Hayek's more recent contributions to social and legal philosophy, which, it might be argued, arose out of his somewhat uncritical extrapolation of these very economic insights to the broader field of social evolution. But, as stated at the outset, a concise evaluation of Hayek must inevitably be a partial one. Moreover, the character of an obituary evaluation justifies, and perhaps even requires, emphasis upon the permanently valuable character of a great scholar's contribution, rather than upon any problematic elements which a critic might claim to perceive within that contribution.

HAYEK'S EARLY CONTACTS WITH AUSTRIAN ECONOMICS

Hayek studied at the University of Vienna under Friedrich von Wieser and Othmar Spann—neither of them a shining exemplar, to put it mildly, of classical liberal thought. It was only after having already earned doctorates in law and political science that Hayek was drawn, in the mid-1920s, into the intellectual circle led by Ludwig von Mises (who had in 1922 published the original German language version of *Socialism,* and who had emerged as perhaps the most influential figure in post-World War I Austrian economics). It seems fair to say that it was primarily after this that Hayek's work in the Austrian tradition matured and developed to permit him to be recognized, by the early 1930s, as one of the foremost representatives of that tradition. Appointed in 1927 as director of the Austrian Institute for Business Cycle Research, Hayek soon published several books expositing the "Austrian" theory of the business cycle, drawing heavily on Böhm-Bawerkian capital theory, and on Misesian insights in the monetary theory of the trade cycle. These contributions rendered Hayek the foremost exponent of the Austrian cycle theory, and led directly to his 1932 appointment, at an unusually young age, to the prestigious Tooke Chair at the London School of Economics. It was during his years at LSE during the 1930s that Hayek was a major participant in celebrated controversies with Keynes, Sraffa and Knight. While these controversies brought Hayek's name into global professional prominence, they also deepened his own appreciation for the methodological subjectivism of the Austrian tradition. This appreciation appears to have been even further deepened in the course of Hayek's arguments, during these same years, in support of the position taken by his mentor Ludwig von Mises in the famous debate on socialist economic calculation.

It seems clear that Hayek's participation in this latter debate forced him critically to reassess the most basic conclusions of twentieth-century economic science. The results of this fundamental re-examination appeared in the form of two related strands of contributions. A number of papers emerged which focused on the role of knowledge in market processes, culminating in the 1945 paper "The Use of Knowledge in Society." These papers were to form the core of Hayek's *Individualism and Economic Order* (1949). A second series of papers, published during the war, focused on the role of subjectivism in the social sciences, and formed the core of *The Counter-Revolution of Science: Studies on the Abuse of Reason* (1952). Together these two strands of contributions constitute, in this writer's opinion, Hayek's most profound explorations of the foundations of economic understanding. Taken together with Mises's contemporaneous work, these contributions represented a most significant deepening and extension of the subjectivist Austrian tradition. There can be little doubt that it was this work that was responsible both for the fact that Austrian economics survived the mid-century dominance of Keynesian thought, and for the renewed late-century interest in Austrian economics, despite the dominance of neo-classical equilibrium theory. Nor can there be any doubt that it was these early and more narrowly "economic" writings on the importance of knowledge and of subjectivism which nourished Hayek's subsequent scholarly work in social and legal philosophy, and which led to his own deepened commitment to classical liberalism as a political program.

THE ECONOMIC BASIS OF HAYEK'S THOUGHT

The accepted core of mainstream price theory from which the new Mises-Hayek insights diverged, was not, in principle, entirely incompatible with these insights. The failure of Austrians up until the 1940s to recognize the need for such rebellious insights is no mystery. Mainstream price theory was, at least since Lionel Robbins's 1932 book, *The Nature and Significance of Economic Science,* clearly seen as rooted in the interaction of individual buying and selling decisions. But the increasing formalization of economics (and especially of the model of perfect competition), and the absorption of Walrasian insights, were converging during the 1930s and 1940s to render mainstream microeconomics primarily a theory of perfectly competitive market equilibrium. Such a theory, embodying in particular the assumption of perfect information, tended to divert attention away from the subjective elements in individual decision-making, from the role of knowledge, ignorance, and uncertainty in the sets of decisions being made, and from the attendant complications surrounding the interactions among decisions. Increasingly it became easy to think of market-clearing prices as being impersonally determined by costs and utility functions, with both of these being perceived "objectively," rather than as colored by the knowledge, expectations, and doubts of decision makers. The mathematics of equilibrium configurations made it appear that market prices are wholly determined by given technological production functions and preference patterns, as if without any intermediation by human, error-prone, market participants. In particular the price theory of the 1930s and 1940s had left little room for any entrepreneurial role. That theory was virtually confined to the analysis of equilibrium states, in which no profit opportunities exist to be grasped by the entrepreneur. The decisions made under such postulated conditions were seen as informed by perfect knowledge somehow acquired before the economic analysis even begins. The global efficiency thought to characterize the fully employed competitive economy came to be seen as implicit in the configuration of interlocking markets, each in perfectly competitive equilibrium. The allocative efficiency perceived to emerge from this hypothesized equilibrium configuration of markets presupposed a level of information-perfection that was mind-boggling in its completeness and intricacy, and sets of mutually sustaining decisions somehow—quite inexplicably—perfectly pre-reconciled before market activity itself began.

It was against this perhaps only dimly discerned core of neoclassical price theory—a core that has, in the half century since then, become carefully and explicitly articulated in mainstream economics along precisely these lines—that Mises and particularly Hayek reacted in the fourth and fifth decades of the century. For both of these Austrian scholars, economic theory needed the injection of a wholesome dose of subjectivism, above and beyond the mainstream acknowledgement of the subjectivism of preferences. For Mises this new subjectivism involved the recognition of the active role of entrepreneurial minds hammering out prices by negotiating in non-equilibrium settings. For Hayek it took the form of a brilliantly unorthodox emphasis on the importance of the knowledge upon which market decisions must be based.

Hayek's recognition of the crucial importance of knowledge in market processes was arrived at in two stages. In his famous 1937 paper "Economics and Knowledge," Hayek (a) interpreted market equilibrium constructs as formalizations of the assumption of complete mutual knowledge on the part of market participants, and (b) demonstrated that hypothesized equilibrating market processes must consist of specific patterns of mutual *learning.* In his aforementioned 1945 paper, "The Use of Knowledge in Society," Hayek identified positive and normative implications of the circumstance that the sum total of knowledge available in society "never exists in concentrated or integrated form but solely as the dispersed bits of incomplete and frequently contradictory knowledge which all separate individuals possess."[1]

That Hayek recognized the deepened subjectivism embodied in these insights is clearly seen in his discussions in *The Counter-Revolution of Science.* There he writes of "the more complex phenomena with which economic theory is concerned and where in recent years progress has been particularly closely connected with the advance of subjectivism." In particular he cited "the new problem of the compatibility of intentions and expectations of different people, of the division of knowledge between them, and the process by which the relevant knowledge is acquired and expectations formed."[2]

It was of course in the Austrian tradition that subjectivism in economic thought had, since 1871, received its clearest emphasis. In identifying his own insights concerning knowledge as embodying an extension of subjectivism, Hayek was consciously advancing that Austrian tradition. But, as later developments in doctrinal history were to reveal, he was advancing the Austrian tradition in yet a different sense, of which he himself could hardly have been aware. His subjectivist advances were helping to lay the groundwork for the subsequent rediscovery, within the economics profession in the last quarter of the century, of the richness of the Austrian tradition in economics, and of its capacity to provide satisfying explanations for phenomena left unexplained by mainstream theory. We have not yet seen the full extent of the impact of this rediscovery; but the contribution to it made by Hayek's scholarly work of the 1930s and 1940s is one which deserves recognition and appreciation.

FROM ECONOMIC TO SOCIAL THEORY

These insights concerning the role of knowledge in economic processes enabled Hayek to appreciate more deeply the nature of spontaneous coordination and its place in the history of economic thought. Particularly against the background of the socialist calculation debate, it became apparent to Hayek that the coordinative properties of markets is made possible by delicate webs of mutual discovery which no single mind could simulate or duplicate. It was not so much that this recognition exposed the fallacies underlying socialist dreams of efficient central planning. More importantly, Hayek realized that coordinative market processes involve the utilization of scattered information which could not, even in principle, be imagined to inform any one decision maker. Hayek was to take this fundamental economic insight and apply it to illuminate spontaneous social processes of all kinds. Hayek's deep and extensive investigations during the 1950s, 1960s and 1970s into the literatures of the philosophy and history of law, and of political and social philosophy, were guided by this central insight. Hayek's understanding of the meaning of spontaneous social coordination was the basis for his critique of constructivist fallacies, the error of believing that institutions and outcomes which emerge spontaneously through mutual discovery, can in principle be arrived at by deliberate design. Clearly Hayek's classical liberalism came, in his mature years, to reflect more and more predominantly the consistent application of this understanding.

Hayek's mature appreciation of a society built on the foundations of individual rights, the rule of law, and limited government can thus be traced directly to his own extension of the subjectivism of the Austrian tradition in economics. It must be emphasized that the economic understanding of markets which emerges from the Austrian tradition differs sharply from the understanding of markets which informs the minimal-statist position of many mainstream economists. Such emphasis is perhaps all the more needed because certain elements of the Hayekian understanding have (especially since Hayek's Nobel prize in 1974) been absorbed into non-Austrian, mainstream thinking. It is now commonplace, in mainstream expositions of the working of markets, to cite Hayek as having taught economists to see prices as signals communicating the information needed for social coordination of individual decisions efficiently and economically. The beauty of the price system, according to this mainstream argument for unhampered markets, consists in its ability, without central direction, to generate mutually dovetailing sets of decisions. Without requiring the necessary information to be concentrated in any single mind, markets are able to stimulate independent agents to act in precisely that manner that will permit their plans to be carried out without disappointment and without regret, since the necessary information is transmitted to the relevant agents by prices. While there is some basis for such a reading of Hayek, we must insist on a more careful interpretation of his position—one much more consistent with his Austrian subjectivism.

The more careful interpretation (confirmed in Hayek's 1968 paper, "Competition as a Discovery Procedure")[3] draws attention not so much to the capacity of prices to communicate *accurate* information, as to the capacity of prices to alert market participants to the need for *better* information. While accurate information is expressed only through equilibrium prices, the beauty of the price system, in Austrian eyes, consists in the potential of *dis*equilibrium prices to stimulate discovery and overcome existing ignorance. Spontaneous coordination, in this view, consists not so much in the possibility of a pattern of fully coordinated decisions without central direction, as in the discovery procedure spontaneously generated by initially erroneous patterns of decisions. It is in the market process of spontaneous learning that the Austrian view places the importance of Hayek's insights concerning dispersed knowledge. It is in this process that Austrian economists find the scope for the critically important role of entrepreneurial discovery and innovation. And it is in this entrepreneurial role, necessarily absent from the centrally planned socialist economy, that Austrian economists see the unique capacity of the market economy to achieve social coordination and prosperity.

* * *

Hayek's scholarly career is remarkable, even extraordinary, in a number of respects. There can be few other examples of such consistently superior intellectual labor sustained for over six decades. Nor can there be many examples of scholars whose work has been so influential in so many diverse fields of social research, including economics, political and legal philosophy, and psychology. In economics itself Hayek's bibliography includes now-classic works in monetary theory, business cycle theory, capital theory, doctrinal history, the theory of socialist planning and economic methodology.

The preceding pages have attempted to identify what this writer believes to be the central thread inspiring much, if not most, of this prolific scholarship. This central thread, we have argued, has nourished not only Hayek's work in economics, but also much of his work in political and legal philosophy. It has, we maintain, supported his mature views on the social usefulness of societal arrangements based on limited government, the rule of law, and secure individual rights. It should be no surprise to discover that this central thread derives from that Austrian tradition in economics in which Hayek was steeped in the foundational years of his career. When we recall Hayek's oft-quoted statement "that every important advance in economic theory during the last hundred years was a further step in the consistent application of subjectivism,"[4] we can appreciate how Hayek's own life's work must be seen as a giant "further step" in that very direction.

NOTES

1. F.A. Hayek (1948) *Individualism and Economic Order*, Chicago: University of Chicago Press, p. 77.
2. F.A. Hayek (1952) *The Counter-Revolution of Science*, Glencoe, IL: The Free Press, p. 33.
3. F.A. Hayek (1978) "Competition as a Discovery Procedure," in *New Studies in Philosophy, Politics, Economics and the History of Ideas*, Chicago: University of Chicago Press, pp. 179–90.
4. Hayek (1952, p. 31).

Source: Friedrich A. von Hayek, *Critical Review*, 1992, 5(4).

3

LUDWIG M. LACHMANN

1906–1990

On December 17, 1990, Ludwig M. Lachmann, one of the most important influences in the contemporary revival of Austrian economics, passed away in Johannesburg, South Africa, after a long illness, just weeks short of his 85th birthday. Ludwig Lachmann spent a long, productive life pursuing the study of the social sciences in general, and of economics in particular, with single-minded dedication, penetrating insight, and utter intellectual honesty.

Born in Berlin in 1906, Lachmann studied in Berlin and Zurich, obtaining the degree of Doctor rerum politicarum from the University of Berlin in 1930. He came to England in 1933, and pursued research under Hayek at the London School of Economics and subsequently at the University of London. A period of service as a faculty member at the University College of Hull was followed by his appointment, in 1949, to the chair of Economics and Economic History at the University of Witwatersrand, Johannesburg, South Africa. In 1972 Lachmann became Professor Emeritus, and spent a substantial part of the subsequent 15 years (until the spring semester of 1987) as a visiting Research Professor in the Austrian Economics Program at New York University, this having been made possible by far-sighted Moorman Foundation financial support. At a gathering held at New York University celebrating his 80th birthday in February 1986, Professor Lachmann was presented with a festschrift (*Subjectivism, Intelligibility, and Economic Understanding,* New York University Press, 1986) in which 24 scholars from around the world paid him tribute. In the course of more than a full half century of vigorous research activity, Lachmann was author of five books and monographs, and scores of journal articles. (A valuable survey of that work up until 1976 was provided by Walter E. Grinder as the Introduction to Ludwig M. Lachmann (1977) *Capital, Expectations, and the Market Process,* Kansas City: Sheed, Andrews and McMeel.)

The editor of the Institute Scholar has suggested that this obituary dwell more on Professor Lachmann's intellectual contributions than on biographical details. Accordingly, we shall endeavor in what follows to capture (with the desperate brevity required by assigned space constraints) certain central elements in Ludwig Lachmann's rich, lifelong exploration of the social sciences—despite our acute awareness that it is far too early to attempt any full assessment of the emergence, development, and completion of Ludwig Lachmann's work. This writer is abundantly aware of the additional difficulties surrounding this hasty, preliminary statement; his feelings of profound affection and admiration for Ludwig Lachmann, recollecting some 30 years of personal friendship and correspondence, render him a most imperfect judge; to complicate matters even further, this writer had, for 20 out of these 30 years found himself locked in a friendly (but quite insoluble) disagreement with Lachmann on certain fundamental points of economic understanding. It will be for future scholars to provide the full scale, dispassionate historical and critical assessment which the prolific work of Ludwig M. Lachmann so richly deserves and demands.

The central thread running through Lachmann's work is, unquestionably, his radical subjectivism—his conviction that economic understanding calls for recognition, not merely that external events influence human action only as they have been filtered through the human mind, but also that each human mind is active and idiosyncratic in interpreting external events and in thus arriving at what it knows and what it expects. It was this conviction that led him, as early as 1959, to assert that as "soon as we permit time to elapse we must permit knowledge to change, and knowledge cannot be regarded as a function of anything else." In his most recent works, Lachmann pursued the implications of this insight with a consistency undeterred by what some have considered the nihilism towards which he appeared to be gravitating. Lachmann was never one to concern himself with conforming to current intellectual fashions and fads. Even where intellectual honesty led him to question the positions maintained by writers for whom he had enormous regard, he never flinched.

In fact there seems to have occurred a steady deepening, or radicalization, of Lachmann's subjectivism during the last 40 years of his life. In 1950, in his inaugural lecture at the University of Witwatersrand, Lachmann was clearly expressing a view of economics largely built upon Mises (whose recently published *Human Action* he was to review enthusiastically a year later in *Economica*). When, in an act of rare kindness to a lonely young Misesian, Lachmann first wrote to this writer in 1961, he was most explicit in his commitment to "praxeology" and to its Misesian character. Yet, as the years passed, it became clear that for Lachmann the subjectivism of Mises (and even more so, the subjectivism of Hayek) came to seem incomplete. The focus of Lachmann's intellectual attention began to shift from Mises to Shackle. In his letters to me of the 1960s Lachmann had described Shackle as an important writer who should be seen as a potentially valuable ally; but after Shackle's *Epistemics and Economics* (1972) it was clear that Lachmann saw its author as embodying that perfection of subjectivist insight towards which Mises provided only the first approach. (See Ludwig M. Lachmann (1976) "From Mises to Shackle: An Essay," *Journal of Economic Literature*, March.) The major shortcoming in the Austrian literature, Lachmann maintained, was its failure to extend subjectivism to encompass expectations. It was Shackle's great virtue, in Lachmann's eyes, that, by underscoring the subjectivism of expectations, he decisively unmoored human action from any deterministic constraints imposed by external events.

Despite his differences with the Austrians, it should be emphasized that his enormous personal and professional admiration and respect for both Mises and Hayek were never in question. And it was with the Austrians that Lachmann found the common ground needed to accomplish what he saw as his overriding intellectual and scholarly duty—the nurturing of a younger generation of economists impervious to what he held to be the blight of late twentieth century economics, the distortions wrought by viewing economic phenomena through the spectacles of deterministic, mechanical, general equilibrium models. This he saw as his life's goal. In the 1960s he could have been pardoned for seeing this goal as almost beyond reach. (In a poignant paragraph written to this writer in 1969, Lachmann wrote: "If we two start quarrelling, what becomes of praxeology?") Yet at the time of his death, barely 20 years later, he could (and did!) look with calm satisfaction at the scores of younger Austrian scholars and colleagues in this country and abroad—including especially, Gerald O'Driscoll, Mario Rizzo, Don Lavoie, and Stephan Boehm—whose economic perspective had been profoundly affected by his patient, sparkling teaching and writing. He could point to the revival, in universities around the world, of appreciation for those subtleties in economic understanding which emerge from a recognition of the need to proceed, beyond "subjectivism as the expression of 'human disposition' to subjectivism as a manifestation of spontaneous action."

Ludwig Lachmann was the eternal intellectual optimist. In his voracious and extraordinarily retentive reading, he discovered nuggets of truth in the writings of thinkers with whom he disagreed most vehemently. Out of these, building on the work of his intellectual heroes, Weber, Mises, Hayek, Hicks, and Shackle, Ludwig Lachmann constructed an edifice of economic understanding peculiarly his own. In erecting this edifice and actively nurturing a sympathetic audience for subjectivist economics until only weeks before his passing, Lachmann made his lasting intellectual contribution to the understanding of society and—perhaps in ways in which he did not himself always quite appreciate—to the understanding of how the market society can systematically foster that social coordination upon which human well-being depends.

We have lost a delightful, encyclopedic colleague who told us the truth with white hot passion discreetly clothed in the most elegant old-world courtesy. How we shall miss this stern but beloved teacher, this warm, but ever-honest friend!

Source: Ludwig M. Lachmann, *Institute Scholar*, 1991, 10(2–3).

INDEX